CW00338343

Woolman's
Greenhouse Gardening

Woolman's Greenhouse Gardening

RONALD H. MENAGE

ELM TREE BOOKS

Produced by Elm Tree Books, Hamish Hamilton Limited
for H. Woolman (Dorridge) Limited, Grange Road, Dorridge,
Solihull, West Midlands, B93 8QB

First published in Great Britain 1974
by Elm Tree Books Limited
90 Great Russell Street London WC1

Copyright © 1974 by R. H. Menage
SBN 241 89032 2

Printed in Great Britain by
Clarke, Doble & Brendon Ltd, Plymouth

Contents

List of Illustrations

Diagrams in the text

Colour Plates

Chrysanthemums: David Burton, Glorietta, Orange Lilian Shoesmith, Yellow Fred Shoesmith and Fred Shoesmith
Fuchsias
Pelargoniums: Solano, Grand Slam, Lavender Grand Slam, Aztec and Grandma Fischer

A*

Preface

THIS book is intended as an introduction to home greenhouse gardening, and as an attempt to provide practical guidance. I hope it may help beginners to start right. It should also give useful information to experienced growers, since every attempt has been made to keep the text really up to date.

In most cases recommendations given are based on my own personal findings, and I have preferred to give these even when differing from the conventional. Some of the information regarding equipment and technique is also published here for the first time.

Everything described in this book is available, and readers should find the list of suppliers' addresses on page 243 extremely helpful.

I have tried to cover all the most popular and rewarding aspects of the home greenhouse in useful detail, rather than gloss over the vast possibilities. Once the basics are mastered, there is no limit to what you can grow and enjoy under glass.

R.H.M.

CHAPTER ONE

Introducing Greenhouse Gardening

ADVANTAGES AND BENEFITS

As soon as you acquire a greenhouse, a new and exciting world of gardening becomes possible. Outdoors in the British Isles plants are subject to many hazards, and extremes of weather alone can bring much disappointment. In the greenhouse you can have almost full control of the environment. You can govern temperature to a considerable extent and provide artificial warmth if necessary. You can decide how much water the plants should receive, and there is better control of feeding, since nutrients are not washed away by rain as in the open. The composition of feeds, fertilisers, and nutrients can be balanced better to suit any individual plant types. Weeds, pests, and diseases are easier to avoid and control, and you can take full advantage of sterilised potting composts which make growing so much more reliable. Even light can be adjusted by the use of shading so that plants can benefit from maximum light when it is in need, and shade to any degree you think desirable when the sunlight might be too intense.

A greenhouse can be enjoyed the year round and the winter can be as colourful and interesting as the summer. It is a delightful place in which to work or potter in winter, and it will be greatly appreciated by the retired, the not-so-young, or the infirm. You can use a greenhouse as a place of beauty, and as a conservatory for the display of decorative plants, to entrap their scent and protect them from weather damage; or you can indulge in more 'down to earth' and utilitarian practices—fruits and vegetables, cut flowers for sale or floral arrangement or decorating the home, winter salads, flower show exhibits, propagation of garden plants, raising bedding plants, and housing special collections of specialist plants like chrysanthemums, orchids,

carnations, alpines, and the like. With a little warmth, plants
from almost the world over can be grown and your scope is
unlimited. Greenhouse gardening can be a never-ending adven-
ture.

Nowadays many people like to make the greenhouse part of
the home. There is nothing new in this. The Victorians used to
delight in very grand conservatories, elaborately built and filled
with exotic plants. There they would entertain friends or take
afternoon tea. Today there is the modern, more modest equivalent in the form of garden rooms or lean-to structures that can
be set against the dwelling. The so-called prefabricated 'home
extensions' are also usually well supplied with large windows
and perhaps a roof letting in some light. These, too, make useful
garden rooms where many house plants will thrive.

Only flat dwellers can be ruled out as possible candidates for
greenhouse gardening proper, although they can still use
windows and have miniature windowsill greenhouses and plant
cases. Small greenhouses are now available to suit the smallest
garden. You don't have to have a garden—a greenhouse can
be erected in a concrete yard or even on a flat roof or large
balcony.

HOW THE GREENHOUSE WORKS

The Romans built greenhouses or plant houses of a kind, but
the structure as we know it in modern times only became possible
with the discovery of glass and the manufacture of glass sheet.
The first building that could be truly described as a greenhouse
was erected in the Apothecaries' Garden, in Swan Walk, Chelsea,
London. This garden, founded in the seventeenth century, still
exists today. The greenhouse was therefore a British invention.
The greenhouse eventually became the hobby of the wealthy
and in the Victorian era everyone of any distinction had a handsome conservatory or 'hot house'. With the passing of the Victorians greenhouse gardening declined and still remained only
possible for the more affluent classes. Since the end of the
Second World War, there has been a dramatic change. More
people have gardens of their own, more spare time, and longer
holidays. At last people are seeing the wisdom of guarding
against the freakish pranks of our climate. There have also

been advances in greenhouse design. It is no longer necessary
to have one built, or to build your own. The market abounds
with prefabricated designs to suit all purposes and situations.
Mass production and bulk buying of materials have made
possible price ranges to suit all pockets, and more recently plastic
has had a further effect in reducing cost. However, at this stage
we must learn a little about how the greenhouse functions,
since glass and plastic have different properties.

At one time glass structures were known as 'sun traps'. This
was owing to the fact that they seemed to catch and intensify
the sun's warmth in some way and hold it for long periods.
This is because sunshine contains rays that we cannot see or
appreciate directly, for example those that give us a sun tan.
When some of these rays (not all) strike an object they may be
transformed into heat energy and be radiated away again as
warmth, or the object may be heated and warm the air around it.
These short-wave rays (of the type easily convertible to heat)
can penetrate glass easily; but the longer waves they are converted into cannot escape back through the glass so readily—
hence the warmth-trapping effect. Most plastics are more transparent to the long waves and radiant heat. Consequently a
plastic greenhouse may change its temperature quickly with the
coming and going of sunshine. Even on sunless days, a certain
amount of radiant energy from the sun is getting through the
clouds and this is often sufficient to be trapped and keep
a glasshouse comfortably warm. In winter when the air is
bitterly cold outside, a glass greenhouse interior may be at
summer temperature if the sun is shining.

COSTS—CAN YOU AFFORD TO BUY AND
MAINTAIN A GREENHOUSE?

As already pointed out, greenhouse gardening is no longer the
sole privilege of the more wealthy classes. There are nowadays
so many firms supplying a range of designs and sizes at very
reasonable prices that it is generally best to select one of these.
Often to make your own greenhouse proves more expensive than
buying a prefabricated type, but in certain cases it may be a good
idea : for example, to fit a difficult site against a dwelling and a
side wall, or between two houses where there is often a narrow

passage. There are firms that make greenhouses and conservatories, garden rooms, etc., to the customer's requirements, but
this is usually quite an expensive business. There is little reason
why anyone should not be able to afford a small home greenhouse—it is certainly much cheaper than owning a television
set!

The question of rates frequently arises. Again, rates need be
no problem. You have to be careful if you are erecting a lean-to
greenhouse, conservatory, or garden room, against a dwelling so
that it becomes part of the house: in this case there may be a
few building regulations to comply with, and nearly always
there will be a *small* increase in your rates. In the case of free-
standing greenhouses in the garden, often they are completely
immune from rates particularly if under 1,000 cubic feet
capacity. Even so, it is always wise to consult your local authority
because regulations differ from place to place. If you are rent-
ing a property it is also wise to consult the landlord before
erecting any garden buildings.

Greenhouse running costs depend on what you intend to do
with your greenhouse. There are numerous possibilities, and a
glance through the following pages will reveal several of them
in greater detail. In very few cases will greenhouse gardening be
a drain on your finances. Often it will save you money and even
bring a profit. This is particularly so if you grow your own
bedding plants for the garden, house plants, cut flowers, and
vegetables and fruits like lettuce, cucumbers, tomatoes, and
strawberries—all of which are quite easy crops to grow, and
expensive to buy in the shops.

You can do more with a greenhouse if you can provide a
little winter warmth, but this need not cost a great deal if gone
about in the right way. The subject of heating costs, saving fuel,
and economical heating apparatus, is dealt with in Chapter
Three, which is entirely devoted to greenhouse heating.

Greenhouse plants are generally quite cheap if bought as
young specimens or rooted cuttings. This is in fact the best
way to buy, and more successful results will be had than by
purchasing large, well-established plants. Older plants are not so
happy about sudden changes of environment. One of the most
economical ways to build up a collection of popular and unusual
plants is by growing from seed. Some of the more rare green-

house bulbs and orchids may be quite expensive. Obviously in these cases a full study should be made of the subject before risking much expenditure and, when possible, cheaper varieties tried first. Some of the exotics that need constant warmth may also be c'ostly, and again you should make sure that you can provide the conditions they require to keep them growing.

A greenhouse is usually acquired with basic essentials like staging. As you progress you will find that you can add refinements and equipment. Few of these are absolutely essential, and the most important are fortunately fairly cheap. (See Chapter Four.) Various gadgets and automatic aids can be added as your finances allow.

GREENHOUSE TYPES AND THE PLANTS YOU CAN GROW

Greenhouses are classified according to the temperatures maintained, as follows:

Unheated greenhouse	No heating at any time.
Cold house	Not allowed to fall below freezing.
Cool house	Minimum about 40/45°F (4/7°C)
Warm house	Minimum about 55°F (13°C)
Stove house (sometimes called 'hothouse')	Minimum about 65/75°F (18/24°C).

These classifications are not too rigid. Sometimes the 40/45°F house is described as a 'cold' greenhouse. The 55°F house called a warm house above may be described as an 'intermediate house'.

The most popular type of greenhouse is the type we describe here as the cool greenhouse. With a winter minimum of about 40°F (4°C) you can grow a vast range of plants from all over the world. Most of the plants from temperate zones will thrive, and many sub-tropical and tropical plants can be kept alive over winter, although they may not actually grow or prove decorative or useful then. The cool house is certainly the one to aim for if you are planning a general purpose greenhouse for growing all the favourite pot plants, and as an aid to the garden in raising bedding plants and for garden propagation. For this reason this book is mainly concerned with cool house work, but plants needing only the protection of glass, and no artificial heat at all, are also dealt with, together with plants demanding only frost protection. At this point it is worth drawing some extra attention to the possibilities of the unheated and the cold greenhouse.

THE UNHEATED GREENHOUSE

The purpose of this greenhouse is to give protection from the excesses of nature only—wind, cold, and rain. It can be used to grow better anything that normally grows outdoors in this country. However, it should be realised that hardy plants often object to being coddled with extra warmth and humidity and perhaps poor ventilation. The function of the unheated greenhouse must be to give weather protection only. It is ideal for all those plants that flower early and may have blooms prone to weather damage. Some examples are camellias, alpines, some of the more tender small shrubs, innumerable spring flowering bulbs, lilies, some succulents and cacti, ferns, fuchsias, hydrangeas, carnations, chrysanthemums, and many garden annuals and biennials grown in pots. In the last-mentioned case, a remarkable standard of perfection can be achieved—often so high that common annuals become something quite exotic!

It should be realised that an unheated greenhouse can always be provided with warmth at any time if convenient or necessary —say in early spring for starting plants into growth or for seed sowing and so forth. It can also be employed for giving winter protection from frost or excessive cold to roots of the more tender garden plants grown in terrace pots, small tubs, and other ornamental containers. Sometimes roots can also be taken up from garden borders and stored in an unheated greenhouse whilst they are dormant over winter.

THE COLD GREENHOUSE (not allowed to fall below freezing)

This type can be used for most of the purposes described for the unheated greenhouse, but often it is best to make use of the warmth for getting earlier flowers or crops and for protecting plants that are invariably killed or severely damaged by frost in the open. In those parts of the country where the winter is severe, all those plants that can be seen thriving outdoors only in the west and south will be very happy. The cold greenhouse is the best for growing many bulbs to perfection, and most of the spring flowering kinds will benefit by being gently forced, and flower much earlier. A very great range of plants that are mistakenly thought to need the cool house can also be grown quite easily in the lower temperature of the cold greenhouse. These include such popular subjects as cinerarias, salpiglossis, calceolarias, and—believe it or not—the exotic bird of paradise flower, *Strelitzia regina* (usually classed as a warm house plant!). There is much scope for further experiment in this respect.

YOU CAN HAVE MORE THAN ONE TYPE OF GREENHOUSE

Although it is usually best to begin with one type of greenhouse, usually unheated, cold, or cool, there is no reason why you should not indulge in, say, all three forms of greenhouse gardening at the same time. The best way to do this is to have a greenhouse divided into compartments, each being maintained to give the right conditions for the plants. Of course, you can always add further greenhouses, separately sited, to your garden if this is preferred. This subject is dealt with fully in the next chapter.

Those plants preferring a fair warmth can be economically grown in warmed frames inside a cold or cool greenhouse, provided they are reasonably low-growing and compact. See also pages 58 and 60.

CHAPTER TWO

The Structure

FROM the last chapter it will be seen that there are very many ways in which you can use a greenhouse. Before choosing a structure it is absolutely vital to be clear in your mind about what you want it for and what you propose to do. If you are taking up greenhouse gardening for the first time, or are still vague about the scope of the subject, it would be advisable to glance through the pages of this book and return later to the matter of choosing a greenhouse discussed in this chapter. The reason for this is that the market now abounds with different designs, shapes, sizes, and constructional materials, and one might suit your purpose better than another. A detailed account of these is given here.

CHOOSING PLANTS TO SUIT A GREENHOUSE AND VICE VERSA

A common mistake made by beginners in greenhouse gardening is that they try to grow too many different kinds of plant under the same conditions. Thought must be given to how much warmth, light or shade, or humidity and ventilation, the plants require, and every attempt made to provide the best environment. Too often, for example, cacti (which like light and a dry atmosphere) are put with shade-loving plants preferring moist air; or you may see fairly hardy plants, needing only frost protection, in a cool greenhouse where the temperature is unnecessarily high for them. Even more absurd examples are plants that may eventually reach a considerable height given a house with a very low roof, and large, high greenhouses used for nothing but low salad crops or the like, which could be more economically grown in frames.

With care and understanding a surprisingly wide range of different plants can be grown in the same greenhouse if proper consideration is given to where they are placed and how they are treated. More information on this will be found in Chapter Six. However, some greenhouse designs may be a better choice for plant collections than others. Also, if you are only interested in growing, for example, grapes, orchids, carnations, or alpine plants, you can get structures specially designed for them.

BASIC TYPES OF GREENHOUSE STRUCTURE

Today there are three types likely to be encountered by the average home gardener (see Fig. 1). These are the partially glazed (having a dwarf wall of timber, brick, concrete, or some

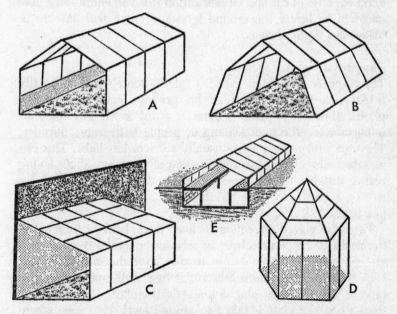

Fig. 1 BASIC MODERN GREENHOUSE SHAPES

A: Plant house. (This may be totally glazed or have a base wall on one or both sides.) B: Dutch light shape. C: Lean-to. D: Round house. E: Sunken house or 'pit'.

other material with the framework on top), the totally glazed
or glass to ground, and the lean-to. The lean-to can be with a
dwarf wall or it can be glass to ground. At one time a sunken
type, called a pit by professional gardeners, was often seen.
This can be used for purposes similar to those suited to a dwarf
wall type. However, the pit is a framework over an excavation
in the ground, and this means there is much less warmth loss
when it is artificially heated and temperatures tend to be more
steady. For this reason it was popular for propagation and
plants demanding a fair warmth. It is not ideal for the small
home garden. It is not easy to install and requires a fair building proficiency, drainage can be a problem on some sites, the
soil dug out has to be put somewhere, and it may take a good
deal of time and effort to build and erect. Even so, provided the
excavation is well constructed, it is still possible to get a framework made to fit over, assuming you are prepared to meet the
extra expense of the special fabrication this will entail—the door
end will be below the ground level and entry will have to be
made via a flight of steps.

The partially glazed greenhouse
This type is sometimes called a 'plant house'. It is generally
fitted with staging and used for growing collections of pot
plants, thus most work is done at waist level. This may be
important for the not-so-young or people with some infirmity.
The area under the staging usually receives less light. This can
be taken advantage of in the growing of the many shade-loving
plants suitable for the greenhouse. It should not be used for
storing rubbish (see page 76). It can also be used for blanching
(see page 207).

Partially glazed greenhouses may have brick, concrete, or
timber bases. Sometimes bases of asbestos or similar compositions
are encountered. These do not usually have the same degree of
heat retention as a more substantial base wall, and one advantage of the partially glazed house is that heat losses are less
than when the glass is taken to ground level. However, where
warmth is concerned much depends on the site. On an open
sunny site, any obstruction to the entry of the sun's radiation
means a loss of free heat. This could be a disadvantage in winter
when the sun can shoot up the temperature under glass even

when it is well below freezing outside on clear days. Green-houses with base walls are not ideal for plants that have to be grown initially from ground level or for tall plants that will need the entire height. Again this is because the lower regions may be considerably shaded by the side walls. Plenty of light is always worth having—you can always shade if necessary.

The totally glazed or glass-to-ground greenhouse
This type is probably the most versatile of all and the best choice if a general purpose structure is required. It can be fitted with staging or not, as preferred. If staging is fitted there is usually sufficient light underneath to keep many plants happy. When shelving is fitted too, it is surprising how many plants can be well grown because there is usually good overall penetration of light. As already stated, it is easy enough to provide shade when necessary. A glass-to-ground house could, if needed, be used in the same way as a partially glazed house if the lower panes were either filled in with timber or plastic or the glass removed and replaced with similar material. However, such treatment might well spoil the structure or its appearance. A glass-to-ground house is excellent for all tall plants and plants like tomatoes and chrysanthemums. Climbers can be accommodated, and there is plenty of scope for baskets and plants in hanging containers. Sometimes it is convenient to have staging only on one side, reserving the other for plants grown from ground level (see also page 74). A possible disadvantage is that when there is glass to ground, and a path alongside the greenhouse, there is the risk of glass breakage through being accidentally kicked or being struck with wheelbarrows or the like.

The totally glazed greenhouse is also a good choice for many plants or crops to be grown on a semi-commercial scale or in quantity such as winter salad crops and cut flowers. Although some of these can be just as well grown in frames which are more economical to heat, where there is much personal attention and cultivation needed it may be more convenient and pleasant to work inside during the winter.

The lean-to greenhouse
The most popular form of the lean-to is the conservatory or garden room and home extension built against the dwelling and

entered via a communicating door. A lean-to can also be built against a garden wall or against some garden building or garage. It is best for a lean-to to face south since there is then more scope because of the wider range of plants that can be grown with plenty of light available. However, even a north-facing lean-to can be useful for many shade-loving plants. In fact, numerous favourite greenhouse pot plants enjoy the shade in such circumstances, and a north-facing lean-to can become quite a successful conservatory if the right selection of plants is made.

Lean-to structures can of course have base walls or be totally glazed according to preference. Most of the garden room type lean-to buildings have base walls to give some privacy and reduce heat loss in winter. It may be of interest to know that an all-glass lean-to is of no use as a sun room if you want it for sun bathing: the rays that give a tan are absorbed by the glass and converted to warmth!

A lean-to is very economical to heat. Often it will derive sufficient warmth from a dwelling to keep it frost free. A lean-to erected against a sunny garden wall may hold considerable warmth overnight. The wall stores the heat it receives during the day and radiates it at night.

For vines, climbers, wall shrubs, and many fruits, the lean-to makes a splendid home. The plants can be trained against the rear wall or up into the roof (see also Chapter Twelve). It is also useful when rather high temperatures are to be maintained the year round.

GREENHOUSE SHAPE AND OTHER STRUCTURAL DESIGNS

The conventional greenhouse shape with vertical sides and gabled roof should not be dismissed just for the sake of being different and modern. For many years it has been found satisfactory and it uses space to its best advantage. The pitch of the roof leads condensation to one side and sheds rain well. It will be noticed that some greenhouses have the sides sloping at an angle—called the Dutch light design. Such structures could be made up from standard frames or Dutch lights also used for protecting low-growing flowers and vegetables, but the advantage of a side with a slight slope is that there is less glass thickness for the sun's rays to travel through. However clear a glass may appear to be to the eye, some light is always absorbed. This can make a slight difference to some crops, but mostly it is of concern to the commercial grower interested in early produce. However, a greenhouse with an excessive side slope can be undesirable for the home garden. It may be difficult to work close to the sides and is certainly not advisable if you want much staging. Some greenhouses are given a slightly circular slope to the roof and sides by placing panes at suitable angles. These designs also permit maximum light. Fortunately they are also designed to be practical in the home garden in most cases, and they can generally be equipped with the usual staging if desired.

In recent years several designs have appeared that have obviously been made for appearance or novelty rather than any serious growing. A bad fault is a roof that is too flat. This often leads to condensation drip which can be a nuisance in the conservatory or home extension type of structure; and it can cause constantly moist conditions at the roots of plants in winter, possibly causing them to rot.

There are a number of circular or hexagonal greenhouses available. This shape is not really new, and was popular in Victorian times for ornamental conservatories. A round house can look very attractive as a garden feature and when filled with decorative plants. It does not use space so well, and if you are looking for a practical design for general-purpose growing it would be advisable to choose the more conventional square or rectangle. A useful design is that which combines glass to ground one side with a dwarf wall or boarded base the other.

Another practical design is the combination greenhouse which has a shed attached. The shed may be alongside so that the greenhouse forms a lean-to, or it may be at one end. The shed can be used for potting and/or the storage of the usual garden tools. It should of course make an ideal potting compartment. It is best if the greenhouse can be entered from the shed, rather than the shed entered from the greenhouse. This means less opening of doors in winter to let cold air into the greenhouse section. The lean-to type of shed/greenhouse should have the glass facing south if possible when sited.

Also of recent appearance are mini-greenhouses. These are little more than plant cases generally mounted on legs for convenience. They are best used for choice plants of the decorative kind, although they can make useful propagators and they can be sited inside the greenhouse too. A plant case or mini-greenhouse inside can be heated to a high temperature economically, so that tropical plants can be grown in them—provided slow growing or small subjects are selected. Small orchids, and plants like African violets do very well in heated plant cases. A modern plant case of recent design is a tall structure mounted on castors. It can be opened up rather like a screen to give easy access to the plants displayed on shelves. It is called by the makers 'the flower tower'.

Compartments and extensions
Attention has already been drawn to the fact that it is important to give plants the environment they prefer with respect to temperature, humidity, ventilation and so on. So that this can be done for a wider range of plants under the same roof, it is most useful to have the greenhouse divided by partitions— one or more—with communicating doors. For example, a greenhouse divided into two compartments could have the first section at the door end devoted to plants needing little warmth or none at all, with the section at the far end used for more tender subjects. Similarly, one section can be well ventilated if necessary with the other maintained at a high humidity for those plants that like it. If you want several sections at different temperatures, the centre section or sections should be kept at the highest temperatures and the outer sections lowest. This way heating is more economical because losses are reduced. It is far better and more convenient than having several separate greenhouses.

Most makers now provide designs that have provision for the addition of partitions which can be easily fitted at any time. If an extension is made to a greenhouse it may be worth considering adding it as an extra compartment.

It is a common mistake for beginners to start off with a greenhouse that is rather small. Before long it is bursting at the sides with plants—and overcrowding often leads to trouble and disappointment. It is consequently wise to buy a greenhouse that can be extended, if and when the need arises, and to leave enough space for an extension when erecting the house.

MATERIALS OF CONSTRUCTION

The warmth-trapping effect of glass structures has already been briefly dealt with (page 15), in comparing glass with plastic. There are some more differences which are of considerable importance and must be taken into account when buying a greenhouse.

Plastic greenhouses

It must be understood that none of the plastics is a substitute for glass. Plastics are by nature very much softer. They can be scratched and abraded much more easily. In some circumstances they may weather badly, particularly on windy sites where there is much wind-blown grit, sand, or dust. Unfortunately, once this happens dirt seems to collect on the surface and become ingrained. It may be most difficult to clean off and attempts may lead to making the scratches and abrasion worse.

Some plastics also change chemically with time and on exposure to sunlight over long periods. They usually tend to become brittle and they may crack and disintegrate.

A further disadvantage is that water does not wet a plastic surface and form a film as it does on glass. This often causes condensation to collect in droplets. These may constantly drip, especially if the roof is insufficiently sloped. The drips can be annoying to anyone working below, particularly in the home extension type of lean-to, and harmful to plants by encouraging excessively wet conditions during the winter months when they should usually be kept carefully watered. The effect is worse when corrugated plastic sheeting is used for a roof and the slope is only slight. Condensation then drips from the entire length of the corrugations.

In their present state of development, plastics are not really a wise choice for a permanent greenhouse intended to be in operation for many years, and probably heated artificially. Only a few plastics of the more expensive type can be compared with glass for aesthetic appearance and clarity—clean, clear, sparkling glass is extremely pleasing. Some of the more flimsy plastics sag and buckle, and move about with the wind. They can look terrible and do anything but enhance the appearance of a garden when used in a structure.

In spite of these severe criticisms—which could well make plastic manufacturers my lifelong enemies!—to be fair they have a number of distinct advantages. They are lightweight and unbreakable. This makes them excellent for temporary plant protection, emergency repair, and for use when glass is impractical owing to breakage risk. They have in fact innumerable uses in the garden and in the greenhouse, which will be brought to the reader's attention later in this book. Used with common sense and understanding, they can be invaluable and may replace glass in many instances.

There are a number of different types of plastic classified according to their chemical composition. Polythene is perhaps the best known and most frequently used. Ordinary polythene is not recommended for outdoor garden work. It soon deteriorates on exposure to sunlight and disintegrates. For making temporary greenhouse structures, use a special grade resistant to ultra-violet light. Even then, don't expect it to last more than about two to three years (much depends on the site).

Flexible but stronger plastics are available, such as acetate sheeting and PVC, often sold under trade names. Some are reinforced with wire. These are of course longer lasting. For more permanent structures, rigid PVC sheets can be used, and these are usually corrugated for strength. One of the best grades for greenhouse construction is the ICI Novolux which is guaranteed for a number of years against weathering. ICI issue plans and designs for several 'greenhouse-type' structures. These are attractive but may have practical disadvantages for serious greenhouse work (see *Greenhouse shape*, page 24).

All plastics used as a replacement or in place of glass should be as clear, colourless, and as transparent as possible. Great care should be taken in cleaning so as not to scratch the surface. Only one shading paint is suitable for application to plastic without fear of scratching on removal. This is Coolglass, the electrostatic type described on page 55. Most plastics should not be put in close contact with creosoted timber, since they may become discoloured or damaged.

A recent plastic, perhaps the nearest to glass in appearance and hardness, is Transpex. This is an acrylic plastic similar to that from which dentures are made. At present it is expensive, but it is a good choice when something unbreakable but as near to glass in appearance as possible is required.

Greenhouse framework and glazing
Very recently there has been a great swing in favour of aluminium alloy framework. This is perfectly justified because it has valuable properties that make it ideal. It is rust-proof and rot-proof and it cannot warp. It is very resistant to oxidation and the effects of weather, and needs no painting, treatment, or maintenance whatsoever. A good aluminium framework will last more than a lifetime with practically no attention. It should be realised that this high praise applies to modern aluminium alloys. Some of the early alloys were far from weather resistant, and later development was greatly influenced by research into finding alloys of aluminium suitable for marine use and resistance to seawater. Aluminium framework is relatively cheap, and it is possible to make very sophisticated glazing bars permitting various simple forms of glazing with clips, and avoiding the application of putty. The various forms of patent glazing found among the manufacturers of aluminium houses all have the advantage of quick and easy glazing and simple removal of glass if necessary. Most aluminium houses are therefore easily taken down and can soon be put up again elsewhere if the need arises.

A new aluminium frame is shiny, but after a time the metallic sheen is lost due to a coating of protective aluminium oxide that forms through exposure to the air. More expensive frames are stove enamelled, and this finish retains its attractive appearance indefinitely. There is no objection to painting an aluminium framework with a gloss paint if desired, but it should be avoided if possible.

Aluminium frames can look out of place in some surroundings. They seem to fit modern gardens laid out in a formal style, and they go well with modern architecture; but in informal settings and when near period buildings, they can appear an intrusion. In such cases mellow timber might blend better, although white-painted frames can also look quite pleasant.

Galvanised steel is also used for framework, although on

comparing price and properties it is difficult to see any advantage over aluminium. Galvanised steel does need painting. If the zinc galvanised layer is damaged to expose the steel below, rust will start corrosion. Steel is also much heavier and less easy to work, and it certainly will need regular painting or maintenance.

All metal frameworks are of course very strong (or should be). They will usually take the weight of hanging baskets or plant containers, and shelving, without fear of the roof collapsing. They can usually be put together quickly and easily with a spanner and screwdriver, single-handed and without the requirement of strength, and even by very elderly or infirm people. Glazing can be done with great ease either because of simple patent glazing with plastic strip and clips, or by the use of a special non-hardening plastic putty. Ordinary linseed oil putty must never be used on metal frames. There are special compositions that never set hard and so allow the frame and glass to expand and contract with temperature so that the glass does not crack or break.

It is sometimes said that metal greenhouses are cold. This is doubtful. It is true that metal conducts heat better than timber, but in a metal greenhouse there is less area of frame and consequently more light entry with greater benefit from the sun's warmth. In any greenhouse the area of frame compared with the area of glass is so small that the difference is negligible in any case. However, in the dwarf wall-type greenhouse, or plant house (page 22), metal panelling for the base walls should be strictly avoided unless they are well lagged. A metal base will become icy cold and like refrigerator plates in winter, resulting in a fantastic heat loss.

All timber greenhouses will need maintenance from time to time, often every year. This constitutes painting or coating with one or other special timber dressings to restore appearance and ensure preservation. Perhaps the most popular wood is so-called western red cedar or similar 'cedar' types. This has an attractive appearance and blends almost anywhere. It is remarkably weather-resistant and has little tendency to warp or attract wood-destroying insects and fungi likely to cause rotting. Teak and oak are some other useful timbers. Cheap timbers and soft-woods are best avoided unless you are prepared to spend considerable time each year in their restoration, and preservation.

The glass used in greenhouses is 24-ounce sheet. It must be clear, colourless, and of good quality. Opaque or coloured glass is not suitable.

WHAT TO LOOK FOR WHEN BUYING A GREENHOUSE

Only you will know how much you can spend, and how large a greenhouse you can accommodate. Attention has already been drawn to the advantages of extendibility and compartments. It may be an advantage to have a structure requiring little maintenance or none at all, depending on the time you can afford. The appearance of the surroundings may have to be taken into account. Check on the advantages and disadvantages of the different greenhouse types outlined on page 20, and do make sure you know what you want to do with your greenhouse.

In general, look for strength of structure and workmanship of high standard. Timber with knot holes and imperfections will not do. If you have a house with boarded base in mind, make sure that it is substantial and not 'matchboarding'. Ordinary putty is best avoided if possible. There are excellent timber houses on the market having frames in which the glass is just slid in through grooves. Believe it or not, this form of glazing does not let in the rain, and the glass can always be instantly slid out for maintenance or access to the roof, or even for extra ventilation. Pre-glazed sections are available too, but don't overlook the need for an adequate roof slope.

Good ventilation is always important. See that the house has adequate vents. A small house will need at least one top and one side vent (see also page 80). Doors and vents must be well fitting when closed and not let in draughts, which will push up fuel bills drastically in winter. Often a sliding door is useful. It can be used for extra air like a ventilator and will not slam—but such doors can sometimes be ill-fitting. Don't buy the first greenhouse you see. Write to a wide range of the firms who advertise and get their illustrated catalogues. If possible follow up by a visit to their showplaces. Greenhouses can also be inspected at many garden centres, and at the national shows at Chelsea and Southport. (See also Chapter Four—vents, fittings, etc.)

SITING THE GREENHOUSE

If possible, choose an open site where it can get all the sun available—unless you are only interested in shade-loving plants. The conventional rectangular greenhouse is best orientated east–west so that the best use can be made of winter sunlight. Also it may then only be necessary to shade the south side in summer. It is wise to put the greenhouse as near the dwelling as possible. This allows convenient running of electricity and mains water to the greenhouse. It also means less walking about in the open for the gardener during rainy or snowy weather and the greenhouse is more likely to get regular visits. Siting the greenhouse near the dwelling is particularly desirable if you have a hot water boiler that needs regular stoking or fuel to carry about.

Make sure the site is well drained. Hollow ground is best avoided since it can attract frost as well as water. On very exposed sites some form of windbreak on the side of prevailing wind is desirable. This can be a belt of conifers (small ones) at a reasonable distance so as not to cast shadow, or something like a wall or fence. Don't have trees anywhere near. They cast shade, make the glass dirty, endanger it by the possibility of falling branches, and may harbour pests and diseases likely to attack greenhouse plants. Their roots may upset foundations too. As already mentioned, a potting shed near at hand is desirable. If the ideal site is not possible, don't be deterred from having a greenhouse. You will merely have to select plants that like the conditions you have to offer—there's always something that will grow anywhere.

ERECTION HINTS AND MAINTENANCE

Putting up a prefabricated greenhouse is simple and it can often be done without help in a weekend or so. Elaborate foundations are rarely necessary, but when a frame is to be erected on dwarf walls of brick or concrete some care must be taken. It is wise to get a professional bricklayer to carry out the work if you are not familiar with such a job. Plans for the base are issued by the makers of the frame.

With most prefabricated greenhouses it is possible to obtain plinths of concrete to set them on. This gives an excellent firm foundation easy to lay. The ground should of course be properly levelled and firm. Don't use freshly dug and cleared ground unless it is well firmed. The manufacturers always issue erection instructions and preparation of the site hints. When it is necessary to make some form of concrete foundation it is usually easily done by digging a shallow trench and filling with a very fluid mix of concrete which can find its own level. Concrete blocks or bricks can be set on top if necessary. All greenhouses with boarded base or glass-to-ground are best given a layer of brick or concrete to raise them just above ground level. If concrete plinths are supplied these will be adequate. This is to prevent the glass becoming splashed with mud from roof drip. It is also wise to make a path of concrete or paving slabs close up to the glass and surrounding the house again, to prevent splash and also so that access for cleaning and maintenance can be achieved.

A prefabricated greenhouse is usually supplied with the glass cut to size. Should it be necessary to cut glass, place it on several layers of newspaper, mark the line of the cut with a wax pencil or ink pen, and score along the line with an ordinary steel wheel glass cutter available from any builders' merchant. Use a straight edge to guide the cutter. A characteristic harsh hissing sound is emitted if the cutter is scoring the glass effectively. Keep the cutter upright and press down firmly. Turn the glass over on the paper and then tap along the score mark with the 'hammer' part of the cutter. The glass will usually crack easily along the line and can be pulled apart. Narrow edges can be removed by levering off with the notches in the glass cutter.

Never put putty over the glass when glazing a greenhouse. The putty is used as a bed for the glass. It should not be used to fill in the angle between the glass and the glazing bar as in domestic window glazing. Always be certain that the surface to be puttied is clean, free from flaking wood or paint, and dry. Cedar is best coated with a solution of shellac in methylated spirit first (knotting). This gives better adhesion and seals in natural oils. Ordinary woods can be painted first.

Lead paints are no longer used or recommended for greenhouses. Lead compounds can dissolve in condensation and the drip may convey poisonous salts to salad and other edible crops.

B

Most modern, quick-drying, hard gloss paints are suitable for greenhouses, but obviously the surface must be properly prepared. For sealing cracks and leaks, glazing tapes are useful, and there are a variety of widths and types on the market.

For cleaning glass a solution of the water softener Calgon can be used. Just brush on with a soft brush and rinse off with clean water. This chemical is relatively harmless to plants and most greenhouse framework. In obstinate cases, a bath stain remover can be used, but this must be applied with care and kept off framework in most cases. It will generally clean off the most difficult grime including lime deposits. It should also not be allowed to contact plants. Use according to label instructions.

CHAPTER THREE

Heating the Greenhouse

PROVIDING just enough warmth to keep out frost greatly
increases the possibilities of the greenhouse, and a little more
widens the scope still further. To heat a greenhouse need not be
an expensive business provided the right equipment is used and
every effort is made not to waste heat. In fact, this is rarely the
case, and much of the equipment on the market could do with
considerable improvement. Here an attempt will be made to
suggest heating apparatus that will prove economical, and the
correct way of using it will be explained as well as ways to
avoid heat waste—and hence reduce fuel bills.

ASSESSING HEATING REQUIREMENTS

It is of the utmost importance that you try to make a rough
estimate of the amount of heat your greenhouse will require.
When the exterior is at a lower temperature than the required
minimum, heat will of course be gradually lost to the outside. A
heater must replace this heat as it is lost and so maintain the
temperature desired. It should not raise the temperature unnecessarily since this will result in waste, but it should be able
to supply heat in sufficient quantity to cope with the most
severe winters. It should be appreciated that the greater the
temperature gradient between the interior and the exterior, the
faster heat will be lost. Every attempt must be made to maintain the lowest temperature necessary to ensure the well-being of
the plants.

The heat lost from a greenhouse can be calculated in terms
of British thermal units per hour (BTU/hr). The heat yield of
fuels and the heat output of heaters can also be assessed in terms

of the same units. It follows that if you know the amount of heat lost from your greenhouse at the coldest time of the year, you can choose a heater that will have sufficient output to make good the loss.

The heat lost will of course depend on the size of the greenhouse, the temperature you want to maintain, the outside lowest possible temperature for the area in which you live, and the materials of construction. Absolutely exact estimates are rarely possible, but the assessment is extremely useful and it will save installing heaters that are totally inadequate or with outputs far in excess of what is necessary.

Since different materials of construction and the surface area they cover will affect the rate at which heat is lost, the calculation involves factors for glass, timber, brick, and so on, and most ordinary gardeners find it somewhat tedious. It is always better to make a small over-estimate, since if the recommendations given later are followed there is no need to run a heater at the maximum output all the time. For this reason it is convenient to make the calculations assuming that the greenhouse is an all-glass structure—which means the maximum heat loss. For greenhouses with base walls and lean-to types, the figures already worked out for you in the table given here will be lower, but they will still be a good guide to the size of heater or its heat output that should be installed, and you will certainly have no need to worry about problems during an exceptionally severe winter.

The following table assumes a possible minimum temperature of approximately 12° frost (20°F or minus 7°C) and the figures should allow the temperature required in the greenhouse to be increased a few degrees if preferred. (See also *Conserving warmth*, page 45.)

Since electricity is an important greenhouse heater fuel, the rating in watts is given for convenience. All good paraffin heaters and hot water heaters fired by solid fuel or oil should have their BTU/hr output ratings stated by the manufacturers. If your greenhouse size does not exactly correspond with the approximate dimensions given in the table it is good enough to choose the nearest. You can also add figures. If, for example, you had a large greenhouse 10 feet by 30 feet long, you can add

APPROXIMATE GREENHOUSE HEATER RATINGS

| Greenhouse size (in feet) | Approximate temperature required | | | | | |
| | 50°F (10°C) | | 40°F (4°C) | | 35°F (2°C) | |
	BTU/hr	Watts	BTU/hr	Watts	BTU/hr	Watts
5×6	6,000	1,800	4,000	1,200	3,000	900
6×6	7,000	2,100	4,800	1,400	3,600	1,000
6×8	8,600	2,500	5,700	1,700	4,200	1,200
6×10	10,000	2,900	7,000	2,000	5,200	1,500
6×14	12,500	3,700	8,400	2,500	6,200	1,800
8×8	10,400	3,000	7,000	2,000	5,200	1,500
8×10	11,700	3,400	7,800	2,300	5,800	1,700
8×12	13,200	3,900	8,800	2,600	6,600	1,900
8×14	14,000	4,200	9,300	2,700	7,000	2,000
10×10	14,600	4,300	9,800	2,900	7,300	2,100
10×15	19,200	5,600	12,900	3,800	9,700	2,800
10×20	23,600	6,900	15,800	4,700	11,800	3,500

the BTU/hr rating given for 10 by 20 feet to that given for 10 by 10 feet. For a minimum temperature of 32°F (a frost-free greenhouse) you would therefore need 11,800+7,300 = 19,100 BTU/hr, or about 5,600 watts if electricity is used. In a case like this two 3,000-watt electric heaters could be installed, for example.

If we consider a small greenhouse, say 5 by 6 feet, and we again use electricity, it will be seen that a 1,000-watt heater will prove more than adequate. Actually if the heater has an efficient thermostat it would not matter if a 2,000-watt heater was used: it would only be switched on by the thermostat when the temperature fell to the figure at which the thermostat is set. No heat or electricity would be wasted. What happens is that if a heater with a higher output is used, it will be switched on less frequently. However, for technical reasons it is less economic to have unnecessarily excessive ratings.

The importance of the thermostat

In case some readers are not familiar with the thermostat and its operation it may be worth explaining more fully. Of vital importance for economic greenhouse heating and for effective temperature control for the plants' well-being, the thermostat is any device that controls temperature by regulating the fuel supply to the heater. It usually works by certain metals expanding or contracting with temperature change, and the movement operating the flow of fuel, the flow of air to solid fuel so that the speed with which it burns is regulated, or electrical contacts. In the case of electricity very accurate thermostatic control is possible, and in some types of heater using other fuels electricity is used only so that its thermostatic accuracy can be taken advantage of, and the current may be used only to operate motors or electromagnets to govern the flow of oil, air, or solid fuel.

Accurate and reliable thermostatic control is a feature to look for when buying a greenhouse heater, but more information will be found under the various heater type headings in the following pages. A thermostat will usually have a dial graduated in degrees and cover a range from just above freezing to about 90°F (32°C). The indicator on the knob should be set to the temperature required. Sometimes the actual temperatures are not indicated, in which case the temperature must be set in the first place by reference to a thermometer. In all cases it is wise to check correct maintenance of the temperature desired by referring to an accurate thermometer, and to then adjust the pointer setting if necessary. (See also page 52.)

COST OF GREENHOUSE HEATING

Nowadays it is impossible to put any accurate cost to heating since the prices of fuels are changing rapidly—unfortunately most often rising. Fuel prices may also vary from place to place and according to the quantity in which they are bought. Bulk buying may cut costs dramatically. If, then, a particular fuel like anthracite or paraffin is being used for domestic heating, it may be worth choosing a similar form of heating for the greenhouse.

If the BTU heat output of a fuel is known, it is possible to make a rough assessment of cost from its current price. This assumes you know the rating of your heater and the amount of heat needed in terms of BTU which you can get from the table already given. The BTU heat output of various fuels is given opposite:

Paraffin :   157,000 BTU/gallon
Solid fuels :   12,000/14,000 BTU/lb
Electricity :   3,412 BTU/unit
Fuel oil :   165,000 BTU/gallon
Liquid propane or butane :   21,500 BTU/lb
Gas fuels :   100,000 BTU/therm

These output figures all assume efficient use of the fuel. Poor heating apparatus and thermostatic control, and bad installation, can waste at least half the possible output. Although the figures may seem to differ widely, in practice there is not an enormous difference in the price of fuels. At the present time, paraffin oil is probably the cheapest, and bottled gas such as propane or butane the dearest. It should, however, be realised that some fuels that may appear expensive may lend themselves to more efficient combustion or use than cheaper kinds, and thus in the long run cancel out the apparent higher cost.

If you know the price of your fuel per gallon, pound, unit, or therm, and the amount of heat you require per hour for your greenhouse, it is only a matter of simple arithmetic to arrive at a rough cost. Don't forget that the heater will be probably out of use during the warmer months of the year. Also costs will vary depending on where you live in the country. In the colder north the heaters may be in greater use than in the south, and the severity of the winter will have a considerable influence.

VARIOUS FORMS OF GREENHOUSE HEATING

Paraffin-oil wick-type heaters
These are still the most widely used. They have the advantage of being inexpensive, of using paraffin which is relatively cheap compared with other fuels, and very convenient to use. All greenhouse owners should have a good paraffin heater handy in case of emergency, whatever other form of heating may be installed. Breakdowns, and particularly strikes, can make electricity and fuel deliveries unreliable. Abnormally cold weather may also make an extra paraffin heater useful.

Unfortunately there are disadvantages, but some can be overcome. Firstly a wick heater is difficult to control by thermostat. There are models available, but they still need improvement.

The main problem at present is to achieve a sufficiently low heat output at the 'off' or pilot light stage. A flue is a desirable feature, since thermostatic models are at present likely to produce fumes harmful to plants.

The ordinary oil heater of course needs frequent attention so that the wick can be adjusted as the weather fluctuates; otherwise there may be much waste of paraffin. It is not the ideal choice if you have to be away from your greenhouse for long periods.

Another important point is that when paraffin burns it produces about its own volume of water released as vapour, and much carbon dioxide. The carbon dioxide doesn't matter—it can be beneficial to plants—but the water vapour can be a nuisance. In winter it is best to keep the greenhouse atmosphere on the dry side, or at any rate not encourage excessive humidity (see also page 79), so ventilation is necessary. Ventilation is also essential to let in air for combustion of the paraffin. If insufficient air gets to the burner, fumes will be evolved. The ventilation means entry of cold air so that the full BTU output of the paraffin is not really used to greatest advantage.

Many people seem to have trouble with paraffin heaters, but it is nearly always their own fault. We have already seen that care must be taken over adequate ventilation. The burner must also be kept clean and the wick trimmed according to the maker's recommendation—or again there will be fumes. Don't spill paraffin on the burner when filling so that it can be volatilised by the warmth of the heater, and never use crude paraffin—only the domestic grades are suitable. Crude paraffin such as 'washings' from garages may contain sulphur compounds and other chemicals that burn to produce gases extremely poisonous to plants. Some plants are extremely sensitive to fumes from paraffin heaters. Tomato seedlings, schizanthus, and some orchids, are examples. Such plants will usually show browning or blackening of the leaf edges and yellowing of foliage. On orchids and thick-leaved plants this may not appear for some time after initial exposure to the fumes.

When buying an oil heater it is specially important to see that you get one with an adequate BTU/hr heat output. Many oil heaters are far too small for the job they are expected to do.

It is not good enough to know that a heater will burn for so many hours on so much paraffin: the heat it yields must be sufficient and you don't get this for nothing. For example, to keep a 6×10 feet greenhouse frost-free you will have to have an oil heater burning about a quarter of a pint of paraffin per hour, bearing in mind the BTU output of paraffin is about 157,000 BTU/gallon (see tables on pages 37 and 39).

Do not use domestic oil heaters for the greenhouse. There are specially designed models. The blue flame type is recommended. Owing to an efficient air supply to the burner the paraffin is more efficiently oxidised and there is less risk of fumes. Catalytic-type oil heaters have been known to evolve fumes in some circumstances, but these are again mostly employed for domestic heating. Greenhouse oil heaters often have pipes or ducts to spread the heat and this is a good feature to look for. Some may have hot water pipes attached as well as hot air ducts. Often a humidity trough is fitted which is intended to be filled with water, but this is not a desirable practice in most cases. As already pointed out, paraffin burns to evolve much water vapour and there is rarely need to increase the humidity still further. Such troughs can, however, sometimes be used for vaporising pesticides.

Other good design features to look for in oil heaters include stainless steel lamp chimney, oil level indicator, and separate oil tank connected to give automatic filling via a constant level device. In any case, an oil reservoir of fair size is desirable to reduce the chore of filling. Copper tanks are best since they are less likely to rust and lead to leaks.

Electrical heating

Electricity has already proved itself to be perhaps the most efficient and effective greenhouse heating fuel. Modern technology has made it extremely reliable and there is rarely trouble from breakdown for long periods. It is regrettable that strikes have tended to bring electricity into disfavour, but we can only hope that the future will resolve such difficulties.

With world shortages of other fuels it seems that electricity will have to become the main fuel eventually, its source being atomic energy. Electrical heating may therefore be a wise investment for new installations. Moreover, electricity can be used in so many other ways that it is of great benefit to lead a power cable to the greenhouse (see also Chapter Four, page 63). Advice notes on electrical installation are given by suppliers.

Undoubtedly the most efficient and convenient form of heater for the average home greenhouse is the fan heater. This, used in conjunction with an accurate thermostat, will control temperature to within about one or two degrees and there is virtually no waste of heat or fuel. The plants also enjoy the air circulation that the fan gives and excellent healthy growing conditions prevail. There is no contamination of the air with products of combustion with any form of electrical heating, and there is no need for any attention whatsoever for very long periods. The air circulation reduces trouble from fungoid diseases dramatically.

Some greenhouse fan heaters have a fan that is constantly running and a built-in thermostat that only switches on the heat when necessary. With this type the warmed air is consequently kept vigorously stirred after the thermostat switches off the heat. This is not an advantage, since the air whirling around the cold greenhouse sides will quickly lose its heat. Still air is a poor heat conductor, but set in motion the heat transfer is rapid. The insulating properties of static air are taken advantage of in double glazing where the trapped air forms the heat barrier. The best fan heater should consequently have a separate thermostat that controls both fan and heat. This way warm air is supplied as needed. When the fan is off the air remains relatively motionless—although there will still be some movement caused by convection. The arrangement gives the benefit of intermittent air circulation, but quick heat loss due to constant circulation is avoided.

Because there is no contamination of the air and no need for extra ventilation, a fan-heated greenhouse can be left practically sealed for several months during severe weather, which further cuts waste. Another important point is that the greenhouse can be lined with polythene to give a 'double glazing' effect (see page 45). With a lining it does not matter if a continuously running fan is used because the warm air cannot come into direct contact with the glass. In large greenhouses it is also possible to use a continuously running fan without fear of too much waste of heat, since the greater volume of air will be circulated less quickly. This of course assumes that the fan is of normal proportions.

The usual rating for fan heaters is from about one to three kilowatts. Switching to allow different levels of heat output is a desirable feature. More than one heater can be used if necessary. The fans are usually designed to render lubrication very infrequent, and maintenance is negligible.

Convection heaters are sometimes used but seem to be uncommon. These consist of a cabinet with holes at the top and bottom. Heating wires inside warm the air which rises to flow out at the top. Cold air is drawn in at the bottom. Another popular electric heater is the tube. Heating tubes are used in a similar way to the old hot water pipes. However, since they are hollow, and have only a heating wire inside, they hold little heat when switched off. Fan heaters and convection heaters share this excellent characteristic. It means that they all respond instantly to a thermostat and accurate temperature control is possible.

Ordinary domestic electric fires of any kind are not suitable for the greenhouse and may be very dangerous where there is water and moisture. The radiant heat some give is damaging to plants.

When it is possible to choose your own thermostat, always select the rod type with variable temperature control. A thermostat should always be checked by reference to a thermometer regardless of whether it has the degrees marked or not. The scale is often inaccurate. Also check after a thermostat has been out of use for some time, before using the heating system again. (See also page 37.)

Hot water pipe heating

Hot water pipes have been used for many years. In their modern form they are still useful, especially when high temperatures are to be maintained. For technical reasons they are more efficient and economical when operating at higher temperatures. Owing to their great heat-holding capacity they respond slowly to thermostatic control, but they react faster at higher temperatures.

Electricity can be used for hot water pipes by means of an immersion heater. This, however, is not recommended because it tends to work out very expensive. Generally, solid fuel or oil-fired boilers are preferred. Natural gas could also be used. There are a variety of boilers on the market. The modern ones are very easy to install and can be put in and operating in a matter of hours. No major alterations to the greenhouse are necessary.

Modern solid fuel boilers are designed to reduce stoking to the minimum and also the clearing of ash. Most have a reasonable thermostatic control, but obviously this cannot be so accurate as with more easily controlled fuels. Oil-fired boilers are of course semi-automatic and need little attention. Small installations use paraffin as fuel, but larger ones may use fuel oil with an electric pump to supply the fuel to the boiler. Oil is usually better controlled thermostatically.

In all hot water pipe systems the maker's instructions regarding installation must be followed exactly. The pipes must rise gently from the boiler. Nowadays aluminium alloy pipes are preferable to heavy cast iron. Boilers are always rated in terms of heat output as BTU/hr (see table on page 37), but manufacturers will advise if given details of your greenhouse. The pipe length necessary to give out sufficient heat must be considered. An idea of the approximate pipe length needed can be obtained from the following table.

Greenhouse temperature	Length of 4-inch piping (in feet) for every 1,000 cubic feet
45–50°F (7–10°C)	36
50–55°F (10–13°C)	42
60–65°F (15·5–18·5°C)	50
70–75°F (21–24°C)	55
80°F (26°C)	60

It is of no use having a large boiler if there is insufficient surface area of pipe to distribute and radiate the heat. Only the fuels recommended by the boiler maker must be used. The pipes are best filled with rain water or other soft water initially. They may have to be topped up via the expansion chamber situated at the far end of the pipe run from time to time. Large installations may have a mains constant level system of the water tank and ball valve type.

Natural gas heating
Coal gas is not easily adapted for greenhouse heating because both it, and its products of combustion, are poisonous to plants. Natural gas is perfectly safe and on combustion it gives the same products as paraffin—carbon dioxide and water vapour. For natural gas heaters, the comments regarding ventilation and humidity made under *Paraffin-oil wick-type heaters* apply (page 39), assuming that the natural gas heater is allowed to pass its combustion products into the greenhouse atmosphere.

It is usually more convenient to use a piped natural gas supply. A special natural gas greenhouse heater is available. This is neat, portable to some degree, and thermostatically controlled, but there could be a better arrangement for heat distribution. Bottled natural gas—propane or butane—can be used but tends to be expensive. Where gas cannot be piped these can, however, prove convenient. Propane is advisable when the storage bottle is to be kept outside the greenhouse. Butane may not volatilise sufficiently quickly in very cold weather. The larger the bottles or cylinders, the more economical these liquefied gases become.

CONSERVING GREENHOUSE WARMTH

Obviously ill-fitting doors and vents and broken glass will let in much unwanted cold air and shoot up fuel bills enormously. All such sources of draught must be dealt with. Many people have found that lining the greenhouse with polythene cuts fuel bills dramatically (as much as 40 per cent is theoretically possible). As mentioned above, electrically heated houses respond well to 'double glazing' of this sort. Use the thinnest polythene available. It must be as clear as possible. Remember that it is the static air trapped between the plastic and the glass that forms the insulation, not the polythene. It must be put up to avoid gaps and it should not be possible for air to flow freely between the plastic and glass. In timber houses the lining is easily put up with drawing pins. A half-inch to one-inch space between the glass and plastic is ideal. In metal houses it is usually necessary to fasten pieces of timber batten to the interior of the glazing bars. An adhesive like Evostick will do the trick if used when the surfaces are dry. The drawing pins can then be pressed into the wood. With some aluminium greenhouses that have an inner flange on the glazing bars it is often possible to fasten the polythene with clothes pegs. Special suckers are also available for making the job of lining easier. The edges of polythene sheet can be held together with a smear of glycerine.

Correct positioning of heaters will do much to avoid waste. No part of the greenhouse structure should be allowed to become heated to a temperature higher than necessary. Don't put heating tubes too near the glass. If possible spread them around the greenhouse to even out heat distribution. Unfortunately they are often sold mounted in banks. A fan heater should go at a central position at one end, and a convection heater slightly to one side at a central position in the greenhouse. Oil heaters should also go slightly to one side to give better heat circulation. During a very severe winter or in an emergency, old blankets or sacking can be thrown over the roof at night to conserve heat. Such covering must be removed for daylight. Dirty glass will radiate heat more readily, so see that the glass is kept sparkling clean in winter. This will also let in as much of the sun's radiation as possible.

Unless dirt has got between the glass and polythene in a lined greenhouse, and provided the polythene is clear and that light entry is good, a lining can often be left up for the summer months. Much depends on how much light the plants you are growing require.

Storage heaters

Some people have used storage heaters with an off-peak tariff for greenhouse heating. However, this type is difficult to control thermostatically. There may be too much heat at times and not enough when it is wanted. They are best used as background warmth with another heat source maintaining the maximum thermostatically.

Oil heaters with electric heaters

As with storage heaters, an accurately controllable electric heater can be used to keep the maximum level of heat with an economical paraffin heater for background warmth. This way the more expensive fuel has less work to do. However, be sure that if fan heating is used with paraffin lamps there is no current of air likely to upset combustion or interfere with a lamp's working.

CHAPTER FOUR

Accessories and Fittings

As purchased, a greenhouse is usually supplied with the bare essentials only, and most interior and exterior fittings have to be added according to your growing requirements.

VENTILATION

A greenhouse should have one top ventilator and one side vent for every 6 to 8 feet of length assuming a width of up to about 10 feet. For alpine plants, and many of the more hardy annuals and cut flowers, more ventilation is desirable (see pages 31, 70, 80). It is an advantage not to have the vents all on one side of the greenhouse so that they can be opened according to wind direction (see page 53). In rare cases ventilators are supplied as extras. Should this occur, do not be tempted to cut costs by doing without a ventilator or two. You don't have to open ventilators if it is not necessary, but it is wise to have them so that they can be used freely when the plants require plenty of air.

The conventional hinged ventilator with stay bar is still fitted to many greenhouses, but there are now louvred vents in some aluminium framed houses, and sliding vents (patent) in Alton greenhouses that can be fitted as optional extras or alternatives in their timber range. Unfortunately some louvred vents do not close to give an airtight seal. This can lead to draught in winter and should be checked when purchasing. The sliding vents on the Alton range are reasonably draught free, and have the advantage that they are fitted as bottom ventilation. This is in the glass-to-ground type of house only. Some other types of greenhouse are also designed to permit the vents to be fitted at staging level or at ground level. There is some controversy about which is best, but to keep the greenhouse cool when the weather is very warm the ground-level vents are preferable. The hot air tends to quickly rise and escape through the top ventilators, and this draws cool air in at ground level, thus giving a complete air change. However, it has been argued that cool air, being heavier than warm air, will fall to ground level on entering from a staging-level vent.

STAGING

At one time staging was nearly always supplied as the conventional slatted type made up from timber battens. It is now possible to have metal frameworks supporting either wire netting (or plastic) or sheet asbestos or similar material. In winter a net or slatted staging is desirable so that air and warmth can circulate, particularly in greenhouses equipped with a fan heater. The more recently introduced net type staging has given excellent growing conditions.

In summer, it may be convenient to cover such staging with plastic sheet or some similar material and spread this with any

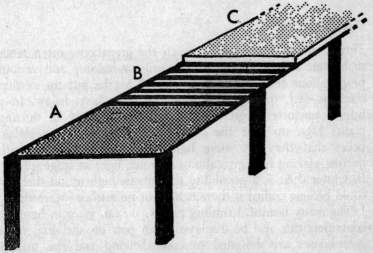

Fig. 2 TYPES OF STAGING

A: Wire or plastic mesh. B: Slats. C: Moisture-retaining material (spread over plastic or in trays).

moisture-retaining substance such as grit, vermiculite, peat, or
the like (see Fig. 2). This aids greenhouse humidity (see page
79; also see *Automation*, Chapter Five, page 70). Some people
prefer to make their own staging from brick or concrete. This
type of staging, being bulky, will hold considerable warmth.
It is quite a good choice for greenhouses where plants demanding moderate warmth are being grown. A substantial staging
will absorb warmth during the day if the greenhouse has been
heated by the sun, and evolve it during the night. Temperatures
tend to fluctuate less easily. It will act in the manner of a
storage heater.

Never take any form of solid or covered staging close up to
the greenhouse sides. Always leave a gap of a few inches. This
is to avoid currents of cold air, that may form in the vicinity
of the glass, from falling and circulating on the surface of the
staging.

The whole greenhouse need not be fitted with staging. Sometimes it is convenient to leave free the side getting the most
light, so that plants can be grown from ground level. This particularly applies to glass-to-ground houses and those with glass-
to-ground one side and a dwarf wall or boarded base the other.

SHELVING

This is useful in the spring when the greenhouse often tends
to become full of plants being raised for bedding and various
propagations from cuttings. It should not be put up so that
shade is cast, to their detriment, on the plants below. In a
bright, uncluttered greenhouse there is no point in putting
plants high up near the glass on shelving in the mistaken
belief that they get more light. Modern greenhouses with
narrow glazing bars give almost as much light at staging level.
In winter there is a possibility that plants high up on shelving
could become chilled if there is little or no artificial warmth.

The many beautiful trailing plants you can grow in hanging
containers can also be displayed from pots on shelving. Most
greenhouses are designed to take shelving and the makers
supply the necessary fittings. For safety these should always be
used, since pots of moist compost can be extremely heavy when
lined up on a shelf.

THE GREENHOUSE FLOOR

This is a very important matter, since so many beginners seem to think that the floor is to be grown in. *If the ground soil of a greenhouse is used there is invariably trouble.* Today we recommend using only properly prepared composts in containers (see Chapter Seven, page 92). The floor is therefore best only regarded as for walking on, or standing things on. If a greenhouse border effect is wanted, a trough can be used to contain the compost. This can be sunk into the ground, the lining being thick polythene with a few holes or perforations for drainage, or the polythene can be draped over a frame of timber boards resting on the greenhouse floor. The depth of the trough or frame will depend on the plants being grown. Alternatively, such containers can be filled with peat and the plants in pots plunged in this. (Fig. 6, page 74. See also Chapter Six, page 74, and *Tomatoes*, page 194.)

A greenhouse floor can be of concrete or similar material. However, this often has the disadvantage that water can collect in puddles. It also holds little moisture over long periods, and this may be a disadvantage in summer because of its poor contribution to atmospheric humidity (see page 79). Generally it is simple and convenient to use the ground on which the greenhouse stands. This can be pressed firm and covered with shingle or gravel, of the type used for drives and paths, to give a clean, neat appearance. To make walking more comfortable, concrete paving slabs can be put down on top where required. A floor of this type will hold plenty of moisture and keep the greenhouse nicely humid in summer. In winter it should be allowed to dry out so as to keep the air more dry. Any total weedkiller can be watered into such a floor freely—sodium chlorate or any of the proprietary path weedkillers—but plants must of course always be stood on plastic or paving so that their roots cannot enter the treated ground.

POTS AND GROWING CONTAINERS

These are discussed in detail in Chapter Seven. Generally plastic pots will be found the more convenient nowadays, but a few clay pots may be useful to have available for some special purposes. Wooden seedtrays are not recommended (see page 233).

For hanging baskets the plastic-covered wire type is useful, but there are some designed for easier watering and to avoid drip. Many other containers for hanging and putting on walls can be found in the shops, but for the greenhouse these should always be critically examined for practicability. In general it is best to avoid highly decorative containers of any kind, and also those in colours likely to detract attention from the plants. Neutral colours, such as terra-cotta, green, and sometimes white, and also black, are the wisest choice.

THERMOMETERS

At least one accurate thermometer is vital to the successful running of any greenhouse. Undoubtedly the best choice is the maximum and minimum type. This has tiny indicators inside the glass capillary which can be set with a magnet or, in the newest designs, by gravity. There are also dial types. The indicators will show the highest and the lowest temperatures that have occurred during the time of inspection and when they were set. For example, by setting the indicators in the evening you can see in the morning just how low and how high the temperature has been overnight. This is really the only way to properly assess any heating system. It is also invaluable in summer to check whether overheating has occurred during an absence, and the effectiveness of shading.

It is wise to buy a good quality maximum and minimum thermometer. Cheap kinds are often made from metals that corrode in the greenhouse atmosphere, the graduations becoming illegible after a short time.

Other thermometers may be required for propagators or for checking soil or compost temperatures in pots, plunges, and the like. Special soil thermometers are available.

It is hoped that temperatures will eventually be given in the Centigrade scale. This is extremely simple, with freezing point being 0° and the boiling point of water being 100°. In this book both Centigrade and Fahrenheit are given. For measuring air temperature numerous dial-type thermometers have come on to the market. These are usually reasonably accurate. For composts and liquids, glass thermometers with mercury, or spirit coloured red, are the most practical.

EXTERIOR FITTINGS

In some cases it is a good idea to make wire frames to go over doors or ventilators to keep out birds or domestic pets, and sometimes small children. All can do much damage in a few minutes. Much depends on individual circumstances and the greenhouse situation as to whether it is worth going to the trouble.

Gutters can be had to fit most greenhouses, or the ordinary domestic plastic guttering can be fitted if necessary. Guttering is useful to lead away water and prevent excessive saturation of the greenhouse floor due to seepage in winter. It also prevents mud splashing on glass-to-ground greenhouses. Unfortunately many people think that the collected rainwater should be used for their greenhouse plants. In fact, to do this is to invite disaster. Rainwater collected from a roof is likely to contain weed seeds, and innumerable pests and diseases. Often the matter is made worse by storage in open butts in which dead leaves and filth accumulates, all adding to the pest and disease build-up. Don't, then, use such water for irrigation in your greenhouse. There is no point in using carefully prepared and sterilised compost if you do (see also page 78).

When a greenhouse is sited some distance from the dwelling house it is often useful to fit a weather vane. This greatly helps in selecting the best ventilators to open for ventilation, seeing which is the lee-side and noticing changes in wind direction. In some areas wind rushing through a greenhouse can create devastation, and in gales can even damage the structure if vents are opened directly facing the tempest. Modern weather vanes are now available in aluminium alloy in many attractive designs that may enhance the appearance of a greenhouse.

BLINDS

Shading when necessary is of the utmost importance, and many beginners in greenhouse gardening fail dismally merely because they do not appreciate this fact. In winter the greenhouse benefits from all the sun it can get, but in summer the sun-trap effect can be too much of a good thing. An unshaded greenhouse in a sunny position in summer can become so hot that everything inside is ruined in a few hours—even tropical plants! Nearly all greenhouses will require shading at some time or other. (See also Chapter Six.)

The purpose of shading is to protect the plants from intense light, especially the shade lovers, and to keep the greenhouse cool.

To keep down temperature, the sun's rays must be stopped *before* they get inside the greenhouse. This means some form of exterior blind or a preparation applied to the glass that will reflect the heat rays away *before* they get through. For many years either blinds were fitted to the greenhouse roof or a shading paint was applied to the glass when necessary. The former is somewhat expensive, the blinds usually having to be made specially to fit any particular greenhouse. However, blinds have the advantage that the shade can be removed easily with changes in weather. Blinds are available made from timber slats or bamboo, and possibly aluminium will soon appear on the market.

Blinds made from solid materials should of course let some light through—hence the slats. Owing to the change in the sun's position, the light passing through on a sunny day will gradually move over the plants so that exposure to the sun is not prolonged. Blinds made from fabric or plastic and in the sheet form should be semi-transparent, and so should shading paints applied to the glass.

Blinds are best fitted on rails so that they do not come into close contact with the roof. This is so that heat absorbed from the sun is not directly transferred to the roof. A few inches of air space between the blinds and the roof is desirable to allow dissipation of the heat absorbed to the air.

It should be appreciated that blinds fitted to the interior of the greenhouse may protect the plants from injury caused by intense sunlight but will not keep down temperature so well. This will be understood by reference to the section on *How the greenhouse works*, on page 14. Roller blinds made from various materials are available for interior fitting where this method is thought more convenient.

For many years green shading materials were applied to glass. This is in fact *quite wrong* and due to complete misunderstanding of the principles involved in shading. *It is of no advantage to have any shading material, including blinds, coloured green.* The green pigment in plants actually absorbs energy—for photosynthesis. It is cool in a woodland glade because this energy is being taken up by the foliage and what is not used is dissipated to the air. When a green substance is applied to glass the situation is absolutely different. Energy will be absorbed and transferred directly to the glass. A green-shaded greenhouse can actually get hotter than an unshaded one !

Research in this country and in Holland has proved that the best colour is white. In fact this has been known to people in tropical countries for centuries who avoid dark-coloured clothing and often whitewash their homes. In sunlight a dark surface becomes much hotter than a light-coloured one. Shading paints applied to the glass should therefore be *white*. In the past shading paints had to be applied and left for most of the summer owing to the difficulty of removal. They were also often troublesome to prepare and apply.

ELECTROSTATIC SHADING PAINT

This has completely revolutionised greenhouse shading and is a quite new introduction. The material is called Coolglass. It is a liquid concentrate that can be diluted with water instantly to give any degree of shading required. It is an intense white and is formulated to reflect back from the glass those rays that cause scorching of foliage and overheating of the greenhouse when the sun is powerful. The diluted concentrate can be brushed on the glass or applied with a spray. The particles are so minute that there is no risk of sprayers becoming clogged.

The curious property of Coolglass is that once applied and dry (it dries almost at once), it cannot be washed off by even torrential downpours. The particles remain attached to the glass by presumably an electrostatic attraction. Coolglass can, however, be immediately removed by wiping off with a dry duster—just like wiping a blackboard. The shading can consequently be applied or removed much in the same way as a blind according to weather changes, but its cost is negligible in comparison to the cost and installation of blinds. It is also an advantage because the degree of shade can be varied and adjusted so easily. For example a weak dilution can be applied early in the year, and this oversprayed or removed and replaced with a stronger concentration as the sun increases in intensity. It is non-poisonous and will not damage structures, but it should be applied with care to red cedar frames so as not to spoil the wood's appearance. It is best applied with a brush in this case.

Coolglass is the only shading safe for plastic, since it will not scratch the surface on wiping off. Some plastics may not wet very easily. This can usually be overcome by adding a few drops of washing-up liquid to the diluted concentrate. Severely scratched or abraded plastic is best not treated with shading paint of any kind, since it may become ingrained and difficult to remove. Adhesion may be unsatisfactory on polythene.

Where the roof is not easily accessible, Coolglass can be applied with a brush or sponge tied to a stout cane or pole. (See Fig. 7, page 81.) It can be similarly removed by attaching a dry duster to a soft broom, for example.

MISCELLANEOUS AIDS AND GADGETS

In all greenhouses potting has to be done at some time or other. If there is no potting shed with a bench, it is worth making a small portable potting bench that can be put on the staging or on some other support when required. The bench is merely a wooden board of tray shape, best made to fit conveniently on the size of staging you have, but with only three sides. (See Fig. 8, page 96.) On this compost can be mixed and pots filled without it getting pushed off on to the surroundings and on to the floor, and scooping is also facilitated. So as to maintain hygienic conditions (see page 76), the surface of the tray is best covered with an easily cleaned material like Formica or similar. An easily portable, lightweight, and clean potting bench tray can be made from sheet aluminium.

To keep compost clean and hygienic, a few plastic bins such as small dustbins, or buckets with lids, are useful. All compost materials should be kept in clean covered containers too (see page 98). A soil steriliser is essential if you are to make your own composts. Although it is possible to improvise one, it is far better to buy a proper steriliser. An electric type is the most convenient. Sizes to suit all requirements are available, and they are not expensive. It is much cheaper to make your own seed and potting composts if you have the time and materials (see page 92). Sterilisers to be used with gas rings or primus stoves are also obtainable. Detailed information on soil and compost sterilisation is given in Chapter Seven.

Humidity of the greenhouse atmosphere is often an important consideration. This is discussed on page 79. To help in seeing just how much moisture there is in the air, a direct reading hygrometer may be useful, especially for beginners. This is a small dial-like instrument costing little. As well as giving readings in per cent relative humidity, it should indicate 'wet', 'normal' and 'dry' air conditions for simplicity.

For assessing watering requirements a moisture meter may be also useful to beginners. This works on the principle of electrical conductivity but the technical explanation is not needed here. The instrument consists of a probe attached to a little meter which gives readings as 'wet', 'moist' or 'dry'. The best form of the moisture meter is the JMA meter. This has the scale graduated in numbers. The meter is supplied with a book of guide tables giving the optimum readings for a wide range of plants and cultural operations. It takes much of the guesswork out of the task of watering and is especially recommended for beginners who tend to be too heavy with the water can (see also page 76).

Another gadget that can often be useful is the frost forecast thermometer. This is actually a kind of psychrometer—another instrument for measuring humidity. Its scale gives a good warning of the likelihood of frost if the instrument is properly placed and maintained. This is especially useful if you have garden frames which can be protected by covering at night, and also draws attention to a check of the greenhouse heating.

FRAMES AND CLOCHES AS GREENHOUSE ADJUNCTS

It is not possible to deal with frame and cloche gardening proper here. It is a specialised subject to which a whole book can be devoted. However, it should be realised that frames, in particular, can take over much greenhouse work. Many of the low-growing subjects and pot plants frequently given greenhouse space could just as well be grown in frames for much of the time. These include favourites like cinerarias, calceolarias, and the like. Frames can be easily, and economically, heated with electric soil warming cables. Dormant plants can be kept in frames, and much propagation and seed sowing can be done in them. All this gives much more free space in the greenhouse, which could perhaps be put to better use for taller plants. It certainly allows the greenhouse to be used for more decorative plants or the stages during which plants become the most suitable for display. Cloche protection can be given to the more hardy plants before they are perhaps taken into the cold or unheated greenhouse for display. They can also be used for protecting bowls and pots of hardy bulbs.

Frame recommendations are given where appropriate in this book. Frame design and the constructional materials follow much the same lines as greenhouses and similar advantages and disadvantages apply. It is frequently useful to have shady frames, and for this reason the north side of a greenhouse is a convenient place to have frame space. Sometimes the frames can be placed or built in contact with the greenhouse side. This helps to conserve warmth. Sometimes frames can be heated from a greenhouse heating system, more usually when hot water pipes are employed. Generally, however, electric soil-warming cables will be found the most convenient. Suppliers of soil-warming cables will recommend suitable types, ratings, fittings, and air-warming cables for frames if given the dimensions and temperatures required. It is also possible to heat a frame with a small paraffin oil heater placed in a sunken pit in the frame. Care is needed with ventilation (see page 40). Oil heaters of the type used for placing under cars are not suitable since they are likely to give out fumes.

The ground covered by a frame should not be used for growing. It can be treated in a similar manner as suggested for greenhouse floors (page 51). It can also be covered with plastic sheeting so that pots can be stood on this out of contact with the soil. Modern lightweight frames are also useful inside the greenhouse for use as propagators (see page 60), and also for covering plunge beds (see opposite).

THE PLUNGING BED

This consists of a bed of moisture-retaining material such as well-weathered ashes, grit, or peat, outside the greenhouse in a sheltered place (see Fig. 3). When it is necessary to stand pot plants outside during summer the pots are immersed up to their rims in the plunging bed, which is kept thoroughly moist. Plastic pots should be plunged so that their rims are just below the surface, but when it is known that certain plants are to spend a fair time in the plunge during some stage of their culture, it is wise to choose clay pots for them. The clay is porous and will allow moisture through. Plunged pots are kept damp and cool throughout the day, whereas if they were stood in the open, on the ground surface, they would soon become baked by the sun and the plants ruined. Plunged pots are also less liable to blow over.

Another use for the plunging bed is in the growing of bulbs, which often need plunging after potting to ensure development of a good root system. This is especially important when forcing (see page 141).

Whatever material is used for the plunge bed it can be kept in position by a rectangle of four boards. Alternatively a pit can be made in the ground if the drainage is good. The moisture-retaining material must be kept moist—not waterlogged. For this reason a frame often makes a convenient plunge bed or a cover for one.

Fig. 3 PLUNGE BED

A: Cover to keep out rain and to prevent waterlogging. B: Layer of grit or gravel to deter worm entry.

PROPAGATING BENCHES AND ELECTRIC PROPAGATORS

The propagation of many greenhouse subjects from seed, cuttings, off-sets, and so forth, requires temperatures considerably higher than is needed for the mature plants. In some cases it is possible to take advantage of the natural warmth of summer for propagation; but summer in the British Isles is unreliable and, in any case, the temperatures required for some forms of propagation may be higher than we could expect to get naturally for any length of time.

For this reason some means of obtaining a localised higher temperature is essential, particularly in the case of the greenhouse gardener wishing to grow plants from seed early in the year.

To attain the higher temperatures for propagation it is necessary to construct a propagating bench or case. This merely consists of a section of the staging supplied with extra heat and covered with some moisture-retaining material, such as sand, peat, pearlite, or vermiculite, and preferably enclosed by a glass frame to retain warmth and a moist atmosphere.

In greenhouses heated by hot water pipes the staging could be lowered in one place to be nearer the pipes, or supplementary oil or electric heating put underneath. In some pipe-heated houses it may be worth running some extra pipes under a section of the staging at one point. In houses heated by paraffin oil lamp it may be possible to place the lamp under the staging and utilise the staging space directly overhead for propagation. Some electric heaters may be similarly adapted (not fan heaters), but with large heaters too much heat may be produced and it will be necessary to obtain an extra smaller heater to warm the propagating area.

Where there is electricity, propagation is easy. Excellent electric thermostatically-controlled propagators are available commercially. Alternatively, an area of the staging can be heated with a soil-warming cable.

With a soil-warming cable it is an easy matter to make your own excellent and effective propagating bench or case. In many cases it is preferable to buying a commercial propagator. A soil-warming cable is embedded in a layer of sand spread out on the bench, the sand is then covered with moist peat, and the pot and pans or boxes of cuttings etc., are then immersed in the peat. A rod-type thermostat (see page 43) inserted in the peat layer is ideal for controlling the temperature (see Fig. 4). When it is desired to propagate a wide range of plants requiring different temperatures, this can often be done on the same warming bench by varying the depth of immersion of the pots or boxes in the peat. Glass laboratory thermometers are useful for checking temperatures.

A soil-warming cable bench can be covered with a glass frame or sheets of glass with advantage. Such an enclosure can be used for accommodating small tropical plants if desired. It can be used for all the usual methods of propagation too, and when a covering is supplied the peat layer can often be dispensed with, the pots and containers being placed on the sand over the warming cables (which is more convenient). In this case the thermostat should be given the job of controlling the air temperature inside the propagator. More information on bench

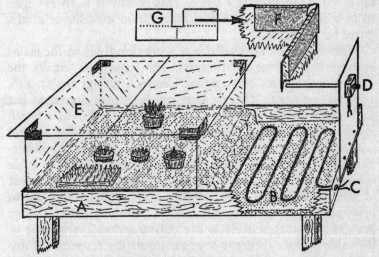

Fig. 4   HOME-CONSTRUCTED PROPAGATOR

A: Base of timber or asbestos sheeting. B: Soil warming cable on layer of sand. C: Warming cable wired in circuit with thermostat 'D' is a useful refinement. E: Glass sheets to retain moisture. F: Metal corner pieces to hold glass are cut as shown in 'G' and bent along dotted lines. (Use sheet zinc or aluminium.)

warming is given in Chapter Fifteen under raising bedding plants, page 234.

In my experience a greenhouse propagating bench needs at least 12 to 15 watts per square foot if it is to reach temperatures in the 70 to 80°F (21 to 27°C) range. Not all greenhouse plants will need this for propagation by any means, but it is advisable to be able to attain this level if necessary. As already explained, with a thermostat that can be adjusted, no heat is wasted even if the source of heat is over-rated and capable of an excess. Unfortunately a number of commercial propagators do not reach a high enough temperature, and this matter must be checked before purchase.

It should be borne in mind that the temperature reached by a propagator or bench depends on the surrounding air temperature. For example, a non-thermostatically-controlled propagator that has been reaching about 75°F (24°C) in winter in a 45°F (7°C) greenhouse may, during spring spells of sunshine, become far too hot when the greenhouse temperature rises into the 60 to 70°F (16 to 21°C) range. This is why it is always wise to fit a thermostat to save fuel (apart from its value as a safe-guard for the plants).

Warming cables are available to work directly from the mains or from low voltage transformers. The former are usually the most convenient for propagators. Common ratings are 75, 120, 150 and 300 watts. Two or more can be used if necessary, but for a small greenhouse a 120–150 watt cable will heat a bench about 5 feet by 2 feet. When laying the cable see that no part touches another or overheating which may damage the insulation may occur. Always keep the material in which the cable is immersed in the moist condition. This gives better conduction of warmth as well as maintaining humidity often important to propagation. Do not immerse electric warming cables in *dry* peat, or peat that is likely to dry out, or serious overheating of the cable is likely owing to the heat insulating properties of dry peat.

WATER SUPPLY

Clean water is essential in the greenhouse (see page 78). A mains water tap in the greenhouse itself will be found most convenient. It is possible to attach a watering lance for manual watering and automatic systems (see page 78). Plumbing can be simply done with modern high pressure alkathene tubing if the local water board approves. This will not burst on freezing, and can be fitted by means of simple connectors.

ELECTRICITY SUPPLY

This is becoming almost essential, since electricity can be put to so many uses, including lighting for the dark evenings. Proper fittings must be used and expertly installed. Greenhouse supply lines and switchplugs, etc., are specially made (see appendix).

CHAPTER FIVE

Automation in the Greenhouse

WITH present-day technology it is possible to automate many of the greenhouse chores that can be a problem to those who have to be away all day—or even for several weeks. This means that business people, weekend gardeners, or those who enjoy long holidays, can still delight in greenhouse gardening without fear of all their work being ruined during absence.

Nowadays automation has become so commonplace that often equipment can be purchased with a greenhouse or at the same time. For this reason this chapter has been put before the one on general routine. Beginners may prefer to read Chapter Six first, and return to this one when the requirements of watering, humidity, and environmental control are understood.

TEMPERATURE

In greenhouses heated artificially temperature is partly controllable by thermostat. This subject belongs with that of heating and has been discussed in Chapter Three. However, temperature depends on other factors such as the amount of sunlight entering the greenhouse, ventilation, and the cooling effect of moisture evaporating from the greenhouse. It should be realised that temperature is controllable by varying these other factors. Which to vary, so that the best conditions for the plants prevail, depends on the nature of the plants, and recommendations are given where appropriate in this book. See also the headings *Ventilation* and *Automatic Shading* in this chapter, and *Blinds*, page 53.

A thermostat can of course be used to control various other forms of automation affecting temperature. Generally the rod type already described (page 43) is the best. However, there are other designs on the market. The moving air type is also accurate. It consists of a tiny fan blowing a *gentle* current of air over the thermostat control device which gives greater accuracy in operation and a better sampling of air temperature. Unfortunately, in constantly running fan heaters, this principle is not an advantage in some cases (see page 42). For fan ventilation a special thermostat is necessary (see under *Ventilation*).

When possible it is always best to site a thermostat as though it were a plant. That is, with respect to the vicinity of the plants to the glass or the coolest position in the greenhouse. For fan heaters and other electrical heaters, it is often recommended that the thermostat should be sited about one-third along the greenhouse, one-third down from the roof ridge, and about 7 inches from the glass. It should not be put in draughts or near the source of heat. When used to operate ventilation or humidity in summer it should not be put in direct sunlight.

WATERING

Although comparatively recent, automatic watering has made fast advances and there are now numerous systems on the market. A choice often has to be made to suit your particular requirements or the type of plants grown.

The capillary sand bench

This very successful method was first introduced by the National Institute of Agricultural Engineering. Its operation depends on the natural phenomenon of capillary attraction—water will rise against gravity through a porous substance. In this case sand is used, and this is kept constantly moist by a water supply. If pots are placed on the moist sand and pressed down so that the compost they contain comes into close contact with the sand, moisture will rise up into the compost. As the plants use water and deplete the moisture in the compost it is replaced from the sand bench, which is in turn kept moist from the mains or a water reservoir.

The system depends on arranging a water supply that will maintain the sand in a moist condition. There is a variety of

C

methods, the most common being a constant-level water supply, the water of which is fed to the sand bench by means of wicks or similar means. To operate the constant level the ball-valve, well known to plumbers, can be used; or a float valve refinement usually made especially for the purpose. Other methods of keeping the sand moist are possible and are described in this chapter.

It is easy enough to make your own capillary sand bench, and the NIAE set-up is illustrated in Fig 5. A number of proprietary

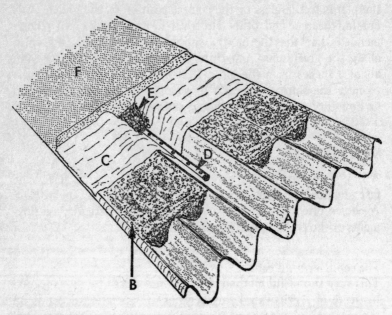

Fig. 5   CUT-AWAY DIAGRAM SHOWING STAGES IN THE CONSTRUCTION OF THE NIAE AUTOMATIC CAPILLARY WATERING BENCH

A: Corrugated roofing asbestos (or plastic). B: Corrugations filled with shingle (with the exception of the centre one). C: Polythene sheeting spread over the levelled-off shingle and depressed into the centre corrugation. D: Plastic pipe with holes drilled at intervals. E: Glass fibre (as used for insulation) to prevent pipe holes becoming blocked with sand. F: Layer of washed sand on which the pots are stood. (The plastic water supply pipe is connected to one of the several constant level float valves on the market.)

kits and apparatus is also available. Some of these have neat float valves and utilise narrow-bore high pressure plastic tubing with simple connections so that plumbing becomes easy and elegant. The tubing is often little thicker than electric cable so that the capillary apparatus can be used for house plants in rooms.

Most of the proprietary capillary units are now in the form of plastic trays that can be connected together to extend the area of watering as needed. Recently a plastic-backed textile material or type of matting has been introduced that can be used in place of sand (see appendix). This has so far given promising results and may well render sand obsolete in the future. The matting is easy to use and is lightweight, and it is easier to sterilise if necessary. The matting can be kept moist by trickle watering via a siphon system, or by the photo-electric method described later. Vermiculite and similar mineral substances of a porous nature can be used in place of sand also. Some proprietary tray systems use these because of their light weight. Some of the smaller systems also use inverted bottle water reservoirs so that a mains connection is unnecessary, but their running time is of course very limited.

The pots used on a capillary sand bench, or on the newer matting, must not be crocked (see page 102). The compost in them must come into close contact with the porous base. The compost must be nicely moist when the pots are put on the capillary bench, or further moisture will not flow up into them. Plastic pots are advisable, although clay can be used. Clay may become slimy and coated with lime or algae in a short time.

Algae are often a nuisance. They can be prevented by the use of Panasand. This product is mixed with the sand used for the capillary bench. It will discourage algae and slime and also help to prevent plants from rooting through the drainage holes and into the sand. Panasand can be lightly sprinkled on capillary matting, if this is used, and it will have the same function.

Trickle irrigation
This can be manual, semi-automatic, or completely automatic. It is basically merely an arrangement whereby water is conveyed to the plants via plastic tubing. Sometimes the delivery tubes are fitted with adjustable nozzles so that the quantity of water each plant receives can be controlled. This arrangement

can be very convenient in frames even if the flow of water is controlled manually. However, an automatic water flow is easily possible. The simplest is a small cistern fitted with a siphon tube to which the trickle line or drip feed line is attached. The cistern is filled by means of a valve with sensitive control knob so that the rate of filling can be easily adjusted. This means that the frequency with which the water siphons over can be regulated to give a flow to suit the plants' requirements. This method has the disadvantage that a good deal of experiment may be needed to get the siphon frequency right, and there is no automatic correction if there should be drastic changes in weather conditions likely to alter the plants' needs for water. The flow of water into a trickle irrigation pipeline can, however, be controlled in a fully automatic way by the use of the so-called 'electronic leaf' or by the very recently introduced photo-electric method. These are described below.

For a greenhouse with many pots scattered about on staging and shelving, the trickle or drip irrigation system may prove inconvenient owing to a network of pipes having to be led to each plant container. However, a system with a reduced number of outlet nozzles can be used to irrigate a capillary sand or mat bench and to distribute water over it uniformly.

The electronic leaf

This is also known by other names according to the makers, but most consist essentially of a porous surface from which moisture is allowed to evaporate. When it reaches a stage of dryness it activates an electric circuit which controls an electromagnetic (solenoid) water valve which then allows water to flow into whatever system is used to distribute the water—generally trickle or mist jets. At the same time the porous surface is re-wetted and the cycle is repeated. The process is automatic because the rate of evaporation of water from the porous surface depends on the humidity of the atmosphere and other atmospheric conditions prevailing in the greenhouse. With most designs of 'electronic leaf', provision is made for personal control of watering frequency and the amount of water delivered so that the method is very versatile. It is also used to control mist propagation (see page 231).

The photo-electric method

This is probably the best automatic control so far introduced. It depends on the fact that plants use water according to the amount of solar energy they receive. On bright days, when the temperature will also generally be higher in the greenhouse, plants take up water for their growth and the higher rate of photosynthesis that then occurs. On dull days and in the dark, very little water is needed since growth hardly takes place. In the photo-electric method the controlling device is a photo-electric cell with a special electronic circuit combined. The amount of light falling on the cell governs the frequency with which a solenoid water valve delivers water to the plants. Thus on bright, warm days the water will be delivered very frequently, but as light fails, or on dull days, the frequency will change accordingly, and in the dark no water will be delivered. Again there is provision for considerable personal control to suit a variety of conditions, and the method can be used to operate the water supplying a capillary bench, trickle or drip irrigation, overhead sprinklers, or misting jets for watering or humidity control, or mist propagation. Unlike the 'electronic leaf', the photo-electric cell is unaffected by slime, algae, or lime deposits from the water supply. It therefore gives reliable and accurate control over very long periods without any attention.

The tidal bench

This system waters pot plants by basal irrigation. The bench consists of a waterproof tray which can be made, if necessary, by draping plastic film over a frame of boards. At intervals that can be controlled by the electric methods already described, water is pumped into the tray so that the bottoms of the pots are standing in an inch or so of water, and then pumped out so that the pots are left without water at their base. The frequency of pumping can be controlled to give a 'high tide' time, long enough for the compost in the pots to take up sufficient water, but not long enough to cause waterlogging. Ordinarily, pot plants must not be allowed to stand in water too long (see page 76). The water supply for a tidal bench comes from a constant-level tank, the water pumped out of the bench being returned to avoid waste. Modifications of this system where, for example, the water siphons out instead of being pumped out, can be made. This method of automatic watering is clean and relatively simple, and worth further experiment, especially where pot plants of similar size and in the same size pots are being grown.

HUMIDITY CONTROL

Manually this is done by 'damping down' (see page 79). The moisture in the greenhouse atmosphere will also be governed by the moisture in pots and on the staging, and by any method of automatic watering employed. With automatic watering the humidity may also look after itself. In some cases it may be necessary to improve humidity or to control humidity but retain manual watering. A high humidity in summer will, in any case, substantially lower the need for manual watering (see page 76). The best way to get water into the atmosphere is by misting jets, and those automatic systems for watering described earlier which can be adapted to supply jets can be used to improve humidity.

VENTILATION

Automatic ventilation is easy and effective. However, it is always advisable to combine automatic ventilation with automatic watering or humidity control. Where there is no way of getting moisture into the greenhouse atmosphere, automatic ventilation—or unattended manual ventilation for that matter —can cause the air to become very dry and increase the water demand of the plants.

Non-electric thermo-expansion devices

There are a few different designs of this device on the market, but all work on the same principle. A special petroleum compound is sealed inside a cylinder. This expands and contracts with temperature change, just like the mercury in a thermometer. Owing to precision engineering and a system of levers, this movement is transferred by operation of a piston to the ventilator. The mechanism can be adjusted to open a vent at any desired temperature, and it is sometimes possible to work both a side and a top ventilator together. Normally one device per ventilator is necessary. Where there are many vents this can therefore prove expensive. Nevertheless, this device has now been in use for many years and has proved reliable and trouble free.

Electric fan ventilation
Fan ventilation is very efficient and ensures a rapid air change in the greenhouse. The fan is best set at one or both ends of the greenhouse in the side high up in the apex. Special greenhouse fans are obtainable. They blow air out of the greenhouse and are fitted with louvres so that wind cannot blow back into the greenhouse when the fan is not running. The arrangement is similar to that used for ventilating in most other domestic buildings or factories. Even so, the louvres are best fastened down during the winter when such automatic ventilation is rarely needed in the greenhouse.

Greenhouse fans are available according to the air change required and the size of the greenhouse. The makers will advise which of their models should be bought if given the greenhouse dimensions. Control is by thermostat, and this must be of a type that switches off with rise in temperature. Some thermostats can be used for heating or ventilation and have terminals for both, but most employed for heating do not have this facility. It is usually best to obtain a thermostat designed to go with the fan. Again, look for reasonable accuracy, but since fans use little electricity there is no need for too great a precision.

AUTOMATIC PEST CONTROL

This is a matter that could lead to problems and that everyone is not happy about. Much depends on the development of pesticides that can be guaranteed harmless to man and animals but effective over long periods in the control of pests. Unfortunately, many pests tend to develop an immunity to some pesticides unless the dose is high enough for an initial complete kill. Automatic pest control seems to rely on the vaporisation of pesticides and it is doubtful whether a concentration certain to kill completely could always be relied on. It would seem that a repellent action might be a better property to look for. Some people do not like the idea of the greenhouse atmosphere constantly containing concentrations of chemicals that might be inhaled. Automatic pest control is therefore a matter of personal choice, and one that should be taken up only after critical and careful consideration of the literature issued by the manufacturers of such products and equipment.

AUTOMATIC SHADING

The photo-electric cell can easily be used to control an electric motor operating greenhouse blinds. The equipment, although extremely efficient, is expensive to install and has to be custom made. There are firms which will undertake this given the greenhouse dimensions.

Recently a combination of glass and plastic sheet has been introduced. Sandwiched between the glass and the plastic is a special chemical material that becomes opalescent on exposure to sunlight, and clears again when the intense light ceases. This is still somewhat experimental and at present very expensive.

Experiments have been made with water alone (or with special chemicals added) to absorb heat radiation when pumped as a film over the greenhouse roof, the pump operating by photo-electric or temperature control. This has proved effective, but there are a number of technical difficulties which at present make it of doubtful practicability for the home greenhouse.

CHAPTER SIX

General Greenhouse Routine

STOCKING THE GREENHOUSE AND DISPLAYING PLANTS

A NEW greenhouse may look bare at first, but it can soon be filled with colour, beauty, and interest. It is wise not to be too impatient though. Best results are had when you start from seedlings or young plants. Large, mature plants that have spent most of their life elsewhere may not take kindly to a sudden change of environment.

A quick way to produce an exciting, colourful display is to sow suitable greenhouse and garden annuals from late winter to early spring (see page 108). Many sowings can be made in autumn too, for flowering the following spring (see Chapter Eight).

Autumn is a good time to procure young plants from nurseries to flower from the following spring to summer. A few examples are auricula, calceolaria, cineraria, cyclamen, fuchsia, impatiens, kalanchoe, primula, schizanthus, streptocarpus, and trachelium.

Nurseries and flower shops specialising in house plants are good sources of greenhouse foliage plants and many flowering plants of a sub-tropical nature. Most house plants will in fact grow much better under glass and reveal their true magnificence. Again, small specimens are the best investment.

For specialist plants like chrysanthemums, orchids and carnations it is vital to patronise those firms with a reputation for high quality (see appendix).

A greenhouse used as a show-place or conservatory will only gain a professional look if there are some climbers and plants in hanging containers. Care should also be taken in displaying the plants artistically, just as you would if composing a flower arrangement (see Fig. 6). Put taller plants at the back of

C*

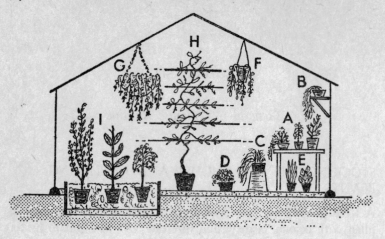

Fig. 6 HOW PLANTS CAN BE DISPLAYED

A: On staging with tall plants at rear and short or trailers at front. B: On shelving (trailers). C and D: In front of staging (short plants can be stood on inverted pots). E: Shade lovers under staging. F: Hanging pots. G: Hanging baskets. H: Climbers trained on horizontal wires. I: Plants in beds of peat with their pots plunged for natural effect.

the staging, and try to get some whose bloom or foliage will tumble over the edge. Climbers can be trained up plastic netting available from most garden shops, the white kind being preferable.

When climbers or plants are trained against the rear wall of a lean-to, the wall should first be rendered and whitened with a waterproof emulsion. This is to maintain hygienic conditions and eliminate hiding places for pests.

On staging plants can be given extra height by standing on inverted flower pots, or tiered staging can be made up and stood on the existing staging. Pots can often be hidden or disguised with pieces of cork or stone, or sphagnum moss, to create a natural effect, and plants grown from floor level can have their pots plunged in a sunken peat trough (see also page 51). Raised troughs or beds can have their sides concealed as suggested for pots.

Some plants lend themselves to being displayed on pieces of tree trunk covered with sphagnum moss. Small ferns, many bromeliads (page 210), and orchids are examples. The tree trunk should be chosen for attractive branching. It should be cleaned and freed from pests if any, and the moss wired on with inconspicuous florists' wire. The plants are then similarly wired on with their roots surrounded with moss and peat. Watering is done by spraying, and feeding with a complete soluble fertiliser like Phostrogen. Very attractive natural effects can be attained.

The bulbs provide a wealth of quick colour. As well as the spring flowering kinds, well known outdoors, there are many exotic greenhouse types flowering in summer and autumn (see Chapter Nine).

Greenhouses used for utilitarian purposes only are best kept free from all extraneous materials and run on strictly scientific lines. There will then be far less bother from pests and diseases, and fewer cultural problems.

Managing the general-purpose greenhouse

Too many home greenhouses are expected to cope with a vast range of different plants and their growing requirements. A certain amount of restraint must be exercised when building up a plant collection. Plants needing extreme conditions that cannot be provided should be shunned, or disappointment is inevitable (see also Chapter Two, page 20).

Care over positioning plants in the greenhouse can take care of some of their simplest requirements (see Fig. 6). Shade lovers can go under the staging or a part of the greenhouse can be shaded for them with a shader like Coolglass, easily removable at any time. Tall plants can be grown from floor level, an area being left free of staging for them. Extra humidity can be provided by a moist base for the pots to stand on—this is a common requirement in summer—or a dryer atmosphere given by siting those plants that like it nearest the ventilators. Temporary compartments for humidity or even temperature can be improvised with the aid of polythene sheeting.

Overcrowding must be avoided at all costs, and it will be found that this can often be dramatically reduced by the use of frames as adjuncts (see page 57).

Greenhouse gardeners are urged to be adventurous. Do not be tempted to grow the same things every year to the exclusion of everything else. Even in the case of specialist plants new cultivars appear frequently, and each year brings a wealth of seed novelties. Familiarise yourself with the catalogues of firms advertising in the gardening press and explore all the treasures they have to offer.

CLEANLINESS IN THE GREENHOUSE

If anything could be said to be the essence of successful greenhouse work it is cleanliness. This is normally associated with neat, tidy, and meticulous working. Anyone who follows these principles cannot go wrong. Greenhouse gardening is an excellent example of a combination of science and art bringing complete satisfaction.

Day-to-day checks for seeing that clean and tidy conditions prevail are not much trouble, and should any pest or disease appear it can be effectively and easily dealt with. When routine care is not given, a chaotic state will eventually have to be faced, and a whole greenhouse full of plants may be ruined. Sickly plants should be removed from the greenhouse, and all dead or decaying plant matter promptly disposed of. Always take a routine look under the foliage of plants where pests often first congregate and diseases first appear.

Do not upset compost on the floor or staging and leave it there. Always wash used pots and seed trays, and do not use the greenhouse to store junk and garden implements—these may harbour pests.

When possible, it is wise to give the greenhouse a yearly clean and sterilisation. This cannot be done effectively with the plants inside or with permanent plants (see page 89). The glass should always be kept as clean as possible (see page 34). Both inside and out should receive regular attention, but more so in autumn.

WATERING

In the outdoor garden plants are frequently underwatered when water is applied, mere sprinklings with a hose or water-can being futile. With pot plants the reverse is the case, and many people tend to maintain perpetually waterlogged conditions. Most horticulturists agree that more pot plants are killed by overwatering than by any other cultural fault, especially among beginners. Pot plants, unless of the aquatic type, must never stand in water for any length of time and the aim should always be to keep a moist compost. The word 'moist' is important: it must be distinguished from 'dry' and 'waterlogged'.

Plants vary water uptake according to their nature, their size and stage of development, and environment such as humidity, temperature and light. A plant cannot be given fixed doses at specific times. Too often one hears someone say, 'I have given my plant a pint of water each morning, but it doesn't seem to grow well.' Try to understand your plants. Those coming from dry countries or places are designed by nature to economise with water and to need little. Small plants that are not vigorously growing and naturally slow growers also require less. Dormant plants, especially in winter, may not want water at all, whereas large plants perhaps bearing flowers and fruit (like tomatoes) may demand considerable quantities during summer. On bright, warm days photosynthesis is rapid and plants are able to achieve quick growth. Then water will be in great demand and can be put to good use. When water is unwanted and unused it can cause root rot and interfere with root function through excluding air from the soil or compost. The absence of air also encourages harmful bacteria. Bulbs, fleshy roots, and similar storage organs are very prone to rotting if they are kept too wet at the wrong time.

Overwatered plants, suffering from root failure that the waterlogged conditions have brought about, usually show leaf yellowing, slow growth, eventual foliage drop and bud or flower drop, and wilting. The compost may appear muddy and sticky, and it may have an unpleasant smell. Unfortunately when this happens the plant is often beyond saving. Sometimes the compost can be washed away, all the sick parts removed, and the remains of the root repotted in well-drained, sweet compost, in the hope that new roots will form.

Anything which upsets the function of plant roots will cause wilting. If the compost is nicely moist there is no need to apply more water. Check that the wilting is not caused by high temperature or bright sunlight. If it is, give attention to shading, but do not apply water unless necessary. Spring pot plants such as cinerarias, and caleolarias, are very prone to wilt. This is because they may not be used to the extra light and warmth as the sun increases in intensity at that time of year. Shading is the answer, and only sufficient water to keep the compost moist should be given.

For assessing the water requirement some simple tricks have been used for very many years. It was at one time common to make a little hammer by fixing a cotton reel on a stick. This was used to tap pots—a high sound indicates dryness, a bass sound indicates that there is plenty of water in the compost. This works well with clay pots but not so well with plastic. You can also lift the pot and see how heavy it is. A moist compost will be very much heavier than a dry one. I prefer to insert a finger into the compost when in doubt, but you can be scientific and use a moisture meter (see page 57).

It is better to water well when you do apply water, but never let it stream from the drainage holes. This will carry away much of the soluble nutrient such as nitrates and soluble potassium salts (see page 82). For this reason plants should not be watered by immersion in buckets of water as so often recommended—and this includes seed trays and boxes.

Nowadays many potting and seed composts are based entirely on peat, and these can be very difficult to wet once they have become really dry. Peat composts must therefore always be kept nicely moist. Fortunately, because of the fibrous texture of peat and the air it admits, the high water content it holds is well oxygenated and root rots are less likely to occur.

Clean water must always be used. It is pointless to employ sterilised composts which encourage excellent growth (see page 92) if filthy water, perhaps containing manure from animal sources, is lavished on your plants. Roof rainwater must not be used (see page 53). Some plants, known as calcifuge—the lime haters—have to be watered with soft water. For such purposes use clean rainwater. It can be collected in clean containers put out just after rain has commenced. It should then be stored in clean closed containers. If much soft water is required, special horticultural water softeners are obtainable—the domestic type may not be suitable. Water can also be partially softened by boiling. It has been found that many plants, including orchids, can be watered with relatively hard water without harm. Less damage is likely than if dirty soft water is used. Most woodland plants, such as primulas, azaleas, many ferns and orchids, prefer water not containing lime.

The temperature of water given to plants is not so important as was at one time supposed. There is no need to leave it to become the same temperature as the greenhouse. On the other hand, some common sense must be used: do not spray icy water over plants growing under sub-tropical conditions.

Probably the water-can is still the most popular method of application. A can with a long narrow spout will make reaching between pots and access to the rear of the staging easier. It is also possible to buy watering lances with a finger-operated valve to attach to a length of hose fitted to a greenhouse tap. Lots of small pots hold water longer if they are plunged in moist peat or water-retaining material contained in seed trays or similar containers. The various automatic watering methods described in Chapter Five should be seriously considered.

HUMIDITY

The term 'humidity' refers to the amount of water vapour in the air. It is often of vital importance to the well-being of plants. When the air is dry, water is lost from the surface of plant foliage more quickly than when the air is moist. This loss is called transpiration. As water is 'breathed out', more is taken up by the roots, and this water, which brings with it soluble plant food from the soil or compost, is used for the intricate chemical processes that take place for plant growth. Curiously enough, the business of transpiration has been found to be very wasteful of water. If the humidity is kept high, transpiration is reduced, and hence the water requirement is diminished. Also, many pot plants seem to prefer a moist atmosphere and soon show signs of sickness when the air is dry. This applies to the many flowers and foliage plants that come naturally from countries or areas where it is moist and humid.

Obviously not all greenhouse plants are of this nature and most succulents and cacti, for example, prefer the air to be on the dry side. Humidity may also have to be adjusted according to the time of year or the stage of the plants' development. In winter it is generally best to keep the air fairly dry. This lowers the chance of trouble from fungoid diseases and various rots that can affect plants making little growth or resting dormant.

Humidity is increased by the process of damping down, which merely means splashing plenty of water about the greenhouse and soaking floor and staging. In summer, plants can often be sprayed overhead with water to wet the foliage. Many choice greenhouse plants demand this treatment. However, it is wise to be careful about wetting blooms which can sometimes be damaged by browning or rotting if they remain wet for long. This has to be borne in mind when positioning automatic mist damping apparatus (see page 70), or any overhead irrigation.

When water evaporates it absorbs heat. Damping down will therefore result in a cooling effect. The principle is that of the old-fashioned milk or butter coolers. Evaporation is speeded up by increasing ventilation. Staging and the effect of greenhouse design on humidity has already been described (Chapter Two). In winter, staging or floors should generally be allowed to dry out so as not to raise humidity.

TEMPERATURE, VENTILATION AND SHADING

Every attempt must be made to maintain the temperature between the limits recommended for particular plants. Extremes for short periods will rarely do much harm and much depends on the nature of the plants. A lot yet needs to be done in assessing just what extremes plants will endure. Some plants classed as warm house subjects at one time, such as Strelitzia, will in fact give splendid flowers if kept in a frost-free greenhouse over winter. Other sub-tropical plants can often be acclimatised to quite low temperatures if the conditions are changed gradually. However, for those plants known to object to freezing, temperatures below should be avoided. In winter it is often easier to maintain temperatures when there is some form of thermostatic heating installed. If the weather is severe or there are fuel troubles and shortages, outside blinds can be lowered at night —during darkness only—to help retain warmth and exclude frost, or sacking or similar textile material thrown over the greenhouse roof.

Damping down, as mentioned earlier, is one way of influencing temperature. Ventilation is another, which can be used to adjust

temperature to some extent in summer. Many home greenhouses have poor ventilation. Perhaps not enough people realise
that air contains carbon dioxide, which is vital to all plants'
growth and may be considered as a food in the same way as
fertilisers absorbed by the roots. The carbon dioxide is used by
the plant to form cellulose, sugars, and starches, from which its
tissues are composed. It is for this reason that carbon dioxide
enrichment of the atmosphere has been used to improve growth.

Good ventilation also deters the establishment of many fungoid diseases, such as the ubiquitous grey mould, *Botrytis
cinerea* (page 85). In winter, always give plenty of ventilation
whenever the conditions outside permit. (See also page 48.)

Very few greenhouses can be left unshaded in summer. Even
with vents fully open and plenty of damping down the tempera-

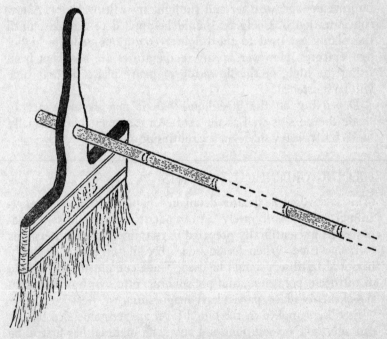

Fig. 7 SHADING BRUSH

A paint brush fastened to a long stick for applying shading paints
to the greenhouse roof. Electrostatic types (Coolglass) can be wiped
off dry with a dry brush (see page 55).

ture is still likely to shoot up if no protection from the sun is given. The great majority of greenhouse pot plants can be ruined by excessive summer temperatures. Moreover, many are from a naturally shady habitat and even bright sunlight may upset them. Foliage plants are especially prone to turn yellow or to lose their variegation. Often a permanent shading can be applied to the glass for the summer months, and the product Coolglass is especially recommended for excellent results and economy. It can be applied with a brush or sponge tied to a stout cane or pole (see Fig. 7). The white light passed by Coolglass also permits flower and foliage colour to be appreciated in its correct rendering, and this is particularly desirable for begonias, fuchsias, and similar show blooms. Special attention must be given to shading in early spring, or sometimes late winter. Plants that have been growing in poor light during winter may react to a sudden improvement in weather and sunlight by wilting badly. A low concentration of Coolglass should be applied to the glass until the plants get used to the brighter conditions and the higher temperatures. However, spring temperatures are best kept from rising too high, or the flowering of many plants at that time will be shortened.

Depending on the greenhouse site it may be necessary to shade the sides as well as the roof. An east–west house usually needs fairly heavy shade on the south side only.

FEEDING GREENHOUSE PLANTS

(This is covered in greater detail in Chapter Seven.) Nowadays animal manures are rarely used, modern potting and seed composts being scientifically prepared to contain all the plant's needs for some time. When feeding does become necessary, properly balanced fertilisers should be used. These contain the right ratio of nitrogen, potassium, and phosphorus, often with other essential elements added, particularly magnesium.

Fertilisers applied in the liquid form are recommended. Plants can only take up solutions and any solid material has first to be dissolved by the moisture in the soil or compost. However, much depends on what you want the fertiliser to do. Liquid feeds are usually fast acting. They should be applied properly diluted and frequently, not concentrated at rare intervals. Solid feeds for pot plants are usually compounded to act over a long period, but there is less control over their release of the elements or the concentration reaching the plant's roots.

Modern, scientifically-formulated fertilisers, such as the product Phostrogen, can be used as soluble feeds by dissolving in water, as foliar feeds by spraying on to the foliage, as a fertiliser to add in the dry state to potting mixtures (see page 93), or again in solution, to grow plants in water without soil or compost—called hydroponics (see page 97). This is because they contain other essential elements such as magnesium, iron, and manganese, as well as the main nitrogen, potassium, and phosphorus requirements.

Plants must never be overfed, or fed when they are in poor health resulting from incorrect culture other than feeding. Overfeeding will result in symptoms similar to those described under overwatering (page 77). Plants can be safely fed when they are making active growth. When dormant there is no point in applying feeds. Whether a plant is fast or slow growing must also be taken into account.

For some plants, special feed formulations have been developed. Examples are tomatoes, chrysanthemums, carnations, and others mentioned in subsequent pages of this book. These recommendations should be followed for best results.

Animal manures are not recommended. They are variable, unreliable, often a source of serious pests and diseases, and unhygienic. Certain sterile fertilisers of a proprietary nature made from natural manures are however permissible if their use is considered necessary. The hit or miss application of 'straight' fertilisers, such as ammonium or potassium nitrate, ammonium sulphate or superphosphate, is also not recommended except in isolated cases.

Top dressing

This is an old term still useful today. It means the addition of a balanced fertiliser or some fresh compost containing adequate fertiliser to a plant that has been in the same pot for a year or more. Top dressing is usually done in early spring or just before the plant is expected to commence growth again. Sometimes the surface compost can be removed entirely and replaced with fresh, but top dressing is usually done when a plant does not like its roots disturbed too much. It can also be done with some long-term bulbs.

STOPPING, TRAINING, AND SUPPORTING PLANTS

Stopping means pinching out or cutting off the growing tip of a plant or plant shoot. It induces more shoots to form from the stem or stems below and hence encourages bushy growth. This may be necessary to produce more flowers or a neat habit. Full details are given where appropriate.

Some plants lend themselves to training into various forms. This can usually be done by a variety of methods including stopping, pruning, and tying shoots to suitable supports, and also disbudding to produce fewer larger blooms (see page 214). Some plants can be trained to form standards. The procedure outlined under *Fuchsia* (page 169) is generally applicable. Other plants that can be grown as standards include pelargoniums, heliotropium, and marguerite.

Pruning is necessary for those greenhouse plants required to be given a desired shape or to be kept neat, to remove dead or diseased shoots or stems, to reduce the space taken up by plants dormant over winter and to keep their size in check, and for various special purposes such as to induce fruiting or flowering. Recommendations are given where necessary; but if in doubt about when to prune flowering shrubs, do it after flowering if considered necessary.

Supports will be needed for plants from time to time. Twiggy sticks can be used for low, bushy subjects, thin split canes for taller plants, and bamboo canes for larger specimens. Various proprietary ties are available, but garden string, cotton, and so forth will also be found useful. Always aim at neatness.

COMMON PESTS AND DISEASES

In the greenhouse pests and diseases are easier to control than outside—provided action is taken in the early stages. If the advice on general cleanliness and greenhouse routine given in this chapter is followed, and sterilised composts are used, there should be few problems. Even so there are some pests and diseases likely to make an appearance even in the best run greenhouses. Special problems (see index) are described under individual plants.

Aphids

This term includes, in fact, many species known by common names such as greenfly, plant lice, and blackfly. In the heated greenhouse these can breed the year round.

The shelves in garden shops abound with proprietary preparations for the control of these pests. I prefer the systemic type, usually based on 'Rogor'. Systemic insecticides are taken up into the tissues of the plant so that the sap becomes poisonous to sap-sucking insects. Many other pests of this type are therefore controlled. Special recommendations may be given on the label of systemics for the treatment of edible plants, and these must be followed. Malathion insecticides give good aphid control, and so does liquid derris, which is a relatively safe insecticide.

Botrytis (grey mould)

This is caused by the fungus *Botrytis cinerea*. It is very common and can ruin an entire greenhouse of plants. Many ornamentals, such as pelargoniums, are prone to it, and so also are crops like lettuce and tomatoes.

The mould can live on dead plant material and can from there spread to living tissues. It is best known as a grey–to–brownish furry mould that releases a cloud of dust-like spores into the air on being disturbed. These spores are ever present in the air and their growth depends on the right greenhouse conditions. Damaged plants are especially susceptible to attack. The mould is encouraged by poor ventilation combined with excessive humidity and low temperatures, and it is consequently very likely to appear in winter. Fan-heated houses rarely have trouble from this fungus.

Strict cleanliness is essential and all affected material must be removed from the greenhouse as well as any decaying plant debris. Attacked plants must have the affected parts cleanly cut out. Control is now relatively easy. The product Benlate, containing Benomyl which has a systemic action, is effective and safe. Routine fumigation can also be given with TCNB smokes (tetrachloronitrobenzene, or Tecnazine).

Damping-off

This is caused by several fungi that attack the base of seedlings and cause them to topple over. It can be very serious and its prevention is now a routine matter, requiring sterilised composts and preventive fungicides. The subject is dealt with under composts (page 92) and the care of seedlings (page 114).

Earwigs (Forficula auricularia)

The common earwig can be the originator of much 'mystery' damage. It is not generally known that this insect can fly and that it does its mischief at night. Cracks and crevices where it can hide during the day, and from which it flies to the plants at night, must be sought out. It frequently damages flowers by eating the petals, leaving them ragged and holed. Many beautiful blooms such as chrysanthemums may be ruined overnight, and seedlings eaten away.

For protecting blooms BHC dusts are effective. Ant bait and killers also destroy the pest and can be put in likely hiding places.

Red spider (Tetranychus telarius)

Unfortunately red spider can be seen with the naked eye only when the infestation has become very serious. It then appears as masses of fine, sticky webbing teeming with minute mites, only easily visible because of the vast number. Any foliage that seems yellow and mottled, and has a tendency to fall, should be carefully examined underneath for the presence of the tiny mites. A small hand lens will make them more easily visible and may also reveal the very tiny, round, whitish eggs. A dry, warm atmosphere encourages red spider, and infestation is less likely to be severe when there is good humidity.

Azobenzene fumigation is an old but still effective form of control, but it may damage some greenhouse plants. Liquid extract of derris can also be used as a spray. Derris dusts are not effective in this case.

Sciarid fly maggots

These tiny worm-like maggots with black heads are the larvae of several species of the fly. The flies themselves are also very tiny and delicate and may not be noticed except when in quantity and when they fly around if plants are disturbed. The maggots are very liable to be found in peat composts and where over-moist conditions prevail. They eat plant roots causing poor growth and eventual yellowing or wilting of the foliage.

An attempt should be made to lower the moisture content of the compost when possible, and initial control can usually be attained by watering with a malathion insecticide. Most general-purpose proprietary sprays or aerosols for the greenhouse will kill the flies.

Slugs, snails, and woodlice
These common garden pests will be a nuisance in the greenhouse if rubbish is left about for them to hide in, and decaying vegetation is not cleared. Modern slug and snail baits are extremely effective, especially in the greenhouse. Woodlice, sometimes incorrectly thought not to cause damage, can be controlled with most dusts containing BHC, for example Topguard Dust.

Thrips (Heliothrips haemorrhoidalis)
The thrips is yet another minute pest difficult to see with the naked eye. It causes white patches to appear on the foliage usually surrounded by tiny black specks. If some white paper is placed below attacked foliage, and the plant shaken, the thrips become dislodged and can be easily seen wriggling on the white surface.

Most pesticides containing the systemics give effective control, and so do derris extract sprays and malathion sprays or aerosols.

White fly
Although also very small, white fly is easily recognised as a triangular-shaped winged insect about 1/25th of an inch long and whitish in colour. The larvae suck plant sap in the same way as aphids and cause foliage to become yellow and sickly. Often a sticky secretion is formed upon which a black fungus grows, making plants very unsightly.

This pest is often difficult to eradicate completely; many pesticides fail to give satisfactory control. Malathion aerosols are probably the most effective. Liquid derris is also worth trying, and derris dusts may discourage the pest.

Application of pesticides and avoiding plant damage

New pesticides are being introduced and recommendations altered and changed all the time. It is as well to realise that it is unlikely that a universal pesticide will ever be introduced owing to the varied nature of pests and plants. Therefore, inevitably, some pesticides are suitable only for certain plants and not for others. It is essential always to read the maker's label very carefully. Plants likely to be damaged by a particular pesticide will be listed on the packaging, and should be removed from the greenhouse or protected with polythene sheeting. Fortunately there are now so many pesticides that it is usually possible to find one that is safe for any particular type of plant. When in doubt the maker should be consulted. Most leading pesticide firms have a technical information department.

Pesticidal dusts are the least effective, but they may have to be used on blooms or where other methods of application may cause damage. 'Puffer packs' are available for most dusts, but there are also special bellows.

Sprays are best applied with a sprayer which delivers a fine mist. Always see that the undersides of the leaves get good coverage. A sprayer with a nozzle that will reach between plants and can be manœuvred is a great advantage. There are many designs and sizes on the market.

Fumigation is the most efficient way of dealing with pests, but it may be impossible to select plants to be treated. The modern aerosol, now well known as a pack for many household cleaning and air-freshening aids, gives a form of fumigation owing to the penetrating mist. Pyrotechnic fumigants, which are lit like fireworks, are also common. Fumigating lamps, in which pesticides are vaporised, are rarely used nowadays, but the principle is employed in automatic methods (see page 71).

To assess the dose of a fumigant the cubic capacity of the greenhouse must be known. The dosage is always given in terms of so much per 1,000 cubit feet or similar. To gain an approximate idea of the cubic capacity of a greenhouse multiply the length by the breadth by the average height. The average height is obtained by measuring the distance from the mid-point between the ridge and the eaves and floor level.

Obviously the greenhouse should be made as airtight as

possible for fumigation. Wet sacking can be used to block cracks. The roots of the plants should be moist, but the foliage dry. The ideal temperature is usually about 65°F (18°C), but this is not essential or perhaps possible in winter. Do not fumigate when there is bright sunshine or when the temperature is excessively high or the plants are under strain. To do so can cause severe damage and blackening of foliage. Sometimes manufacturers recommend removing flowering plants from the greenhouse or picking blooms. Flowers can sometimes be bleached by fumigants. The best time to fumigate is in the evening, the greenhouse being left closed overnight and well ventilated the next morning. Full instructions for the best use and application of fumigants are given on the makers' labels or in leaflets supplied.

Sterilising greenhouses

Greenhouses left derelict for many years, or greenhouses that have been neglected or become pest- and disease-ridden, are often best cleared and sterilised and a fresh start made. This is often done after, say, tomato and chrysanthemum culture and/or if there is a period when the greenhouse can remain empty for a few weeks. It is not possible to properly sterilise a greenhouse containing plants, since all plants are killed by any sterilising agent which is really effective.

A simple way to sterilise is to burn sulphur which produces sulphur dioxide gas—pungent and *poisonous*. About one pound should be burnt per 1,000 cubic feet. Flowers of sulphur can be used (obtainable from chemists) with a few wood shavings to aid ignition. Sulphur dioxide may damage some instrumentation such as thermometers with metal scales, and automation instruments. These should be removed beforehand.

The structure and ground can be sterilised by treatment with formalin. This is sold for horticultural use by garden shops. It should be diluted to give a 2 per cent solution according to label instructions. This solution can be used for washing down the greenhouse interior and for watering into the ground. If the ground soil of the greenhouse is used for growing it can be employed to give some measure of temporary sterilisation. The solution can be used also for sterilising pots, boxes, and other containers and tools used in greenhouse work.

It is absolutely vital that all fumes of the formalin (containing formaldehyde gas) have disappeared before the greenhouse is used again. This may take from four to six weeks if the ground soil has been treated.

The pesticide safety code
Pesticides should not be used unless you know exactly what you are doing, and using, and have reference to the maker's instructions or other responsible information. They must not be inhaled or allowed to come into contact with the skin unnecessarily. They must be kept absolutely out of reach of children. They should be properly labelled and any unlabelled containers with doubtful contents discarded. Pesticides must not be poured into water courses or ponds and the like.

A booklet called *Chemicals for the Gardener*, published by the Ministry of Agriculture, is available from any good bookseller at a very modest price. This will keep you up to date with approved pesticides. Those approved by the Ministry of Agriculture are most strongly recommended. These pesticides have a large 'A' topped with a crown clearly marked on their labels, with the words 'Agricultural Chemicals Approval Scheme' below.

DURING THE GARDENER'S ABSENCE

When the greenhouse has to be left for holidays or absence for long periods, it is nearly always best to get a friend or a professional gardener to come in and keep an eye on things from time to time. Any special instructions should be written down and left with the helper. Failing this, and for shorter periods, the greenhouse is best shaded in the summer, a fairly heavy shading with Coolglass being safest. Some ventilation should be left, but not too much or drying out will be hastened. A thorough soaking and damping down should be given before departure in an attempt to keep up humidity as long as possible. If there is a solid floor, trays or bowls of water scattered around will assist atmospheric moisture. Obviously one or more of the automatic aids described in Chapter Five is the real answer to problems caused by absence.

Flowers should be cut or removed before departure when

possible, so that they do not mature and rot during absence, and a routine treatment with a systemic pesticide given if conditions and plants permit. Often, plants can be kept in excellent condition for long periods if covered with polythene bags.

CHAPTER SEVEN

Composts, Pots and Potting

MUCH of the success and popularity of the greenhouse in recent years is probably due to the development of modern seed and potting composts. These replace the old hit-or-miss mixtures of messy manures and variable ingredients that at one time made the growing of pot plants almost a mystic practice.

In case some beginners are not clear about the meaning of the word 'compost', it is necessary to point out that it has nothing to do with *garden* compost made by rotting down vegetable matter. In greenhouse gardening potting and seed composts are specially formulated mixtures in which to grow plants, and they have now been given much scientific development and study. With their proper use failure can be almost completely ruled out, and even the most inexperienced gardener should be able to grow superb plants. Seed germination is excellent, and damping-off (see page 114) very rare.

JOHN INNES AND UNIVERSITY OF CALIFORNIA COMPOSTS

The growing of pot plants was revolutionised by the introduction of the John Innes seed and potting composts, developed after much research and experiment by W. J. C. Lawrence and J. Newell of the John Innes Horticultural Institute. Their book on the subject, *Seed and Potting Composts* (George Allen and Unwin), should be read for full details.

The John Innes composts showed that composts could be standardised to a considerable extent to suit a very wide range of plants. This means that a few composts can replace the very many different kinds at one time employed and that results are more reliable. The John Innes composts also showed that trouble from pests, diseases, and weed seeds could be eliminated entirely by partial sterilisation, which allowed beneficial soil organisms to survive but killed all those which were undesirable. Further, they showed that it was possible to add the ideal balance of fertilisers to maintain excellent healthy growth for a long period.

To make the John Innes compost properly some care is needed. Also, in recent years, it has sometimes been found difficult to obtain loam suitable for the formulae. For this reason various loamless composts have been introduced. Some are based on peat entirely and others on peat and grit. There are many proprietary ready-made composts of this type on sale in the shops, and most can be relied upon to give satisfactory results. However, I still personally prefer the original John Innes, especially for plants to be kept in pots for long periods. The peat and peat/grit composts are better for short-term work as for annual pot plants and bedding plants (see Chapter Fifteen). The John Innes composts can be bought ready-made too, but it is important to buy from a reputable source since the compost *must* be properly prepared.

Composts based entirely on peat have the disadvantage that the pots are lightweight and that pot plants more easily become top-heavy. Also the peat is difficult to wet once it has been allowed to get too dry. Peat compost must always be stored slightly moist and never permitted to dry out completely. To overcome the difficulty of water uptake, some modern proprietary peat composts have a wetting agent added.

Peat/grit composts are better, in my opinion, and a good one has been devised by the University of California. This in its seed and potting form, and the John Innes formulae, are given here:

John Innes seed compost
(used for seed germination, page 112)

Parts by volume	Per bushel	Per cubic yard
2 loam (sterilised)		
1 peat		
1 coarse sand		
Calcium superphosphate	1½ ounces	2 pounds
Chalk	¾ ounce	1 pound

John Innes potting compost

Parts by volume	Per bushel	Per cubic yard
7 loam (sterilised)		
3 peat		
2 coarse sand		
John Innes base	¼ pound	5 pounds
Chalk	¾ ounce	1 pound

John Innes base fertiliser

Parts by weight
  2 hoof and horn ⅛ th inch grist, 13 per cent nitrogen
  2 calcium superphosphate, 18 per cent phosphoric acid
  1 potassium sulphate, 48 per cent potash
These specifications must be complied with. The base fertiliser is
available ready-made, also a Chempak equivalent substituting
Nitroform for the hoof-horn. (Nitroform is a modern synthetic
long-acting nitrogen fertilizer of reliable composition.)

The John Innes potting compost above is the No. 1. By
doubling the fertiliser and chalk added the No. 2 is obtained,
which is the most generally useful. Three times the quantity of
fertiliser and chalk will give No. 3, and so on. This is to allow
for the different possible requirements of plants. Slow-growing
plants will be happy with No. 1, whereas fast and vigorous
growers should have No. 3. Recommendations are given on
the pages which refer to culture.

The University of California composts
The basic composition is an equal mixture by volume of peat
and washed sand or grit.

University of California seed compost
Add to each bushel: *15 × 15 × 10" Box = 1 Bushel*

Ammonium sulphate	½ ounce
Calcium superphosphate	1 ounce
Potassium sulphate	¾ ounce
Ground chalk (or limestone)	4 ounces

University of California potting compost
Add to each bushel:

Ammonium nitrate	3 ounces
Potassium sulphate	1 ounce

Hoof and horn	3 ounces
Magnesium limestone	2 ounces
Ground chalk (or limestone)	4 ounces
Calcium superphosphate	2 ounces

(For suppliers of horticultural chemicals, see appendix.)

With the University of California potting compost, feeding has to begin rather sooner than with the John Innes. However, the peat and peat/grit composts have the considerable advantage that no sterilisation is necessary. Peat and coarse sand or grit, provided they have been properly stored, are relatively free from pests, diseases, or weed seeds. Sand is also easily sterilised if necessary by heating.

Making your own John Innes composts
It is not difficult to make your own John Innes composts according to the formulae given. For some purposes it may be possible to substitute ordinary good garden soil for the loam. The soil should be sterilised as described on page 98. In certain cases it may be possible to use a good garden soil without sterilising, but this is *not* generally recommended. However, a John Innes compost made up from unsterilised loam or compost will still probably give better results than any other hit or miss mixture if the soil used is fertile and clean.

For most home gardeners it is convenient to make up a bucketful of compost at a time, and in any case it is better not to keep the made-up compost too long. For a large bucketful the amounts of fertiliser and chalk to add are the following:

Seed compost
Calcium superphosphate	⅓ ounce
Chalk	⅕ ounce

Potting compost No. 1
John Innes base	1 ounce
Chalk	⅕ ounce
(omit for calcifuge plants)	(see page 97)

Weighing can be done on a small 'diabetic' balance obtainable from chemists. A measure for the loam, peat, and sand can be made by cutting a plastic bottle to give a measure with the capacity of 26¾ fluid ounces (1/48th bushel) when filled level with the top. Use a household measure to run the required

Fig. 8   PORTABLE POTTING BENCH
A three-sided tray of wood or sheet aluminium is useful for mixing
composts and potting and can be placed on staging when needed.

amount of water into a plastic bottle, mark off the level, and
then cut round with scissors. This measure can be filled, level
with the rim, twice with sterilised loam, once with peat and
once with sand, for the seed compost, Fill seven times with loam,
three times with peat, and twice with sand, for the potting
compost. You will find that this will fill a large bucket in the
case of the potting compost. Usually less seed compost is
required.

Make sure the peat used is damp. Black, poor quality decom-
posing peat must not be used. Mix the fertilisers and chalk with
the *dry* sand, and sprinkle this over the mixed peat and loam
spread out over the potting bench (see Fig. 8). Then mix all
together thoroughly. Use the compost slightly moist, and store
in polythene bags or in closed containers.

*Making your own University of California compost and loam-
less types*
The University of California composts are similarly easy to prepare. The proportions in the formulae given can be scaled down
according to personal requirements. To help in this it may be
useful to know that bushel measures can be constructed as
follows:

1 bushel = a box 15 × 15 × 10 inches
½ bushel = a box 10¾ × 10¾ × 9½ inches
¼ bushel = a box 8½ × 8½ × 7¾ inches

Proprietary ready-mixed packs of fertiliser chemicals (such as Chempaks) can be bought for mixing with your own peat or peat/grit. This will save weighing out and having to order several separate chemicals initially. Certain complete fertilisers containing the necessary trace elements can also be used for loam-less composts. For example, Phostrogen can be used to make up a peat/grit compost. The basic mix the makers recommend is three parts by volume of moist peat and one part of sharp sand or grit. To every 5-inch pot of this should be added one level teaspoonful of Phostrogen and one level teaspoonful of ground chalk. The chalk should be omitted for calcifuge plants (see below). For subsequent feeding of plants grown in this compost the same fertiliser should be used, dissolved in water according to the manufacturer's recommendations. Phostrogen can also be used for hydroponics—the growing of plants in solutions of chemicals without soil at all. An instruction leaflet can be obtained from suppliers (see page 243). A useful book giving full information on hydroponics is *Beginner's Guide to Hydroponics* by James Sholto Douglas (Pelham Books).

COMPOSTS FOR SPECIAL PURPOSES

Although the composts so far described can be used for a vast range of plants, there are—as one might expect—some exceptions. These are mostly dealt with under the entries relating to individual plants in Chapters 8–13. The most commonly encountered 'special case' is that of calcifuge plants. These are plants which object to lime and which originate mostly from acid soils, leafmould soils and woodland areas. In such cases the composts already mentioned can be used provided that the chalk is omitted from the formula. There are also special lime-free proprietary potting composts on the market in the ready-made form. Some mains tap waters contain excessive amounts of lime (hard water) and should this be the case plants potted in a lime-free compost must be watered with *clean* rainwater or specially softened water (see page 78); otherwise lime will soon build up in the compost and possibly raise the alkalinity (pH). The ideal pH (a measure of acidity and alkalinity) for a normal potting compost is pH 6·4–6·5 which is very slightly acid. (pH 7·0 is neutral.) The acid potting composts can go considerably

below this figure, but less than pH 5·5 is not recommended for
the acid-loving plants most frequently cultivated. For a few
renowned acid lovers, such as ericas, a special John Innes acid
compost is worth making.

John Innes acid compost

2 parts loam, 1 part peat, 1 part sharp sand all by volume. To
each bushel add 1½ ounces calcium superphosphate and ¾ ounce
flowers of sulphur.

For plants that prefer specially good drainage, like cacti and
many succulents, extra washed grit can be added to any of the
normal potting composts. For plants of a semi-aquatic nature a
good proportion of charcoal in crushed form will help prevent
souring. Lilies and ferns may enjoy leafmould additions, but
this should be sterilised. However, generally it is unnecessary
and undesirable to add materials to the standard composts, and
additions should not be made unless there is very good reason
or special recommendation.

STERILISING SOIL, LOAM, AND OTHER COMPOST INGREDIENTS

The loam used for John Innes composts should be prepared by
the method described in *Seed and Potting Composts* (see page
92). Sometimes suitable loam can be purchased from garden
sundriesmen, or failing this a good garden soil can be used—
but in all cases it must be *sterilised* if it is to be used for a true
John Innes compost.

The sterilisation is actually *partial* sterilisation. It is designed
to destroy pests, diseases, and weed seeds, but not beneficial soil
organisms and bacteria which make nutrients in the soil available to plants. Although chemicals can be used for sterilisation,
steam treatment is undoubtedly preferable.

Small steam sterilisers can be bought from horticultural sundriesmen at prices that will soon save the cost in compost. The
steriliser is merely a water container in which the water can
be boiled by flame heat or by an electric kettle element. The soil
or loam is placed in a box with a perforated bottom that fits
over the water reservoir, and steam is allowed to pass through.

The loam or soil must be *dry* to begin with. The water should be boiled until a thermometer near the top of the soil reads about 180°F (82°C) and this temperature should be maintained for about ten minutes. The temperature should not be allowed to rise above 200°F (93°C). Ideally, this temperature should be reached within a period of about forty minutes.

Afterwards the loam should be tipped out on to a clean surface and allowed to cool. It can then be used to make up compost immediately, but the compost made with freshly sterilised loam is best kept for a few days before use.

For small quantities a domestic saucepan can be employed. The John Innes Institute suggest boiling half an inch of water in the saucepan and adding dry sifted soil nearly to the brim, and then simmering for fifteen minutes.

Peat does not need sterilising. Leafmould, if sometimes used for special composts, can be sterilised by pouring boiling water over it. Leafmould often contains innumerable weed seeds.

Fertilisers for the standard composts

For feeding plants in the John Innes composts a special liquid feed has been devised as follows:

John Innes liquid feed

Parts by weight	
15	ammonium sulphate
2¾	potassium nitrate
2¼	mono ammonium phosphate
Rate of application:	½–1 ounce of the mixed powdered crystals per gallon of soft water.

The ready-made mixture can be obtained from garden shops or sundriesmen. If it is dissolved in hard water it should be used immediately or some of the phosphate may become insoluble.

The other composts can be used in conjunction with most proprietary pot plant feeds of the liquid or soluble type, such as Phostrogen. However, the composts contain enough fertiliser to get the plants to a fairly advanced stage. When to begin feeding depends on the nature and vigour of the plant, but a good time is just before flower stems or flower buds are expected. Some liquid feeds can be applied direct to the foliage provided the maker's recommendations are followed. Absorption will take place through the leaves and give very quick response. Some feeds may scorch the foliage and should *not* be applied in this way. These include the John Innes liquid feed. (See also page 82.)

For plants grown in John Innes composts the John Innes base fertiliser can be used as a top dressing if required. About one teaspoonful to each 5-inch pot, with a little more or less approximating to pot size, is the amount to use.

POTTING, POTTING-ON, AND REPOTTING

In most greenhouses these operations are carried on at intervals the year round. Clearly it is of the utmost importance to do them properly. If this is learned at the start it becomes automatic, and you will soon get to know your plants' pot requirements.

Choosing pots

Most people now use plastic pots, which are easy to clean and relatively unbreakable. Clay pots seem to be slowly disappearing, which is a pity. A few are useful for plants needing to be plunged because clay is porous and lets moisture through. Clay pots should be thoroughly soaked before use. They can be cleaned by soaking overnight and then scrubbing.

Owing to their non-porous nature plastic pots have the advantage that watering needs to be less frequent. If you have been used to using clay pots and change to plastic, be careful not to overwater. The growth and development of plants in clay pots and plants in plastic pots seems to differ little.

It is wise to stock a selection of various sizes of pot. Pot size is now measured by the diameter at the top. The most useful sizes for general work are 2½-inch, 3½-inch, and 5-inch. A few very small 1¾-inch pots may sometimes be useful, as well as a few 10-inch pots. What are known as 'half pots' can sometimes be a most suitable choice. Half pots are the same as ordinary pots with respect to top diameter, but they are only about half the depth. This makes them useful for low growing subjects and plants that are naturally shallow rooted. Sometimes half pots are called alpine pots, because alpines and rock plants are usually grown in them. All flowerpots should be well supplied with drainage holes. (See also page 103.)

For plants to be subsequently bedded out or transferred to permanent large pots, various temporary pots of polythene or waterproofed card can be used. There are also composition pots, which are designed to be planted with the plant and to rot down afterwards to produce humus for the plant roots. Unless conditions are kept nicely moist, these composition pots may not always rot as they should and will then restrict the roots.

Never use flowerpots which are larger than necessary. Plants that remain small in excessively large pots look ridiculous. Moreover, the excess compost may lose its nutrients with continued watering and before the plants' roots can penetrate into it. Sometimes slight under-potting is helpful in encouraging plants to flower.

Hanging pots and baskets
Many plants may be beautifully displayed in hanging containers and trailing plants may be suited only to them. Pots can be hung by attaching wires. Clay pots can be treated as shown in Fig. 9. Plastic pots can be easily drilled around the edges and wires put

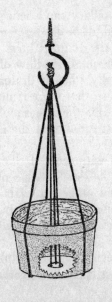

Fig. 9
HANGING A CLAY POT
WITH WIRES

through the holes. Baskets are frequently used, and there are now types with a saucer-shaped bottom that holds water for a short time, making watering easier and preventing mess from drips. Ordinary wire baskets have to be lined with moss before filling with compost. They tend to dry out quickly and consequently to demand more watering attention. It can be an advantage to place a few pieces of polythene sheet over the moss lining, leaving a few slits for drainage, before filling with compost. This reduces water loss, but the moss tends to go brown quickly. This may not matter. It should be remembered that many vigorous trailers will in any case soon obscure the hanging container from sight.

Take care that hanging containers can be safely supported by the roof. They may be very heavy when watered.

Large hanging containers can be filled with peat and three or four pots of trailing plants plunged in this. It is then possible to replace them easily, and is a particularly suitable method for plants with a short decorative period.

Potting (see Fig. 10)

Clay pots must be used soaked, but not wet with free water, or compost may stick making repotting troublesome. All pots must be scrupulously clean.

Unless pots are to be stood on a capillary sand bench (see page 67), they may need to be crocked. This old term means placing a few pieces of broken pot over the drainage holes. This prevents compost falling through and permits free flow of any excess water. For plants needing specially efficient drainage a few pebbles can be put over the crocks so that there is no risk of the compost causing clogging. Actually the aim should be never to apply so much water that it streams from the drainage holes (see page 76).

Pots with only one drainage hole, as with most of the older clays, should always be crocked when necessary. Some of the newer flowerpots made from plastic and other materials have several drainage holes and slightly raised rims at their base to allow free escape of any excess water. These can usually be left uncrocked.

For pots to go on a capillary sand bench it may be helpful to place a tuft of peat in the drainage hole or holes. Some gardeners

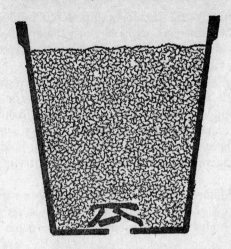

Fig. 10   CORRECTLY FILLED FLOWERPOT
Note that a space is left at the top for applying water. Drainage
hole(s) must be crocked or otherwise treated to allow free drainage.

use glass wool. This will admit water by a 'wick' action, but
prevent compost soiling the sand of the bench.

There is no need to use broken clay pot for crocking of
course. Plastic or clean stones of suitable shape can be sub-
stituted. There are also perforated zinc disks and circular plastic
or wire mesh available, but sometimes the perforation or mesh
is too fine for good drainage and pebbles still have to be put
over the top to avoid clogging.

With fast-growing plants soon to be repotted, crocking is
usually unnecessary (see also Chapter Fifteen, page 233). Several
designs of self-watering pot, which hold a reserve of water for
semi-automatic watering, are on the market. These are fine for
the isolated specimen plant or small group, but far too expensive for general use.

For potting, a compost must always be moist—not wet. It
should have sufficient moisture to enable it to be 'poured' from
a scoop or trowel, but not to cause it to stick to the hands or
surfaces. For greenhouse work never pot plants too deeply. The
point where roots and stem meet should generally be at surface
level. There are a few exceptions such as the stem rooting lilies
pointed out later in the book. Many plants and storage organs,

bulbs, etc., that would require a fair depth outdoors can be potted with their tops well exposed when there is the protection of glass. This gives plenty of pot depth for their roots to penetrate. (See also Chapter Nine.)

The standardised compost should never be excessively firmed down. A gentle tap of the pot on the bench as the compost is poured in around the plant's roots is all that is required. With the all-peat composts, a further gentle firming, when all the compost has been put in, may be necessary to hold the plant firm. Too much compression will impede the entry of water and air.

A pot should never be filled to rim level. Leave a space between the compost surface and the rim to allow for watering. Such a space is also useful to help in judging how much water has been applied.

After potting it is usually necessary to water carefully. When there has been much root disturbance it may be better not to water immediately, since damaged roots can rot in wet conditions.

Potting-on

This means moving a plant on from a smaller to a larger pot (see Fig. 11). For best results plants should be grown in pots just big enough for them. When the roots fill their pots, they are moved on to another slightly larger pot. This means fairly frequent potting-on, but it is good greenhouse culture. The practice ensures that a plant has fresh, fertile compost with the right fertiliser balance available for its roots all the time as it develops, and you will be amazed at the excellence of the plants that result. Generally the new pot should give about an inch extra of compost around the root ball.

To pot on, first remove the plant from its pot as described below. Place sufficient compost in the new pot to ensure that when the root ball is rested on it the plant is brought into the new position required—do not forget to remove any crocks, which should be gently disentangled from the roots if necessary. Then run in more fresh compost round the sides. If this compost is moist—not wet—it should run freely from a scoop. A tap of the pot on the bench will usually be sufficient to settle it down, but some of the peat composts may require gentle push-

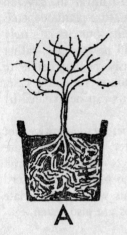 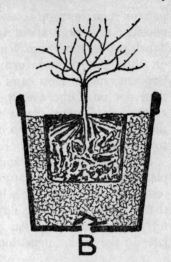

Fig. 11 THE PRINCIPLE OF POTTING-ON

A : Plant to be potted-on. B : The same plant with root ball intact shifted to larger pot.

ing down with the fingers. Very fibrous compost may require pushing down around the sides, and between roots, with a short stick known as a potting stick. It may have to be used when potting orchids and when dealing with plant roots where it is difficult to get compost between them. Remember that modern potting composts rarely, if ever, need ramming down firmly.

In many books and articles you will see the instruction 'pot on as required'. This means when the plant has filled its pot with roots, which can usually be checked by gently tapping the plant out of its pot in the following manner. After first watering to ensure the compost is moist, cover the pot top with the hand, allowing the plant stem to pass between the fingers, and invert it; the rim of the pot can then be tapped on the bench edge or tapped gently with a *small* hammer, when the root ball will generally slide out cleanly.

The need for potting-on does however vary, and the knowledge of what to repot and when will come after you have had practical experience. Recommendations are of course given in this book. Generally plants raised from seed will need frequent potting-on. For example, a seedling may begin in a 2½-inch

D*

pot (or sometimes in a seed tray, see page 113), and require potting-on through about two pot sizes to finish in, say, an 8-inch pot for flowering. When to pot on mature plants depends on their nature and further development; but it is rarely frequent, and in most cases the aim should be to repot, rather than pot on. Otherwise it would obviously be impossible to accommodate many plants in the greenhouse. In many cases the repotting or potting-on of mature plants can be avoided by top dressing (see page 83).

Many annual plants, and a fair number of decorative pot plants of a perennial nature, flower better if their roots are restricted. Presumably this has something to do with survival, the restriction hastening flowering and the production of seed for propagation. Attention is drawn to this where appropriate later in the book. Suggestions for pot sizes are also given.

Repotting
To repot is to transfer a plant to another pot of the *same* size, at the same time removing as much of the old compost as

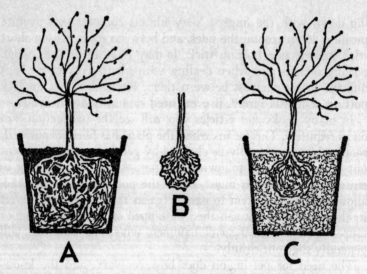

Fig. 12   THE PRINCIPLE OF REPOTTING
A: Plant to be repotted. B: Plant removed from pot and root ball and root reduced in size. C: The plant repotted into same size pot with fresh compost.

possible and replacing it with fresh (see Fig. 12). This can be done with many dormant perennials just before they are expected to commence growth again. In such cases there is little risk of upsetting the plants, but again it is not possible to generalise. Recommendations for the best time for repotting, and for which plants this can be done, are given in this book when necessary.

CHAPTER EIGHT

Growing Plants from Seed

GROWING from seed is one of the most exciting ways to acquire plants and it is also the cheapest. Nowadays there is an excellent supply of rare seed as well as many delightful novelties which are the result of plant breeders' expertise. It is essential for the reader to consult the catalogues of the firms listed in the appendix. These will be sent free on request and are always well illustrated. Do not be content to patronise just one seed firm. Various firms have different specialities and all should be explored.

GERMINATION REQUIREMENTS

For best results the seed must be bought from a reliable firm. Even then, with rare seeds a chance may often have to be taken. Successful germination depends on the age of the seed, how it has been stored, and its condition when harvested. Seeds collected from distant or difficult parts of the world may not always give good germination and sometimes they may not germinate at all. Conversely, the seed of most popular plants, such as those used for bedding and greenhouse display, generally gives germination approaching 100 per cent. Such seed is usually specially produced by the seed firms and is tested by them before sale.

Always keep a look out for F1 hybrids. These are obtained by special crossing of selected parent plants and the resulting plants are always much more vigorous. Also of note is tetraploid seed produced by a special chemical treatment. Tetraploids have much larger flowers and usually greater vigour too.

To germinate properly a seed must have a suitable temperature, moisture, and air or oxygen.

A rough idea of temperature requirement is from about 45°F (7°C) for the more hardy plants such as garden plants and annuals for bedding, to about 80°F (27°C) for sub-tropical and tropical greenhouse plants. For most of the seed germination in the average greenhouse you will find about 60° to 65°F (16° to 18°C) adequate.

If the temperature is too low, seed will take a long time to germinate, fail completely, or rot. At excessively high temperatures seed can be killed, or it may germinate too quickly and produce long, spindly, weak seedlings that often prove useless. Follow the germination temperatures suggested in this book.

Air, or the oxygen it contains, is essential to the seed as it germinates. It is necessary for the chemical processes that take place inside the seed. Waterlogging after sowing, or sowing too deeply, will suffocate the seed.

Obviously water is necessary too, but it should be present as *moisture*. During germination seed must not be allowed to dry out. This is another common cause of failure.

SEED SOWING TECHNIQUE

Sow seed as soon as possible after it has been received. Do not store packets in damp places such as the greenhouse or where they may be exposed to extremes of temperature. Specially sealed packeted seed with controlled humidity is now available and was introduced by Sutton's, the well-known seed firm.

To aid germination some large seeds can have a tiny part of the outer skin or covering peeled away with a razor blade or very sharp knife. This assists penetration of moisture and air. Soaking in water overnight may also help to get moisture into some large seeds with woody coverings, but soaking should never be carried out for too long.

To aid the handling of some very small seeds it is now possible to obtain them in the pelleted form. The seeds are coated with an inert mineral material, like Bentonite, a type of clay, to increase their size considerably. Sometimes a fungicide is included in the coating. Pelleted seed is usually about the size of small beads and is easy to pick up with the fingers. It can be sown individually and spaced well in containers so that pricking out (see page 112) may not be necessary. The coating, being designed to give protection but allow moisture and air to penetrate, generally helps to give good germination.

For seeds known to take a long time to germinate, it is sometimes wise to employ a seed dressing. This is a fungicidal powder, a little of which can be put in the seed packet with the seeds and distributed over them by shaking. The coating will protect the seeds from various rots caused by fungi which may contaminate the seed compost after sowing. It should be realised that although a clean, sterilised seed compost may be employed initially, after a time it is liable to contamination from the air and surroundings.

Seed must always be sown in a disease- and pest-free compost. For most seeds a special seed compost is preferable and details will be found on page 92. However, some large seeds, which have a considerable supply of plant foods already supplied by nature, can be sown direct in potting compost.

For most small seeds it is usual to sow on the compost contained in small seed trays or pans. Nowadays plastic trays measuring about 8½ inches by 6 inches and about 2 inches deep are freely available and are a convenient size, fitting most of the small propagators sold in the shops. For large sowings the standard seed tray, measuring about 8½ inches by 14 inches and about 2 inches deep, can be used. These seed trays are supplied with drainage holes distributed over the bottoms which are ridged to allow free escape of any excess water.

For the majority of seeds 1 to 1½ inches depth of compost in the tray is sufficient depending on the size of the seed. For fine seed it is wise to put a layer of seed compost in first and then a thin covering of seed compost pressed through a sieve of about 10 mesh. The compost should be firmed down very gently—not compressed—and given a level surface. For levelling and firming, a simple tool made by bending a piece of metal sheet into an 'L' shape will be found useful, one side of the 'L' being used as the handle.

The compost must be moist—not wet—before sowing. The seed should be sown thinly so that the tiny seedlings are not overcrowded when they appear. You don't have to sow all the seed in a packet at once. If there are plenty it is a good idea to save some in case the first attempt should fail or meet with an accident. In some cases, especially with the seed of annuals, it is also wise to 'stagger' sowings so that a succession of batches of plants are obtained at different stages of maturity. This means that plants can be had in flower over a much longer period.

To assist in the distribution of very fine seed it can be mixed with a little clean silver sand. Large seeds can be set over the compost surface with the fingers or with a pair of finely tipped tweezers leaving plenty of space between each seed. A rough idea of the space to leave is from about ½ to 1 inch, but it will depend on the seed size.

For most average seeds the sowing can be done by tapping the seed out of the packet with the forefinger moving the packet over and just above the compost surface as you do so.

After sowing the seed should be just covered with some more fine compost—except in the case of very fine seed which should be left uncovered. A deep covering is rarely necessary and it could be undesirable. A rough guide to the covering depth is to cover with a layer of compost about the same diameter as the seed. Thus a seed measuring about ⅛-inch across would have that depth of compost put over it. Some seeds germinate better if exposed to light, and should not be covered.

TABLE ONE

SEEDS NEEDING EXPOSURE TO LIGHT FOR GERMINATION
(These should not be covered with compost)

Anthurium species	Iris species
Bellis perennis	Lettuce
Bromeliads	Lobelia cardinalis
Cacti and succulents	Mimulus species
Calceolarias	Nicotiana
Crossandra species	Petunias
Ficus species	Philodendron species
Gesneriaceae (many species)	Primula species
Gloxinias	Saintpaulias
Gramineae (grasses)	Streptocarpus

Having sown the seed the next step is to see that there is adequate moisture present in the compost. It is usually necessary to apply more, and this is best done with a sprayer delivering a fine mist of water. Do not water seed trays by immersion. The excess of water running away will take with it valuable soluble fertilisers.

To retain the moisture in the seed compost a sheet of glass should next be placed over the seed tray. However, before doing this I prefer to first cover with a sheet of clean white paper. By putting paper under the glass condensation that collects on the glass does not fall on to the seed and cause very wet conditions of the surface compost. Another advantage of the paper is that it lets some light through, which may be an advantage for some seeds (see table), but not enough to accelerate the growth of slime or algae. This could be important in the case of seeds that take a long time to germinate, since such growth can interfere with germination. Instead of sheets of glass, the seed trays can be slid into polythene bags or merely covered with a suitable transparent plastic.

SEED GERMINATION, PRICKING OUT, AND AFTER-CARE

For most greenhouse plants grown from seed some form of propagator to supply the necessary warmth for germination will be required. Most bedding plants sown early for summer display in the garden will also need artificial warmth. Home-made propagators have been described (page 60), but a look around any garden centre or shop will usually reveal a number of proprietary designs to suit a wide range of requirements. The serious greenhouse gardener will find it a wise investment to get the best that can be afforded. Thermostatic control to give a range of temperatures and a high maximum temperature are two important features to look for. Some greenhouse plant seeds may require about 80°F (27°C) for initial germination, although afterwards it is often possible to gradually reduce temperature until the plants are happy in much cooler conditions.

After placing the seed trays in the propagator and giving the temperature recommended, an inspection should be made each day, to see that the compost is still moist and whether germination has commenced. If the same propagator is being used for several batches of different seed it should be seen that all have reasonably the same temperature requirement. As soon as germination begins the paper covering should be immediately removed. Sometimes germination is erratic, but do not wait for all or most of the seeds to germinate before removing any covering and giving them light. However, very tiny seedlings can be left with the glass cover over to help retain moisture in some cases. If the propagator is equipped with a cover, the glass or plastic seed tray covering may usually be removed completely, but the propagator cover should be left in position until germination is complete. After germination light is essential or the seedlings will bcome drawn, spindly, and pale in colour. All the same, good light does not mean direct powerful sunlight.

It has been found that best results are had when the seedlings are pricked out as soon as they are large enough to handle. The term 'pricking out' means removal of the seedlings to more permanent quarters such as small pots for growing on and potting-on as described on page 104, or to large seed trays in the case of bedding plants (see page 233). For slow-growing greenhouse and pot plants it is also often convenient to prick out into large seed trays rather than into small pots. Watering is then generally easier, and the young plants can be moved out of the seed trays and into pots when large enough.

To handle very small seedlings during the pricking out process I prefer to use a pair of long, finely tipped tweezers such as can be obtained from most chemist's shops. Some people use a thin piece of flat wood or plastic with a 'V' cut at one end to insert into the compost and lift the seedling out. After removal the seedling should be lowered into a small depression made in the compost in the new seed tray or pot and *gently* firmed in position by repositioning compost around it. Be very careful not to damage roots, especially when a seedling has a long tap root. The sooner pricking out is done, the less likely it is that severe damage will be caused. The seedlings will consequently grow away much more quickly.

In some cases when seed is plentiful and inexpensive, or when the seedlings are too numerous and too small to make pricking out very practical, the seedlings can be thinned out by removing and discarding the surplus. However, with most greenhouse seeds this is wasteful.

Some large seeds can be sown directly into small pots if preferred. How many should be sown, and the best pot size, will be found suggested in this book where appropriate.

When modern composts are used the once dreaded damping-off of seedlings is not common. However, the spores of the various fungi that cause the toppling over of newly pricked-out seedlings are quite likely to be present in the air. It is wise therefore to water-in all pricked-out seedlings as a routine with Cheshunt compound. This copper fungicide can be bought from garden shops and should be applied according to label instructions. Application is best done with a fine spray as suggested for watering seed trays, and this operation can replace the normal watering-in of the pricked out seedlings that would be necessary to settle the compost around the roots.

After pricking out, the seedlings can generally be transferred to the greenhouse staging or to shelves. Be careful not to expose them to strong sunlight at first and to check that adequate moisture is present each day. However, good light is essential, as already pointed out. Some seedlings of plants preferring higher temperatures may be better returned to a propagator until well rooted and established.

FAVOURITE GREENHOUSE PLANTS FROM SEED

Abutilon hybrids (flowering maple)
These are easily grown perennials flowering the first year. If the plants are stopped, by pinching out the growing tip when a few inches high, they will branch to form a bushy pot plant. If left they may grow tall but flower sooner. Old plants may become scruffy and lose lower foliage. The leaves are maple-like and the flowers pendent on short stalks and about 2 inches in diameter. Colours are shades of pink, crimson, orange, and yellow, and the petals are often attractively veined. A large cluster of yellow stamens enhances their beauty. Germination is easy at about 60/65°F (16/18°C), one plant per pot. Pot on to final 5-inch for first year flowering. Best in cool greenhouse, but will survive frost free. From March sowings, flowers can be had from summer to winter.

Acacia (mimosa)
The most popular acacia is *Acacia dealbata* which is the mimosa of the florist. It is an easily grown pot plant but is usually grown for its graceful foliage, since the flowers usually only

come after some years when the plant is well established in small tubs and takes up considerable room. The yellow fluffy balls of flower are well known, and in a large, frost-free greenhouse with good light they will be borne freely in spring. For foliage, first-year plants can have a 5-inch pot. Germinate at about 65°F (18°C). Plants that have become inconveniently large can be tried permanently planted outside in the milder sheltered parts of the country. Other species of acacia are listed in the seed catalogues and some of these make more compact pot plants, but few flower quickly. Sow any time from spring to summer.

Annuals (hardy garden types)
Choice varieties of many garden annuals make excellent pot plants. The extra care and potting compost with the protection of glass produces the most spectacular results. A cool airy greenhouse is essential so that the plants can be raised under almost hardy conditions. Best results are had by sowing in autumn and growing on over winter. Very early flowers can be had. Generally it is convenient to prick out the seedlings several to a 5-inch pot. Recommended to grow in this way are *Phlox drummondii* (most varieties), *Clarkia elegans* ('Salmon Bouquet'), calendula ('Golden Gem'), nemesia ('Unwin's Hybrids', and 'Funfair'), nicotiana ('Idol'—this is compact and remains open all day), and larkspur ('Dwarf Hyacinth Flowered'). The several F1 hybrid types of antirrhinum make fine pot plants. The large flowered forms can have all side shoots removed to produce single enormous specimen spikes. For this put one plant to each 5-inch pot. 'Double Column' stocks, which produce a single spike, can be grown similarly. 'Beauty of Nice' stocks are useful for winter flowering. For stocks get the Hansen's type. The seedlings have light and dark green leaf colouring to indicate which will be double flowered; keep only the light green seedlings. Best germination temperature is about 50°F (10°C) for these stocks, which gives the most noticeable colour contrast in the seedlings. Some of the taller annuals will need thin canes for support as they grow, but here I have suggested the more compact and dwarf forms which should always be selected for pot work.

Asparagus (so-called 'asparagus ferns')
These are not ferns (see page 186). Most usually seen are
Asparagus sprengeri which has pendent fine needle foliage and
is popular to go with flowers in hanging baskets, and A. *plumo-
sus* with even finer foliage but of erect habit. The foliage of
the latter is often used with buttonhole flowers like carnations.
However, more recently a delightful species, A. *meyersii*, has
become available. This has foliage similar to A. *sprengeri* but it
is very neatly erect and much more compact. It can be given a
3½-inch pot the first year and a 5-inch the second. It is much
slower growing than A. *sprengeri*. All these species are suitable
for a frost-free greenhouse. Germinate the seed in early spring
at about 60°F (16°C).

Begonias (see also pages 144, 162, 183)
All begonias are best sown as early as possible to get early
flowering and a long period of bloom. The fibrous-rooted kinds
popular for bedding make excellent pot plants. The large
flowered forms of these, such as Muse Rose, are especially suitable. 'Colour Queen', a variety with green and cream variegated
foliage, is also interesting. There are many F1 hybrids giving
a wide range of flower and foliage colour.

Exhibition double begonias can be grown only from tubers of
named varieties (see page 144). However, quite decorative
tuberous sorts can be had from good strains of seed. The multiflora doubles, such as 'Double Fiesta', are particularly recommended. These will flower—prolifically—from summer to
autumn if sown early, the flowers being about 3 inches in
diameter. It is also possible to grow from seed several types of
pendulous begonias for hanging baskets. These, too, flower the
same year from early sowings. A species simple to grow from
seed and of special merit is *Begonia bertinii*. Again this is quick
flowering although tuberous. The flowers are brilliant scarlet
and very striking indeed although single. A compact form and
a strain of seed giving white, yellow, and orange colours as well
as red shades is also available.

B. *rex* is a handsome foliage plant with variously coloured
and marked large heart-shaped foliage, but it does best in a
warm, shady and humid greenhouse.

Begonia seed is very fine and can be mixed with some dry

silver sand to assist even sowing. Do not cover with compost. Germinate at about 65°F (18°C). Keep the seed trays in a warm propagator until the seedlings are large enough to handle, after which the fibrous sorts can be transferred to large seed trays until ready for potting.

Browallia

Browallia speciosa is a free-flowering perennial which gives a splendid show of winter bloom in the warm greenhouse. In the cool greenhouse the plants are best allowed to remain dormant by keeping only slightly moist over winter, when they will flower from spring to autumn. The blue flowers are small but generously produced. Sow in early summer, when no extra warmth will be necessary for germination. In the cool greenhouse keep the plants in small pots over winter. Do not worry if some deterioration occurs. In spring new growth will begin, and it is then advisable to nip out any remains of previous year's growth to within about 4 inches from the base, otherwise straggly plants will result. In a warm greenhouse growth will continue over winter and the plants should be potted-on as required. Generally a 5-inch pot is suitable for flowering plants. The seedlings are best stopped several times to encourage branching growth and prevent a tendency for tall straggly development.

B. *viscosa* is a pretty annual with blue, white-centred flowers in great profusion. Sown in spring, flowering will occur in autumn. Put several seedlings to each 5-inch pot and stop them when about a few inches tall to induce bushy growth.

Calceolaria

Herbaceous calceolarias are among the most important greenhouse pot plants for an easy dazzling display from seed. There are a number of varieties giving dainty neat plants with masses of small flowers to huge specimens with enormous pouchlike flowers in great clusters. The varieties can be chosen to suit your greenhouse size, but where possible some of each can be displayed together. In spite of their exotic appearance, with the inflated flowers often speckled or spotted with contrasting colours, calceolarias can be grown in merely frost-free conditions. However, it is imperative that frost is kept away or the plants will be blackened and rendered useless. For earlier bloom a cool greenhouse may be necessary. The time of flowering also depends on variety and time of sowing. It is possible to have flowering plants from November to late spring.

Generally seed should be sown from May to June. Compact and small flowered multiflora varieties usually flower sooner than the huge exhibition types. The F1 hybrid, 'Glorious Formula', is especially early. No extra warmth will be needed for germination. Prick out the seedlings into large seed trays spacing them well. Put the trays in a cool, shady place over the summer months, such as a north-facing cold frame. Keep watered and watch for aphids (page 85), to which the plants seem to be prone. When the plants are large enough for potting, transfer to 3½- or 5-inch pots depending on size. Take care not to damage the brittle foliage. The F1 hybrids can be flowered in 3½-inch pots. Large varieties can be potted on as required to 5- to 7-inch pots. As the plants gain height, provide a cane. Feed with a liquid feed just as the sign of buds can be detected. During winter watch for botrytis attack (page 85). From late winter onwards Coolglass shading may have to be applied at times to the glass. The plants are likely to wilt with an increase in the sun's intensity. Cool, shady conditions with good ventilation are essential. Do not use pesticidal smokes on these plants, and avoid spraying the flowers. After flowering the plants should be discarded.

Calceolaria rugosa 'Sunshine' is a new F1 hybrid shrubby type. Before it was introduced shrubby calceolarias could only be satisfactorily raised from cuttings. The F1 seed yields splendid sturdy plants for summer bedding from February sowing, but the plants are also excellent for pots. In 5-inch pots in the frost-free greenhouse they will form large specimens evergreen in winter and continuing to flower from early on the following year.

Campanula (see also page 166)

The most popular greenhouse campanula is *Campanula isophylla* (page 166). This cannot be grown from seed. However, a very similar species, *C. fragilis*, is easily grown from a spring sowing with generally no extra warmth required in the greenhouse. It

has large, pale blue flowers and can be used for the same purposes as C. isophylla.

Very spectacular when well grown is C. pyramidalis, the
chimney bell flower. This can be sown in May with no extra
warmth. Prick out the seedlings first into seed trays, and then
into 5-inch pots. Keep them in a shady cold frame until autumn.
Then plant into 8-inch pots individually or three to a 10- to
12-inch pot and keep in a frost-free greenhouse over winter.
From spring on the plants will quickly increase in height until
by summer tall spikes of flowers will be produced making an
impressive sight. Both blue and white forms are available, and
the ultimate height is from four to five feet.

Capsicums and solanums
Although two very distinct species of the same family, the
culture of these can be described together. Capsicums usually
have green to red elongated or slightly elongated fruits. Solanums,
better known as winter cherries, usually have spherical berries
of similar colour. Solanum berries can be poisonous however,
especially if eaten by children, which is not generally realised.

For a good crop of berries it is important to sow early. Late
February to early March is best. Germinate at about 60/65°F
(16/18°C) and prick out into small pots in the cool greenhouse.
Some varieties may need stopping when a few inches high to
promote bushy growth. Pot on as required to final 3½-inch pots.
During summer keep down temperature to the minimum. When
flowering takes place stand the plants outside or plunge the pots
in a tray of moist peat outside. Solanums especially need good
pollination or the berries will not form. Outside, insects will do
this, but it also helps to spray the open flowers with a fine
mist of water to distribute pollen. If this fails to result in attain-
ing a set of berries, try using a tomato set (see page 198).
Capsicums usually set much more easily than solanums.

Solanums are prone to magnesium deficiency. For this reason
it is wise to add Epsom salt (magnesium sulphate) to the potting
compost, about ½ ounce per bushel. Magnesium deficiency will
result in leaf yellowing and fall.

In October return plants to the greenhouse. Solanums will
usually be beginning to form the red colour in their berries.
Capsicums may develop much earlier depending on variety,

and some can be ready for decoration by late summer. Good varieties of capsicum, sometimes incorrectly listed in catalogues as 'peppers', include 'Red Fangs', 'Fips', and the multi-coloured 'Chameleon'. A notable large berried solanum is 'Red Giant' with bright orange fruits.

Chrysanthemum (see also pages 214 and 235)

The greenhouse chrysanthemums usually grown from seed are the 'Charm' and 'Cascade' types. The former is easy, the latter needs care and training. Both have masses of small starry flowers in a variety of beautiful colours, and both can be started from seed sown in February with a germination temperature of about 60°F (16°C). Transfer seedlings first to large seed trays, then to small pots and pot on as required. The seedlings should be stopped by removal of the growing tip, when about three leaves have been formed, to promote bushiness. During summer the plants can be accommodated in cold frames and some time during summer they will need the final potting into 8- to 10-inch pots depending on their development. Flowering will take place from late summer to autumn. The Charms will form large cushions of bloom up to about 2½ feet in diameter on plants about 1½ to 2 feet high. The Cascades will be taller and those plants with poor flowers in colour or form should be discarded. The best ones are retained for taking cuttings and subsequent training into the cascade form.

During late autumn basal shoots will form on those Cascade plants saved. These should be taken as cuttings (see page 224) about 3 inches long, and rooted as described in Chapter Fourteen. When rooted, pot into 3½-inch pots and grow on over winter in the cool greenhouse. By spring the plants will need 5-inch pots of John Innes No. 3 compost or similar. When the plants are about 1 foot tall they should be removed to outside the greenhouse after hardening off. When about 1½ feet tall pot on to 12-inch pots, and insert a stout cane in the ground in such a way that it has an angle of about 45° and the plant stem meets it at a height of about 6 inches from the plant's base. The plant is then tied to the cane as it grows. In the lower leaf axils side shoots will form as the plant develops. These should have the tips removed when about three leaves have formed. This encourages more shoots to form on the new side

shoots and these are again stopped as already described. The
process should be repeated until about late September. As a
result of the stopping the plant should then be bushy at the
base and tapering at the top, and the leading shoot will in the
meantime have been tied to the cane as it develops. The final
stopping should be arranged so that the lower parts of the
plants are pinched out during about mid September, the middle
parts at the end of this month, and the upper parts about a week
later. This is to ensure that flowering is subsequently evenly
distributed over the whole plant and does not begin at the top
before flowers appear at the base.

In October the plants will be ready for removal to the protection of a frost-free greenhouse—an operation needing great
care to avoid damage. The plants should be from about 3 to
5 feet long and covered with buds. The cane must be carefully
removed and the plants lowered gently so as not to snap the
stem. At this stage it is useful to gain the assistance of a helper.
Take the pot, with the plant being supported by your assistant,
into the greenhouse and place it on a shelf or on the staging
where the hanging plant will be able to 'cascade'. To prevent
breakage of the stem it is best to bend a piece of very stiff wire
into a 'U' shape and insert one end of this into the compost at
the pot's side. The base of the plant's stem can then be tied to
this. In some cases it may also be necessary to slope a cane from
the staging or shelf to the floor to support the plant. It has
only been possible to give a rough outline of the training procedure here. Success comes with practice and your technique
may have to be altered to suit your particular growing conditions. The plants should be fed as described on page 215.

Cineraria

This is another pot plant valuable for outstanding colour and
it can be easily grown along the lines suggested for calceolaria
on page 117. The two are often grown together. The same
germination temperature and pot sizes apply. Cinerarias bear
masses of daisy-like flowers in many colours and sometimes the
petals are banded in white. Colours can be rich and vivid, or
pastel and delicate. There are many varieties embracing multiflora types with lots of small flowers, intermediate kinds, and
huge exhibition forms. There are also stellata types that have

masses of small, starry flowers. An important new variety is 'Spring Glory'. This has large flowers but the plants are compact. It is notable for exceptionally long flowering over up to about ten weeks. It can be sown in June for Christmas flowering or later for spring use. 'Gubler's Double' is a double flowered variety, but it is somewhat clumsy looking and limited in colour.

Cinerarias are even more prone to flagging than calceolarias. In late winter the sun may be intense enough to cause considerable wilt of the foliage. Should this happen, apply Coolglass to the glass and wipe off during dull weather. Do not apply more water to the plants if the compost is already moist. In more shady and cool conditions the plants will quickly recover. Cinerarias are also liable to serious aphid infestation and it is wise to apply a systemic insecticide as a routine precaution. Generally the plants do not need canes for support unless being transported. Discard after flowering.

Coleus (flame nettle)

This popular foliage plant with gloriously coloured leaves is simple to raise from seed sown from any time up to early summer. However, to save fully grown plants over winter, a congenial warmth is necessary or the foliage will fall. For this reason it is best to sow early and discard the plants at the end of the year. Germinate at about 60/65°F (16/18°C) and prick out into seed trays. Allow the plants to develop sufficiently to show their true colours—the tiny seedlings may not look very exciting. The best colours can then be potted and the others discarded. Pot on as required and remove flower spikes as they form. The flowers are not particularly decorative and may even give an untidy appearance. Many beautiful varieties are now available including fancy kinds with frilled or laced foliage. Of special note is the new F1 hybrid 'Carefree'. This seed gives an outstanding range of contrasting colours of great richness, many unusual to the normal coleus strains. The plants are compact and vigorous.

Cuphea ignea (Mexican cigar plant)

Ths is a delightful neat pot plant with numerous small elongated scarlet flowers with black and white tips. It is very quick flowering and even as a seedling is impatient to bloom. Sow in early spring at 60/65°F (16/18°C) and prick out into 3½-inch pots in which they will flower. This species is good for a bright greenhouse or sun room, but it is also tolerant to shade. The plants can be kept over winter if desired, but they are so easy to raise from seed it is hardly worth while.

Cyclamen (see also page 146)

From a September to November sowing, good flowering specimens of cyclamen can be had in about fourteen months. A number of varieties will be found in the seed catalogues ranging from miniatures to large flowered sorts. Some strains are noted for scent, but not all cyclamen have this desirable quality. Some varieties are also of special interest for particularly attractive foliage.

Place the seed on the compost surface and cover with about ½ inch of fine moist peat. Germinate at about 65°F (18°C) and maintain this temperature steady. Germination may be erratic, but when the seedlings have formed two leaves prick out into 2½-inch pots. Keep the temperature at about 65°F for the seedlings until they are well rooted and then lower to about 60°F. During about April pot on to 5-inch pots. For summer transfer the plants to a shady cold frame. When potting cyclamen at any stage see that about one-third of the corm protrudes above the compost surface, since this lessons the chance of rotting. In September take the plants back into the greenhouse and treat them as described for growing from corms (page 146). Remove any premature flower buds to preserve the resources of the plants for the main display from December to spring.

Recently, varieties with frilled petals have been introduced, and some of them are very attractive. Very new is the F1 hybrid double. However, this has not really the charm and grace of the single cyclamen flower. A dainty new miniature to be recommended is 'Puck'. This is very free flowering, has a good colour range, pleasingly marked foliage, and grows to only about 8 inches tall.

Exacum affine

This has small but freely produced lavender-blue flowers with orange yellow anthers. In the cool greenhouse it can be sown in spring for autumn flowering. In the warm greenhouse it will flower in winter. It is of special interest for its delightful fragrance, but unfortunately I have found that some new so-called improved varieties have lost their scent. These are the varieties developed for compact habit. Sow from February onwards, germinating at about 65°F (18°C). Prick out several seedlings to each 3½-inch pot and grow on in warmth for early results. Transfer to the greenhouse staging in spring when the temperature is rising generally. Exacum like shade, warmth, and humidity for best results.

Ferns (see also page 186)

Ferns are grown from spores which are botanically quite different from seed in structure. Most seed catalogues offer spores of mixed ferns suitable for cool or warm greenhouses. The spores are very fine indeed and can be mixed with a little silver sand for sowing to get better distribution. Sow in spring on a compost that is lime free. The peat/grit composts are best. The compost should be in a well-drained half pot (page 100), and this stood in a shallow dish or tray of water so that the compost is kept really moist. After sowing cover the half pot with a sheet of glass and place in a shady part of the greenhouse. Germination may take some time and the tray of water must be kept topped up during this period. (Two months is not unusual.) After this time the compost surface may appear to become covered with a greenish lichen-like growth. This is the first stage in fern growth, the prothallus stage.

Close inspection will reveal that each prothallus consists of a tiny heart-shaped filmy growth. It is at this stage that fertilisation takes place and for this to happen a film of water on the prothalli is essential. Leave the glass cover in place on top of the half pot to keep in moisture. After fertilisation the tiny first fern frond will begin to rise from the prothallus. The sporeling can then be pricked out in the usual manner into small pots and potted on as required. For composts and general culture, see page 187.

Freesia (see also page 147)

From a January sowing freesias can be expected to flower from summer to autumn. They do not make tidy pot plants, but the blooms are useful for cutting and the corms formed can be saved from any specially good plants for size, colour, or fragrance. Sow about seven to eight seeds, which are quite large, to each 5-inch pot and give a temperature of about 60/65°F (16/18°C). Cover with about their own depth of compost. Germination is hastened if the seeds are soaked overnight in tepid water before sowing. After germination leave the pots in the propagator for a week or so. Then move to the staging of a cool greenhouse where the temperature preferably does not fall below about 50°F (10°C) for long periods. A few thin canes and some inconspicuous thin tying material will be needed to keep the foliage neat when the plants grow. After flowering, continue to water and feed from time to time until the foliage begins to die down. Then allow the pots to dry and separate the corms from the compost. Spread out the corms in the sun for a few days to dry and 'ripen'—a treatment which improves flowering. The corms can then be stored in a dry, frost-free place and potted as described on page 147.

Gerbera jamesonii (Transvaal daisy) (see also page 171)
An early spring sowing will often give plants flowering from autumn into winter. It is essential for seed to be reasonably fresh. It should be sown on end (it is elongated in shape) or at any rate only covered very slightly with compost. Germinate at about 70°F (21°C), prick out into small pots and pot on as required. Generally, 5-inch pots are suitable for flowering specimens in autumn. Although the Jamesonii hybrids are interesting to grow in that some good colours can be found and the finest plants saved, there are two other important new introductions. The first is the 'Ramona' strain which has very broad petals and very strong stems for cutting. The second is 'Thurman's Double'. This has a wide colour range and the flowers are often surrounded with a ring of thin petals becoming very double towards the centres. Since 'Thurman's Double' is specially produced for the seed trade, by hand pollination and prompt harvesting of seed, the seed is extremely fresh and germination is usually 100 per cent. This is just as well because the seed is expensive.

Gloxinia (see also page 149)
At one time beginners often had difficulty in growing these

magnificent plants from seed. However, the introduction of F1
hybrids with their increased vigour has now made the job quite
easy. Sow in January. Do not cover the seeds with compost since
germination is better if some light reaches them. Germinate at
about 70°F (21°C) and keep the seed trays in the propagator
until the seedlings are large enough to handle. Germination is
usually very good, so sow thinly. The seedlings can be pricked
out into large seed trays or into small pots if preferred. The
young plants are best kept in the warmth and humidity of a
propagator until the general rise in greenhouse temperature
allows their transfer to the staging. Gloxinias like warmth,
shade, and humidity. Pot on as required, taking care to leave the
tops of the small corms just above the compost surface. A final
5-inch pot is suitable for flowering, which should occur from
late summer to early autumn. After flowering dry off the
corms as described on page 149, and thereafter treat as for growing from corms. The finest flower display will be had the second
year.

Grevillea robusta (Australian silky oak)

Although this ultimately grows to a considerable size, it is a
decorative foliage plant in its young stages. It can also be kept
more compact by stopping when it has reached an inconvenient
height. Sow from early spring to summer, germinating at about
70°F (21°C) and transferring the seedlings to 3½-inch pots. A
lime-free potting compost must be used for best results. Pot on
as required. In winter the plants may deteriorate unless cool-
house conditions can be maintained, but plants that lose their
foliage due to chill may grow again with the approach of warmer
conditions in spring.

Heliotropium peruvianum (cherry pie)

Often used for summer bedding, the new varieties of this sweetly
scented plant are excellent for pots. The best is 'Marine' which
is compact and has deep-blue flowers. Sow from January to
spring, germinating at about 60°F (16°C) and pricking out into
3½-inch pots. Pot on as required to 5-inch pots. Generally no
stopping is required for this variety. Flowering is from late
spring to autumn depending on time of sowing. The plants can
be saved over winter in the cool greenhouse when they should

be cut back. Growth will begin again in spring, but nowadays it is probably best to raise new plants from seed each year.

Hibiscus

There are numerous beautiful hibiscus for the greenhouse, but the one to raise from seed is the F1 hybrid 'Southern Belle'. This remarkable plant has enormous flowers the size of dinner plates in beautiful shades of carmine, pink, and rose. Also pure white with carmine centre. Sow as early in the year as convenient—preferably January. Germinate at about 65/70°F (18/21°C) and prick out into 3½-inch pots. From then on pot on as required to a final 10-inch pot. Growth is rapid and it should be borne in mind that the plants will eventually grow to a height of from 4 to 5 feet and bear their great flowers from summer onwards. The plants can be retained over winter, but I have found that for best flowering it is preferable to raise new plants from seed each year. This is a splendid plant for the cool conservatory, and one that will amaze the grower.

Impatiens (busy Lizzie)

This is probably one of the most commonly seen of all pot plants, but often it is either not very well grown or is allowed to become straggly. There are many excellent varieties now available and best results are achieved if frequent sowings are made so that young plants can be used for decoration instead of old ones. The dwarf forms are the most suitable for pots and they are very quick flowering, even very young seedlings bearing bloom. Sow almost at any time of the year if a cool or warm greenhouse is available for the winter. Germinate at about 65°F (18°C), pricking out into 3½-inch pots. Plants will flower in this size pot quite well and form neat growth almost hiding the pot from view. Notable new varieties include 'Zig Zag' which has white flowers striped with pink, salmon, scarlet, and orange, and is very striking, 'Minette' which is of very low and spreading habit, 'Elfin' which is also dwarf and with very bright colours, and 'Treasure' which has exceptionally large flowers. All these are F1 hybrids.

Jacaranda mimosaefolia

Like grevillea this makes a handsome foliage plant. Although less frequently seen it is probably more decorative. It can be raised from seed in exactly the same way, but there is no need for a lime-free compost in this case. The foliage is delicate and ferny in appearance, and a large, well-grown specimen is very beautiful.

Kalanchoe blossfeldiana

In recent years this has become a popular house plant. It is easy to grow and even suffers some neglect without apparent ill-effect. Being a succulent, it does not mind if you occasionally forget to water. Numerous varieties are available, with scarlet, orange, magenta, and yellow flowers borne in large panicles. The foliage is dark green, thick, and succulent. Sow in spring germinating at about 65°F (18°C). Prick out into 2½-inch pots and pot on as required. The plants will flower in winter in the cool greenhouse or as indoor pot plants, but the finest results will be had the following year. Flowering is sometimes unpredictable with regard to time of year and is affected by the day length and amount of light the plants receive. After flowering the plants are usually best cut back to some extent, otherwise straggly specimens may result.

A trick to get early flowering is as follows: Sow in January and grow on the seedlings until June at 45/50°F (7/10°C). Transfer to a cold frame which is blacked-out. Remove the blackout each day so as to regulate the daylight to only nine hours per day. Continue until flower buds form—usually after about ten weeks. Since old plants can become woody and straggly, it is wise to propagate from small cuttings or raise new plants from seed frequently.

Lobelia tenuior

This species is a tender but very glamorous form of the well-known garden lobelia and has very large showy flowers of a beautiful blue colour. It is useful for hanging baskets or for trailing from shelves or from the staging edge. Sow as early in the year as possible, germinating at about 65°F (18°C). Prick out into large seed trays and return to the propagator until well established. To encourage bushy growth, stop the seedlings when a height of about 3 inches is reached. Transfer the little plants to 7-inch half pots or other containers, setting about four or five plants to each 7-inch pot. If you do not want it to trail, use a few twiggy sticks to keep the plants upright. Flowering begins in summer and continues until autumn. This species enjoys warmth, and if sown too early under cool conditions may fail. If no suitable propagator is available leave sowing until later. Flowering will then of course also be later. During summer, shade the greenhouse where this lobelia is placed and keep up humidity. Discard the plants after flowering.

Mimosa pudica (sensitive plant)

This is an exciting curiosity that everyone should grow at some time or other. Children find it especially interesting. The attractive foliage is made up of numerous leaflets. These fold up dramatically on being touched, and a more vigorous disturbance causes the whole plant to collapse. The plant recovers after being left alone for half an hour or so and is then ready to repeat a performance. Sow in spring, germinating at about 65°F (18°C), and prick out into 3½-inch pots in which they can remain for the year and in which they will produce their small, solitary, pale purple to pinkish mimosa-like flowers—by no means showy. A height of about 9 to 12 inches is usually reached by autumn. The plants can be kept and grown on over winter in a warm greenhouse. However, young plants are more sensitive and it is a better proposition to raise new plants each year from seed. The seed is fairly large and can be soaked overnight to improve the speed of germination.

Nierembergia caerulea

This is almost hardy, and useful for the frost-free greenhouse. It grows to a height of about 9 inches and bears masses of blue campanula-like flowers, about ½ inch in diameter, with yellow centres. Sow in spring, germinating at about 60°F (16°C). Prick out the seedlings into 7-inch half pots, setting about four or five to each pot. The plants will flower during summer; but if they are saved over winter after being cut back to within about 2 inches of the compost surface, and given just sufficient water to keep the compost moist, they will make new growth the following year and flower much more profusely. The variety 'Purple Robe' should be obtained if possible.

E

Palms (see also page 189)

A number of palms are easy to grow from seed. One of the easiest is the magnificent *Phoenix canariensis* which is hardy on the Isles of Scilly. Two hardy palms are *Trachycarpus fortunei*, and *Chamaerops humilis*. Useful for the small greenhouse is *Phoenix roebelinii*, the dwarf date palm. *Butia capitata*, a near relative of the coconut, *Howea belmoreana*, the curly palm, and *Howea forsteriana*, the thatch palm, are among others worth growing. The seed is very large and is best germinated by immersion in moist peat at a temperature of about 80°F (27°C). When the seed shows signs of germination by sprouting or cracking, plant in 5-inch pots. For general culture, see page 189. For ease and tolerance to cold conditions I recommend *Phoenix canariensis*, although this will eventually become too large for the greenhouse. It can then be tried outside in sheltered mild places.

Pelargoniums (see also page 174)

Regal pelargoniums are usually best bought as named varieties. Until recently zonals ('geraniums') were also best bought as such. However, the recent introduction of F1 hybrid seed has altered the situation. Very fine plants can now be very simply raised from seed to flower the same year as sowing. The 'Carefree' hybrids give a range of beautiful colours including white, pink, and scarlet. The flowers are handsome and the plants strong and vigorous. Separate colours are also now obtainable. Two F1 hybrid dwarf forms are also to be highly recommended: 'Dwarf Carefree' which has a variety of colours, and 'Sprinter' which has well-formed flower heads. Both are very early. From January sowings plants can be ready for summer flowering. Sow in a temperature of about 65°F (18°C). Transfer to 3½-inch pots and then pot on to 5-inch pots. For general culture, see page 174.

Petunia

There is little point in growing the ordinary multiflora bedding petunias in pots under glass. The grandiflora types and the doubles, often spoilt by weather outdoors, are ideally suited. The doubles are also often delightfully scented like carnations with a similar clove-like fragrance. The double 'Giant Victorious', an F1 hybrid, makes a magnificent pot plant. Sow as early in the year as possible at about 60/65°F (16/18°C). Do not cover the seed with compost since light aids germination. Prick out into large seed trays and transfer the seedlings to 3½-inch pots when large enough. For flowering, a final 5-inch pot is adequate. For best results, petunias like plenty of light and an airy greenhouse. The doubles will, however, tolerate some slight shade.

Pharbitis tricolor (morning glory)

This is one of the most beautiful of the easily grown climbers. It is usually listed in catalogues as *Ipomea rubro-caerulea* although this name is not correct. The plant is typical of the Convolvulus family, but the flowers are often at least 4 inches in diameter. Although several colours ranging from crimson to white striped blue are now available, I still think the original intense blue is the finest. The flowers are seen at their best in the morning—hence the name morning glory. By afternoon they have usually faded, although there will be plenty of buds ready to open the next day. Sow in early spring, germinating at about 65°F (18°C), and prick out the seedlings into 2½-inch pots. Prompt pricking out, before a long tap root is formed, is essential, or the seedlings may die or deteriorate. Try to maintain warm conditions for the seedlings in the early stages. Pot on to a 5-inch pot for flowering, providing a cane for the plant to climb up. Alternatively, put several plants in a 10-inch pot and train them up wires, strings, or plastic netting fastened to the wall of a lean-to or the greenhouse side. Morning glory will enjoy a position in good light. If grown in a 5-inch pot, stop the seedling when a few inches high to encourage several shoots. This will reduce the ultimate height which can be as much as 8 feet and absurd for a small pot. In recent years a disease believed to be of the virus type has affected pharbitis. The seedlings fail to develop a green colour and appear pale, whitish, or white striped, and lose vigour. If this happens, a higher temperature sometimes helps to boost the seedlings so that they recover. Seed should be tried from another source. The variety 'Heavenly Blue' is an old favourite. 'Early Call' is a new rose-pink form. 'Flying Saucers' is white with blue stripes. To hasten germination, soak seed in water overnight.

Polyanthus

The brilliance of the polyanthus for outdoor spring colour is
well known. It also makes a splendid pot plant for the greenhouse and is especially useful where there is little or no artificial warmth. Under glass the pleasing fragrance of the polyanthus
will also become better appreciated. There are many exquisite
forms available, and again the F1 hybrid seed is recommended.
Particularly fine is the recently introduced F1 'Regal Supreme'
which has flowers larger and of finer quality than the more
popular 'Pacific Giants' as well as a wonderful scent. Of the
separate colours the blue strains are perhaps the most beautiful,
especially with the central yellow eye being the complimentary
colour. Other fancy types can be had too, including 'laced'
forms where the petal edges are delicately bordered with a contrasting colour.

Sow during February to March, germinating at about $55/60°F$
($13/16°C$). A higher temperature than this is undesirable. Prick
out into large seed trays allowing plenty of space around each
seedling. The trays can be kept in a shady cold frame until such
time as they can be transferred to 5-inch pots—probably from
late summer to autumn. In autumn take the potted plants into
the frost-free or cool greenhouse where the temperature should
not rise higher than about $45/50°F$ ($7/10°C$). Over winter slow
growth will continue and sufficient water should be given for
this without waterlogging the compost. In early spring when
the flower buds are first detected, begin feeding with a liquid
feed. After growing the plants as pot specimens they can be
transferred to the garden where they will usually multiply.
However, for the finest pot plants it is better to grow freshly
from seed rather than to divide up existing outdoor plants.

Primula

From a very large number there are three most commonly grown
primulas for the greenhouse: *Primula malacoides*, *P. obconica*,
and *P. sinensis*. If sown in May these flower from early winter,
starting with *P. sinensis*, the Chinese primula, to late spring.
P. obconica often continues to flower for many months, becoming a perennial. *P. kewensis* is also worth growing because
it provides the colour yellow which does not occur in the
others.

Beginners often fail in growing primulas from seed. If the following instructions are followed disappointment should be avoided. See that your seed is from a reputable firm and reasonably fresh. Do not cover the seed with compost since light is necessary for the best germination. Germinate at about 60/65°F (16/18°C) and promptly prick out into large seed trays. Keep moist and well shaded during the summer, and the temperature down. In autumn pot into 3½-inch pots. P. *malacoides* can be left in this size for flowering, but the other two will need potting on to 5-inch pots. When potting do not press the compost down firmly round the roots or plant too deeply, or rotting at the base is likely. Do not use hard water for watering. It is best to use *clean* rainwater—not collected from roofs or stored in dirty butts (see page 78)—if the mains water is hard or limey. The compost should also be checked for alkalinity. A pH of about 6.5 is ideal, but in some cases an acid compost (see page 98) may give better growth. In alkaline compost, containing too much chalk or lime, growth may be very slow and weak and the foliage will turn yellow and sickly. The minimum temperature for these primulas should not fall below 45°F (7°C).

Numerous varieties of these primulas will be found described in the seed catalogues. It should be noted that both P. *obconica* and P. *sinensis* can cause an unpleasant skin rash in people allergic to them. If redness or irritation of the skin is noticed when handling them, it is best to have nothing more to do with these two species. P. *malacoides* and P. *kewensis* appear to be harmless.

Saintpaulia (African violet) (see also page 176)

This is another plant that the introduction of F1 hybrids has made worth growing from seed. Mixed colours are available in the F1 form giving blue, pink, and white, as in the variety 'Fairy Tale', or there are 'Blue Fairy Tale' or 'Pink Fairy Tale'. Sow as early in the year as convenient to yield plants flowering the same year. Germinate at about 65/70°F (18/21°C), but sow thinly because germination is usually very good. Do not cover the very fine seed with compost. Prick out the seedlings when large enough to 2½-inch pots and return them to the propagator until established. In the cool greenhouse it may be wise to leave

the seedlings in the propagator until warmer weather arrives.
Pot on as required, but take care not to snap off the brittle
foliage. It is usually best to pot on just before the leaves protrude over the pot rim. Young plants will flower well in 3½-inch
pots, but they can be potted on to 5-inch if required. Since the
plants are not deep rooted they can often look better in half
pots. For general culture see page 177.

Salpiglossis

This extremely colourful annual, which bears a multitude of
richly-hued trumpet flowers often exotically veined with golden
yellow, is very easy to grow. If sown in autumn, very early
flowers on large plants can be had the following spring. If sown
early in the year, flowers can be had from summer onwards.
There are a number of fine varieties listed in the catalogues, but
the one to get for a fantastic display is the F1 hybrid 'Splash'.
This is also more compact, early, and vigorous. Germinate at
about 60°F (16°C) and prick out into 3½-inch pots. When the
seedlings are about 2 to 3 inches high stop them to encourage
branching growth. Vigorously growing plants from autumn
sowings can have the shoots formed after the first stopping
again stopped, but early spring-sown plants may not need this
second stopping. Pot on spring-sown plants to 5-inch pots for
flowering. Autumn-sown plants may need a little larger pot
since they make larger plants. Height is from about 1½ to 2½
feet and a cane will usually be needed to safely support the
plants. Good light and airy conditions are important. A frost-
free greenhouse will give excellent results.

Schizanthus (butterfly flower, poor man's orchid)

This easily grown annual is outstanding for free flowering and
colour over a very long period. Sowing can be done in autumn
for spring flowering and early in the year for early summer to
late autumn bloom. The flowers, although small, are exceed-
ingly pretty and come in all manner of wonderful colours. In
addition they are beautifully marked and veined and borne in
vast numbers almost obscuring the foliage. The foliage itself is
highly decorative, being ferny and delicate. Germinate at about
60°F (16°C). For autumn sowing the large flowered varieties are
recommended. 'Pansy-Flowered' and Sutton's giant hybrids,

which used to be called 'Cattleya Orchid', are outstanding and will give exhibition results. For sowing early in the year these, and also several dwarf varieties, can be selected. 'Hit Parade', which grows to a height of about 1 foot, is remarkable for easy culture. It needs no stopping and flowers with amazing speed. This variety should be given staggered sowings so that it can be seen in flower over many months. Prick out autumn-sown seedlings into large seed trays and transfer to 5-inch pots when large enough. Three seedlings can be put to each 5-inch pot, or one seedling can be put to each if you are prepared to carry out more stopping. Stopping the seedlings is important to get as much branching growth as possible. Stop when about 2 inches tall, and all side shoots at a similar length. Further stopping can be carried out depending on the vigour of the plants and how soon they are wanted in flower. Pot on if necessary to 7-inch pots depending on their requirement. A cane will be needed for support since autumn-sown plants can reach a height of 3 feet. From sowings from January to spring the plants can usually be put three to each 5-inch pot. One stopping may be sufficient for the taller varieties. The dwarf types can be left alone. Over winter schizanthus are susceptible to botrytis (see page 85) and they are also sensitive to paraffin fumes. Give good ventilation, and shade in spring. Ideal for cool house.

Streptocarpus (Cape primrose) (see also page 178)

Raising from seed sometimes presents some difficulty to beginners. The following method should reduce failure. Sow as early in the year as possible at about 65°F (18°C). Use sifted John Innes No. 2 compost and do not cover the seed. The seedlings grow very slowly at first and should be left in the seed trays in the propagator until large enough to handle and well rooted. For this reason sow thinly so that there is plenty of compost around each seedling which can be removed with the seedlings on transference to 2½-inch pots. Do not plant the seedlings in the pots too deeply or they may tend to rot at the base. Keep them in a propagator after potting, maintaining about 65°F (18°C) until they are well rooted and making obvious healthy growth. Often the seedlings may appear slightly distorted and one leaf may grow more than others. This is not unusual and need cause no alarm. Once established the plants usually grow quickly and can be potted on and transferred to the staging. From January sowing good plants can be had in flower by autumn. 'Triumph' hybrids are recommended. These have an excellent colour range and the flowers are borne well above the foliage on strong stems. Pelleted seed is now available. For general culture, see page 178.

Thunbergia alata (black-eyed Susan)
This is another very easily grown quick-flowering annual that will charm everyone with its orange to cream flowers with contrasting matt black centres. It can be used in hanging baskets although its nature is climbing. It is by no means rampant and can be trained up a fan of canes set in a 5-inch pot. Sow from about February onwards at about 60/65°F (16/18°C) and prick out directly into 5-inch pots. One to three plants can be put to each pot or they can be set around the edge of a hanging basket. A good strain of seed should give a high percentage of flowers with black eyes, but sometimes this desirable feature is missing. This species will do well in bright conditions or in shade. However, in a dry atmosphere it is very prone to red spider attack (see page 86). It can be expected to reach an ultimate height of about 3 to 4 feet.

Torenia fournieri (wishbone flower)
The flowers of this species are of unusual shape and of deep blue colour contrasting with a golden yellow throat. Although small they are freely born and the plant is neat and compact. Sow in spring at about 65°F (18°C) and prick out the seedlings into 2½-inch pots, or if preferred to large seed trays for the early stage of growth. Subsequently put about three to four seedlings to each 5-inch pot. As the plants grow a few twiggy sticks will be needed to give support if the plants are required to grow upright. However, the plant can be used as a neat trailer and for hanging containers if required. In the warm greenhouse this species can be had in flower almost the year round by staggering sowings. Since a congenial temperature is required for best growth it is best not sown in the cool or frost-free greenhouse too early unless it can be kept in a roomy propagator in the young stages. It grows to about 1 foot.

TABLE TWO

MORE INTERESTING PLANTS TO GROW FROM SEED
(Recommended)

Sow during spring. Germinate at about 65°F (18°C) unless otherwise stated. Pot sizes are for flowering size plants.

Ardisia crenulata   Shrubby plant with bright red berries. 7-inch pot.

Ascelepias curassavica   Attractive heads of orange flowers. 5-inch pot.

Ascelepias physocarpa   Spiky inflated seed pods second year. 7-inch pot.

Boronia megastigma   Scented purple-yellow flowers second year. 7-inch pot.

Brunfelsia calycina   Scented lilac flowers. Evergreen. Sow 70°F.

Cardiospermum halicacabum   Inflated pods. Trail or climb. Foliage.

Caesalpinia gilliesii   Small shrub. Showy scarlet stamens. 10-inch pot.

Caesalpinia pulcherrima   Shrub. Showy orange-yellow flowers. 10-inch pot.

Clivia miniata (see page 167)   3/4 years to flower from seed. Sow 75°F.

Coffea arabica   Shiny foliage. White flowers in warmth. Sow 75°F. 5-inch pot.

Cordyline terminalis tricolor   Foliage tinted red or rose. Sow 75°F. 5-inch pot.

Crossandra undulifolia   Pink flowers over long period. Evergreen. 5-inch pot.

Cyperus alternifolius   Foliage arranged like umbrella spines. Aquatic. 5-inch pot.

Datura suaveolens   Short tree. Scented white trumpets third year. Warm. 10-inch pot.

Desmodium gyrans   Terminal leaflets move. (Telegraph plant.) Very curious. 5-inch pot.

Dracaena indivisa   Palm-like foliage. Sub-tropical bedding plant. 5-inch pot.

Eccremocarpus scaber   Easy climber. Showy orange/scarlet flowers. 10-inch pot.

Eucalyptus citriodora   Lemon-scented foliage. Minimum winter temperature 50°F. 7-inch pot.

Eucalyptus globulus   Glossy eucalyptus-scented foliage. Almost hardy. 7-inch pot.

E*

Gossypium herbaceum   Cotton. Yellow flowers short-lived followed by fluffy cotton balls. 5-inch pot.

Heliconia hybrids   Handsome foliage. Small flowers like Strelitzia. 8-inch pot.

Hippeastrum (hybrids and species)   Handsome flowers, see page 150.

Hypoestes sanguinolenta   Foliage spotted red. Very pretty. 5-inch pot.

Luffa cylindrica   Elongated gourds – bathroom loofa. Curious. 10-inch pot.

Musa coccinea   Handsome foliage like banana. Sow 80°F. 10-inch pot.

Nertera granadensis   Cushions of bead-like orange berries. 5-inch pot.

Passiflora caerulea   Vigorous climber. Hardy. (Passion flower.) 10-inch pot.

Passiflora quadrangularis   Exotic version of above. Warm only. 10-inch pot.

Petrea volubis   Climber. Long racemes, blue flowers. Sow 75°F. 10-inch pot.

Philodendron bipinnatifidum   Glossy foliage plant. Sow 70°F. 5-inch pot.

Rechsteineria leucotricha   Tuberous. Silver-grey leaves, salmon flowers.

Rehmannia angulata   Bright red flowers over long period. 5-inch pot.

Rosa miniature   Easy from seed, flowering first year, 5-inch pot.

Schefflera digitata   Large shiny pale-green foliage. 5-inch pot.

Sesbania punicea   Racemes of salmon pea-like flowers. 7-inch pot.

Sparmannia africana   White flowers in winter. Minimum temperature 45°F. 5-inch pot.

Statice suworowii   Long pink tail-like flowers. Everlasting. 5-inch pot.

Vinca rosea   Glossy foliage, pink or white flowers. 5-inch pot.

All these plants are generally easy and give quick results from seed except where stated. However, those taking several years to flower are so beautiful they are worth waiting for.

CHAPTER NINE

Growing Plants from Storage Organs

MAKING PURCHASES

IT is not possible to enter here into the botanical explanation of the differences between bulbs, corms, tubers, rhizomes, tubercules, pseudobulbs, and so forth. However, all these have in common that they store plant food in the form of chemicals such as starches, sugars, and the like. They are consequently collectively known as 'storage organs'.

It will be appreciated from this that when you buy a bulb, or storage organ of some kind, its quality will depend on how it has been grown. It is vital to patronise reputable firms or nurserymen. Never buy storage organs that are soft or spongy, show signs of rot, have holes, or are covered with 'corky' tissue as is possible in the cases of cyclamen and gloxinia. Bulbs that may be covered with loose scale, such as narcissus or tulip, and bulbs like lilies composed of segments, should be closely examined for signs of mould or mildew. Generally a good size is desirable in bulbs, since they are more likely to be of flowering size. However, some corms and tubers can deteriorate with age and their size may not be significant (see under individual species headings).

The time of year of planting is often important. A good nurseryman will not despatch material until the proper time. Planting should then be done as soon as possible.

GENERAL CULTURAL HINTS

Bulbs or other storage organs should not be grown in 'bulb fibre' which contains no nutrient. The potting composts described in Chapter Seven should be employed. The storage organs grown in the greenhouse fall into two classes—spring flowering 'bulbs' (not all are true bulbs) grown in pots and often forced, and half hardy or tender types. The culture of these is different and is described here separately.

Spring flowering 'bulbs'
Nearly all the spring flowering bulbs commonly seen in outdoor gardens can be grown in pots in the greenhouse. Grown thus their beauty can be better appreciated and their fragrance becomes more noticeable. They can also be had in flower earlier. Some are given special treatment by the growers so that they flower considerably earlier. These are called 'prepared' bulbs and can generally be flowered for Christmas or soon after. To get earlier flowers some ordinary bulbs can be 'forced'. This means giving a slightly higher temperature for a time. However, not all bulbs can be forced, and some so treated may go 'blind'— produce no flowers at all. Varieties that can be forced are always marked in the catalogues of the bulb suppliers.

Ornamental pots and bowls are often used for potting bulbs. Care must be taken with undrained containers to see that they do not subsequently become waterlogged. A few pieces of lump charcoal at the bottom may help aeration and keep the compost from 'souring'. For the greenhouse, clay bowls or half pots are usually best.

The number of bulbs to plant per pot or bowl varies with type and personal preference. The larger bulbs like hyacinths can be individually planted if desired. When planting more than one, try to select bulbs all near enough the same size and quality—otherwise they may flower at different times. Any loose debris adhering to the bulbs should be removed before potting and any dead roots trimmed off. Pot so that the tops of the bulbs are just level or slightly above the compost surface (see Fig. 13). Large bulbs like hyacinths and narcissi can have at least half protruding above the compost. This is to give a good depth for the roots to penetrate. It should be remembered that since the bulbs will be grown under frost-free conditions there is no need for deep planting.

After potting, the containers must be put in the cool and in darkness. They should be immersed in the 'plunge' described on page 59. See that the compost is kept moist, but on no account allow waterlogging. Plunging is essential to stop top growth being formed before an adequate root system has developed.

If it is not convenient to plunge the containers heap as much moist peat on top of the container as can be persuaded to stay put and then cover with a polythene bag or piece of polythene held in place with an elastic band. Stand the covered pots outdoors in a sheltered place free from frost. Whilst frost and freezing must be avoided, high temperatures at this stage are harmful. Inspect the containers from time to time to see that they are moist. It usually takes from six to eight weeks for shoots to appear. If the bulbs appear to be rising out of the containers it is probably because the containers are too small, the bulbs have been put too deeply, or the compost has been firmly pressed

Fig. 13 POSITIONING GREENHOUSE BULBS

Most greenhouse bulbs should be potted with at least half above compost surface to give maximum depth of compost for roots.

around them. This fault, if it occurs, can be corrected now by repotting in a larger container. Attempts to push the bulbs down will damage the roots.

When shoots have appeared, all covering should be removed and the containers stood in a shady, cool place. After about a week they can be gradually introduced to full light and then given as much light as possible to prevent pale, drawn foliage. For flowering from early spring onwards, most spring flowering bulbs should be potted from September to November. In spring every attempt must be made to keep temperatures in the greenhouse down, and slight shading with Coolglass may be required.

Forcing spring flowering bulbs
Forcing does not mean subjecting bulbs to hot, humid con-

ditions as so many beginners seem to think. If this is done most bulbs will fail. At first the potting and plunging procedure already outlined must be carried out so as to get a good root system. When there are signs of top growth and there are plenty of roots, transfer the containers to a greenhouse where the temperature does not exceed about 60/65°F (16/18°C). This temperature is best allowed to develop slowly over a week or so, and at the same time the bulbs can be introduced to full light. To see whether there is adequate root growth, the bulbs can be tapped out of their pots if necessary. If the compost is moist it should come away cleanly without disturbing any roots that have formed. Unless there are adequate roots it is unwise to begin forcing. When flowering occurs the temperature can be considerably lowered to extend the life of the blooms. Bulbs to be forced should be planted from August to September.

Prepared bulbs
Full instructions and the best temperatures are usually provided by the suppliers of the bulbs. Sometimes plunging is necessary for a time, and sometimes it is not. Since the preparation of bulbs for early flowering needs care and experience, they are necessarily more expensive. If saved after flowering they can be potted the following year or transferred to the open garden. However, they may fail to flower until they have settled down to a normal sequence of growth again.

Greenhouse and summer flowering storage organs
These are potted much in the same way as already described. They are left in the greenhouse and not plunged. Specific cultural notes are given later in this chapter.

Often these bulbs, corms, tubers, rhizomes, and so on, have to be 'started' into growth. This is usually done by immersing them in moist peat in suitable containers in a warm propagator. When there is a sign of life in the form of shoots or roots, they are then potted in potting compost. In some cases starting in this manner ensures that planting is done the right way up, for it is often difficult to locate the tops of—for example—gloxinia corms.

After-flowering care of storage organs

After flowering, the foliage of bulbs, corms, and the like should be looked after. Then is the time to water and feed well, for it is usually then that food for future growth and flowering will be stored in the organ and development there will take place. With true bulbs the flowers will usually be formed inside in the 'embryo' state. As the foliage deteriorates watering should usually be gradually reduced until the pots are allowed to go dry. There are exceptions (see below) for which it is necessary to give just a little water when the organs are dormant. However, in general the organs can be stored dry during dormancy or over winter, and suggestions for storage are given under the individual species headings.

TABLE THREE

SPRING FLOWERING BULBS, ETC., FOR POTS

Many of the following have small storage organs and should be planted 5 to 7 per 5-inch pot or *pro rata* according to size. They are generally best grown in half pots except for the larger bulbs like hyacinths, narcissi, and tulips.

Allium (1–3 per 5-inch pot)	Leucocoryne
Anemone	Leucojum
Babiana	Muscari
Bulbocodium	Narcissus (includes Daffodil)
Chionodoxa	Puschkinia
Crocus	Scilla
Eranthis	Tulip (there are many species)
Erythronium	Tecophilea
Fritillaria	Urginea
Galanthus	
Hermodactylus	
Hyacinth	

BULBS AND OTHER STORAGE ORGANS FOR GREENHOUSE DECORATION

Achimenes

There are numerous species and varieties of these charming flowers embracing many colours. Some are upright growing and

others are trailing and ideal for hanging baskets. Some can be
grown either way and if wanted upright can be given a few
twiggy sticks for support. They are grown from tubercules
which are small catkin-like storage organs. These can be started
into growth from late January to April by immersion in moist
peat in a propagator at 60/65°F (16/18°C). As soon as they
are seen to sprout, set about three to five plants to a 5-inch pot,
just covering with compost. Half pots can be used if desired for
the upright types. If put in baskets, about ten to fifteen will
be needed for one of average size. After planting, the temperature should be allowed to fall as little as possible. In the cool
greenhouse, planting is best left until March or April. When
growth is proceeding well, water generously and in summer see
that humidity is kept up. Slight shading from direct sunlight
will be required. Flowering usually begins in June and may continue until late autumn. When the foliage begins to die down
reduce watering and gradually allow the pots to become dry.
The tubercules can be stored with the pots on their side and
quite dry over winter in a frost-free place. The following January
the compost can be separated from the tubercules, which should
have increased in number considerably, and started again and
potted as already described.

In most catalogues will be found listed the Michelssen hybrids
which have large flowers in bright colours and a neat habit. A
fine variety for hanging containers is 'Cattleya' with blue and
white flowers. 'Purple King' is an old favourite of dwarf habit
and easy for beginners. Also easy is 'Paul Arnold', violet-purple
with strong stems. 'Peach Blossom' has rich pinkish flowers with
dark eyes. Very many beautiful forms can be obtained from
specialists.

Begonia (see also pages 116 and 183)
Among the tuberous begonias can be found some of the most
impressive greenhouse blooms. A catalogue from a specialist
firm should be obtained for descriptions of named varieties, of
which there are very many. New varieties are introduced frequently. These choice varieties have enormous blooms in wonderful colours but are necessarily expensive. The beginner would
do well to start with some of the cheaper, but quite good,
varieties offered in the catalogues of seed firms. They are usually

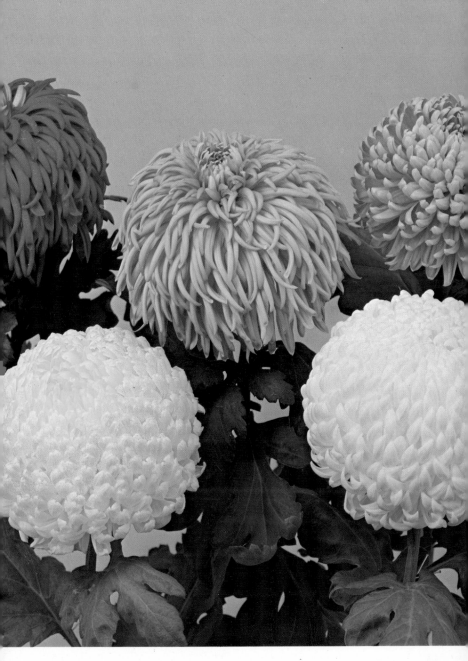

CHRYSANTHEMUMS: DAVID BURTON, GLORIETTA, ORANGE
LILIAN SHOESMITH, YELLOW FRED SHOESMITH, AND
FRED SHOESMITH

FUCHSIAS

PELARGONIUMS:
SOLANO, GRAND SLAM,
LAVENDER GRAND
SLAM, AZTEC AND
GRANDMA FISCHER

A BENCH OF PRIMULAS:
P. MALACOIDES,
P. OBCONICA AND
P. KEWENSIS

A CORNER OF THE
AUTHOR'S GREENHOUSE
IN SPRING, SHOWING
ORCHIDS (CYMBIDIUMS)
WITH BULBS AND
OTHER POT PLANTS

THE AUTHOR'S CONSERVATORY:
GROUP OF PLANTS INCLUDING CINERARIAS, CALCEOLARIAS,
CLIVIAS AND SCHIZANTHUS

GLOXINIAS AND IMPATIENS IN THE AUTHOR'S GREENHOUSE

listed at the end among miscellaneous bulbs, tubers, etc., and include pendulous and multiflora sorts.

Start the tubers by immersion in moist peat at a temperature of about 65°F (18°C). This should be done as early in the year as possible for summer to autumn flowering the same year. If possible maintain a temperature of about 55°F (13°C) after transferring the tubers to 5-inch pots when they show signs of growth. The top should come level with the compost surface. The top is usually the concave or flat side. If large exhibition blooms are wanted allow only one shoot per tuber to develop. Others can be used as cuttings and should be carefully broken off where they meet the tuber. As the plants grow the stems will be very brittle and a cane should be given for support. When buds begin to form feeding should commence. The male flowers are the showy ones, and to encourage the resources of the plant to be directed towards these, the female buds should be removed. The females usually form each side and can be easily identified by the winged seed pods attached. Summer shading is important, especially when the plants are in bloom. Coolglass is ideal for begonias since, as well as giving excellent light for growth without the risk of scorch, it gives good colour rendering of the blooms.

After flowering reduce watering until the pots are dry, but while the foliage is in good condition do not be in too much haste to withhold water and reduce feeding. When the pots are dry at the end of the year the tubers can be removed, freed from adhering compost and top growth, and stored in a frost-free place in a box of clean, dry sand over winter.

Canna (see also page 237)
The best canna for pots in the greenhouse is the low growing 'Canna Lucifer'. This variety is very neat and sturdy, reaching only about 1½ to 2 feet in height. The huge gladiolus-like flowers are a brilliant vermilion and orange. This variety and other taller named varieties, some of which have beautiful bronzy-coloured foliage (see also page 237), can be started from fleshy rhizomes, again immersed in moist peat early in the year at about 60/65°F (16/18°C). When seen to be growing, the rhizomes should be transferred to the smallest pot that will take them comfortably and kept as near about 60°F as

possible. 'Canna Lucifer' will flower well in 7-inch pots, but the larger varieties will need 10-inch pots. The earlier the rhizomes are started the longer will the plants be decorative— from summer to late autumn. Water and feed well during summer and gradually reduce watering in autumn. Cut off the faded top growth and store the pots in the greenhouse under frost-free conditions. It is best if the pots are not allowed to go absolutely 'dust dry' in winter. If the rhizomes dry out completely they sometimes die or do not start well again. The following year the rhizomes can be removed from the pots and started again. It may be possible to separate them into several segments to increase the number of plants. In general, cannas like plenty of warmth, light, and feeding, but they are easy summer greenhouse plants.

Cyclamen (from seed, see page 123)

Beginners find it easy to grow cyclamen from the corms of young plants offered by specialist nurserymen. Old 'corky' corms may flower badly or not at all, although there have been exceptions when plants continue to flower for many years. Start the corms from July to August, but planting in 5-inch pots of potting compost. The convex side of the corm should be put downwards in this case and about a third of the corm allowed to protrude above the surface of the compost. No extra warmth is necessary at this time of year and the pots can be conveniently accommodated in frames shaded well. Water cautiously at first and more generously as the plants make active growth. Bring the pots into the greenhouse in September and try to keep a minimum temperature of about 50°F (10°C). Premature flower buds can be removed if they form too early and the main display is wanted during winter and early spring. The corms can be kept for further flowering for one more year if desired. To do this, continue watering and feeding after flowering for a time. Then gradually reduce until the pots are only sufficiently moist to retain the foliage in good condition. Rest the plants in a shady cold frame standing the pots on a layer of shingle to prevent entry of worms, and return to the greenhouse in September, then treating as before. Some people recommend drying off the corms completely after flowering, but I have had better results through cultivating the plants as described here. The corms usually offered are choice greenhouse varieties mostly with large flowers. However, some of the hardy cyclamen species are worth growing in the cold greenhouse (see page 18), and also in an alpine house (see page 209).

Eucharis

The species usually grown is *Eucharis grandiflora*. It is a very large, long-necked bulb which should be potted as described for hippeastrum (page 150). This bulb is not suitable for chilly conditions and is most likely to succeed in a warm greenhouse. The large, powerfully fragrant flowers are white and reminiscent of those of the daffodil in shape. In warm conditions they are borne several times a year including winter in a warm greenhouse. Minimum temperature should be about 60°F (16°C). This bulb likes a fibrous compost, and if the John Innes is used some extra peat can be mixed in. In summer give plenty of water and feed when active growth is being made. In winter also water enough to maintain the foliage in good condition. This bulb must never be allowed to become completely dry. A certain amount of potting-on can be done, but top dressing will eventually become necessary rather than disturbing the bulb.

Eucomis (pineapple flower)

The species grown is *Eucomis bicolor*. Its common name is derived from the strange pineapple-like cap of foliage at the top of the flower spike. The bulbs are easy in the cool greenhouse. Pot direct into 5-inch pots early in the year, leaving the nose exposed. Water cautiously until growth is seen. In the cool house no extra warmth is necessary, since the bulbs are almost hardy. The flower spikes are sent up from July to August. The flowers, borne hyacinth fashion, are greenish with lilac edges, and on about 1 foot stems. Although the flower is attractive and bound to catch attention, it can sometimes emit a very offensive carrion-like odour and is then best put outside. This fact rarely seems to be brought to the growers' attention.

Freesia (from seed, see page 124)

Corms planted during summer, about six to a 5-inch pot, should flower during winter. The large flowered hybrids, which are not hardy, should be obtained. No extra warmth is needed in summer, but a winter temperature of about 55°F (13°C) is desirable. After flowering the culture outlined as for growing from seed should be followed (see page 125). Freesias like plenty of light or the foliage will become pale and inconveniently long. Very choice named varieties are available as corms, and some are specially noted for fragrance, such as 'Blue Banner' and 'Souvenir'. 'White Swan' is an excellent cut flower, and 'Pink Giant' is exceptional for free flowering. Not all are scented.

A further planting can be made in late September if desired for winter to spring bloom. In this case the pots should be plunged as for spring flowering bulbs (see page 140).

Gladiolus

The ordinary garden gladioli are not very successful in pots and there is little point in growing them in this way. An exception is 'Nymph', a variety of the dwarf species *Gladiolus nanus*. Other named varieties of this species can, however, also be tried if desired. Plant about three to each 5-inch pot in late autumn, just covering with compost. Keep in a frost-free house or frame until March when they can be put on the staging and given gradual extra warmth. Water freely only when growth commences and becomes vigorous. *G. colvillii* 'The Bride' can be grown similarly and is early flowering. Both these varieties are white, but 'Nymph' has bright carmine streaks.

Gloriosa (gloriosa lily)

The most readily available and most commonly grown is *Gloriosa rothschildiana*, a delightful species that can be easily grown from large elongated tubers. It is by nature a trailing plant and can look very effective in hanging containers provided that there is enough height to the greenhouse—the plant may hang down at least 5 feet. Generally, it is more convenient to grow it as a climber. The leaves have tendrils at the ends to assist support, but a cane and tying will usually be necessary. The flowers are like those of reflexed lilies—brilliantly coloured crimson and yellow, freely borne, and very attractive indeed.

The tubers are often very long. Start them into growth by immersion in moist peat at about 60/65°F. If you have a warm greenhouse this can be done as early in the year as convenient for early flowering. If conditions in the house are cool, delay starting until later. April to May starting will result in flowers from late summer to autumn. Check the tubers each day and at the first sign of rooting, transfer to 7-inch pots. Set the tuber so that the rooting end is centrally placed. Maintain warmth and water well as soon as top growth becomes vigorous. Just before flowering start feeding and continue until the end of the year. When the foliage begins to deteriorate—this may not be until early winter—let the pots go dry and remove top growth remains. The following year the pots should be carefully tipped out—the tubers are brittle and easily damaged— and it will usually be found that at least one extra tuber has been formed. Shade the greenhouse slightly in summer and maintain a good humidity. A similar species sometimes grown is G. *superba*.

Gloxinia (see also page 125)

These wonderfully exotic and showy flowers with pleasing velvety foliage are easily grown from tubers started in early spring, or earlier if there is general greenhouse warmth. It is often difficult to distinguish which is the 'right way up' for the tubers, but if they are started by being plunged in moist peat at about 60°F (16°C) it soon becomes apparent where roots and where shoots form. Pot in 5-inch pots, in which they can be left for flowering. If potted early the pots are best left in a warm propagator. The plants like warm, humid and shady conditions. Water well when growth is rapid but try to keep water off the foliage if possible. However, a fine mist of water, that does not allow water to collect on the foliage in droplets, is beneficial in improving humidity. After flowering, which is usually from late summer to autumn, gradually reduce watering and allow the pots to dry out. Then tip out the tubers, free from compost and remains of top growth, and store in a dry, frost-free place until starting time the following year. Two-year-old tubers usually give the finest results. After this they may become 'corky' and are best discarded. Propagation of plants that you wish to retain can be done from leaf cuttings (see page 227). Catalogues list a number of named varieties.

Haemanthus

The species generally grown is *Haemanthus multiflorus*. This has an extraordinary flower like an enormous crimson dandelion clock, and bright green attractive foliage often coming after the flower. Pot the bulbs in spring as for hippeastrum. Give little water until the bulb is seen to be shooting. Once this occurs, growth is usually remarkably rapid. Flowering is usually late summer and this is followed by the luxuriant foliage. Then is the time to feed and water well, gradually reducing this as the foliage deteriorates. During winter keep the bulbs almost dry or they may rot, and at a temperature of not less than about 40/45°F (7/10°C). If potted in spring, no extra warmth is usually needed to get the bulbs growing.

Hedychium (gingers)

Several species can be grown from rhizomes. The most usually seen are *Hedychium coccineum* with scarlet flowers, H. *coronarium* which is white and scented, and H. *gardnerianum* also powerfully fragrant, and with red and yellow flowers, and probably the best. Height is from about 3 to 4 feet and the flowers are borne in spikes during late summer to autumn. Pot the rhizomes in March, choosing pots large enough to take them comfortably. Pot on as required. Ultimately very large pots or small tubs will be required. Best results are had by letting the plants become established in these and leaving them undisturbed. Water well in summer, sparingly in winter. The plants may take a few years before they flower freely, but the foliage is attractive and tropical looking. Although they are called 'gingers' and belong to the ginger family, these species are not the source of commercial ginger.

Hippeastrum (so-called amaryllis)

This is an important and impressive indoor bulb that has now become extremely popular. It can be had in the 'prepared' form for Christmas and early flowering, and is available in a number of named hybrids with enormous trumpet flowers in beautiful colours. Bulbs for normal flowering should be potted in early spring. The very large bulbs should be given a 7-inch pot and potted so that about two-thirds protrude above the compost surface. The flower bud may soon appear and grow rapidly.

During this time watering should be cautious, since it is not until the foliage begins to appear that there is substantial root growth. For this reason great care must be taken when the great flowers are formed, at the top of the stem, to see that the whole plant does not topple out of its pot—there may be no roots for anchorage. When the foliage forms, watering can be generous. If potted in spring, the natural greenhouse warmth may be adequate for growth. Earlier planting will demand more warmth, and often an indoor windowsill can be used to grow excellent plants. A first quality bulb may produce two flower stems each bearing four flowers. Sometimes a later flowering will occur in autumn.

Hippeastrums, like many other members of the Amaryllidaceae, prefer to remain undisturbed for as long as possible. For this reason repotting should be delayed for at least three years if possible and top dressing carried out. Although some people dry off the bulbs over winter, I find that far superior results are had if the bulbs are given just sufficient water to keep them maintaining the foliage in good condition. However, this can be done only in a greenhouse where the temperature minimum is about 40/45°F (7/10°C). Prepared hippeastrums are potted from October onwards usually for Christmas flowering. Full instructions are supplied with the bulbs. Hippeastrums can be grown from seed, although flowering may take from three to five years. They can also be propagated from offsets or, in other words, from the small bulbs that often form around the side of the large parent. These bulbs can be separated when repotting (see page 229).

Hymenocallis (Ismene) (Peruvian daffodil)

The species usually grown is *Hymenocallis calathina* and the variety usually available is called 'Advance'. This can be treated exactly as for hippeastrum, to which family it belongs. The flowers are very like daffodil in structure and have a delightful fragrance. Sometimes available is *H. festalis*, the variety 'Zwaneburg' being particularly fine. The flowers of these species are white, but a very pale yellow form is sometimes seen. Hymenocallis is frequently listed in catalogues as 'Ismene'. Pot up early in the year and maintain a temperature of about 55/60°F (13/16°C). The temperature requirement is somewhat higher than for hippeastrum so it is not so suitable for the cool greenhouse. Flowering occurs from March to April. A good-sized bulb will flower year after year, but small bulbs will have to be grown on before satisfactory flowering takes place. Keep almost dry in winter and leave undisturbed for as long as possible.

Ixia, Tritonia, Sparaxis

Since the culture of these is similar, they are described together here. They are grown from small corms and have dainty, many-coloured flowers borne several to a spike on stringy, wiry stems. They make good early cut flowers but are pleasing when grown for decorative pot effect and are rather like freesia. They can be planted similarly. The best time is in October after which they should be treated like spring flowering bulbs and plunged. During about January the pots can be transferred to the cool greenhouse and very gently forced if desired. Culture is similar to freesia (see page 147). Flowering can be expected in spring. There are many named varieties of ixia and the nurserymen's catalogues should be consulted for details. The tritonias usually grown in the greenhouse are *Tritonia crocata* varieties, 'Orange Delight' being recommended. *Sparaxis tricolor* and *S. grandiflora* are mostly grown in the greenhouse and the variety 'Fire King' is an old favourite. These corms are not expensive, and after flowering it is a good idea to plant them out in the garden. Outside they should be well covered with soil and given a warm, sunny site.

Lachenalia (Cape cowslip)

Several species are grown from small bulbs. These are of special interest because they can be a good choice for baskets and their flowers are long lasting. The best for baskets is *Lachenalia bulbifera*, usually listed as *L. pendula*. The flowers are coloured in a combination of yellow, red, and purple. The bulbs can be planted through the sides of wire baskets, set with 2 to 3 inches between each bulb. Alternatively the bulbs can be put on top of the moss lining, with their tops pointing downward, before the compost is put in. A few more bulbs should be put at the top and around the edge. Such a hanging container will become a globe of colour when the flowering occurs from December onwards. Other species can be given bowls or pots with about

five or six bulbs to each 5-inch container or *pro rata*. Just cover
with compost. Potting is best done from August to September.
Put the containers in a cold frame or cold greenhouse and transfer to the cool greenhouse where the temperature does not fall
to below about 40°F (7°C). Temperatures in excess of about
55°F (13°C) must however be strictly avoided or flowering may
fail. After potting see that the compost is moist but do not be
too free with water until the foliage is well away. Best for pot
culture is 'Nelsonii', a variety of *L. aloides*.

After flowering put the containers in full sunlight and when
the foliage dies down allow them to go dry. They may be left
dry until the next potting time when any off-sets can be
separated for propagation.

Lily

Most lilies are excellent for pots. In recent years some wonderful hybrids have been introduced, some of which are expensive
and could constitute a risk in the open garden. Under-glass
success is usually ensured provided simple cultural care is taken.
The majority of lilies grow well in the potting composts recommended in Chapter Seven (page 92). However, they do not
seem to like richly manured or fertilised soils or composts. A
simple, special one which is easy to make consists of 4 parts
fibrous loam, 3½ parts sterilised leafmould, 2 parts grit, and
½ part of crushed charcoal (¼-inch lumps). Some lilies form
roots at the base of the stem. To provide compost for these as
they develop it is possible to increase the depth of the pot
by adding a collar of metal sheet or plastic, or by cutting a
plastic pot to suitable shape (see Fig. 14). When potting lilies,
the 'nose' of the bulbs can be left slightly protruding from the
compost, so as to give maximum useful depth for the basal
roots (if such a collar is used); if any stem roots appear they can
be given compost immediately by tipping it into the extra space
provided by the collar. Autumn to spring is the best time for
planting. After potting, the bulbs must be kept cool by plunging as described for spring flowering bulbs (see page 140). Care
should be taken that there is not too much moisture present, or
rotting may occur. When growth begins, the pots can be
brought into the cool greenhouse, but high temperatures must
be avoided. Usually, the most useful pot size is from 6 to 8

inches, depending on the size of the bulb. The larger lilies can
be set one to each pot, but some of the smaller types can
be put three together. For descriptions of the enormous range
of lilies available, the catalogue of a specialist firm should be
consulted (see appendix). Specially recommended are 'Mid-
Century' hybrids, 'Oriental' hybrids, and 'Fiesta' hybrids. The
following species and their varieties are also excellent:

Lilium auratum. Very exotic and powerfully scented. Stem
rooting. Has some fine named varieties with rich colouring.
L. brownii. White trumpet flowered with outside shaded choco-
late brown. Stem rooting.

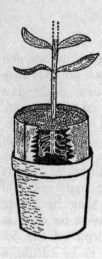

Fig. 14 LILY COLLAR

Stem roots of lilies can be given more compost by adding a collar of bent zinc or
aluminium (or plastic).

L. japonicum. Trumpet flowered, white tinted pink, fragrant,
about 2–3 feet high. Plant three or four to each 8-inch pot.
L. longiflorum. The Easter lily forced by professional growers
for Easter. Stem rooting. A good variety is 'Holland's Glory'.
L. regale. Very well known in gardens, but also good in pots.
Stem rooting to some extent.
L. speciosum. Reflexing petals, fragrant and often flushed pink
or crimson. Flowers in autumn when many others have finished.
Most are stem rooting.
L. tigrinum. The tiger lily, an old favourite. 'Splendens' is good
for pots, and there is also a double form.
L. umbellatum. A low-growing lily for limited space. Erect,

colourful flowers, often very exotic. There are many named varieties.

L. *formosanum pricei*. This trumpet-flowered lily is remarkable for its ability to flower the first year from seed. It is best to acquire your stock this way, because the bulbs that form the first year can be saved for even better bloom production the following year. The first year, about five seedlings can be given a 10-inch pot. In subsequent years, plant about three bulbs to the same sized pot. Normally, other lilies take some years to reach flowering size. Sow L. *formosanum* as early in the year as possible. Germinate at about 55°F (13°C), and prick out into small pots and pot on. You will be delighted with this lily which is so easy, free flowering, and fragrant.

Nerine

For the greenhouse the exquisite named varieties of nerine should be obtained, not garden forms. Beginners often fail through incorrect culture of these bulbs. They should be potted immediately they are received in August, one bulb to a 5-inch pot. Pot as for hippeastrum, leaving the top of the bulb above the compost surface. Place the pots outdoors in a sunny frame and give no water until there are signs of growth of flower spike or foliage. At this stage give water generously, ensuring that the compost is thoroughly moistened all through. I suggest the John Innes No. 2 or a peat/grit compost. The all-peat type are difficult to wet once dried out. Bring the pots into the cool greenhouse for flowering from autumn to December. The flowers are borne as umbels of six to ten, on stems about 1 foot high, and have graceful, slender petals. The colours are glorious shades of rose, pink, and salmon, and a glistening metallic lustre often enhances their beauty.

After flowering cut off the dead umbel and continue watering until the foliage yellows. Then reduce watering, allowing the pot to go dry, and store dry in a frost-proof but sunny place until next starting time. Do not repot for several years—the bulbs prefer to remain undisturbed. Top dress before starting into growth; and when repotting is necessary, do it in August.

Polianthes tuberosa (tuberose)

This is noted for its sweet scent, and it also makes a fine cut flower, but it tends to be an untidy pot plant. The variety 'The Pearl', which is double flowered, is usually grown. The species itself is single and quite pretty. Both are white with the flowers borne as spikes. Pot the bulbs as soon as received with the tips just protruding from the compost. One to a 5-inch pot or three to a 7-inch pot. Water cautiously at first and try to maintain a temperature of about 55/60°F (13/16°C). If the bulbs are obtained in spring this will not be difficult in the cool greenhouse. However, the tuberose can be forced at almost any time of the year if this temperature is attainable. The bulbs often fail to flower if saved for another year. This could be due to the fact that most are imported from Mexico and it is difficult to give the best ripening conditions here. After flowering, try exposing the bulbs to as much sunshine as possible, then store dry over winter in a frost-free place.

Smithiantha

Modern smithiantha named varieties embrace some of the most beautiful combinations of flower and foliage colours to give often very dramatic effects. The leaves are also of delightful velvety texture. The flowers are borne as spikes and are reminiscent of foxglove in structure. Colours embrace shades of salmon, pink, cream, orange, yellow, red, and purple. Foliage colour may be rich shades of green, olive green, red or purplish, and there may be an iridescent sheen.

Start the rhizomes in late winter at 55°F (13°C) by immersion in moist peat. When growth is seen, immediately pot one rhizome to a 5-inch pot or three to a 7-inch pot. Cover with just a thin layer of compost, and make sure they are placed flat. Return the pots to the propagator if the greenhouse is cool until the plants are well rooted. Then water generously. Where early conditions are cool it is best to delay starting until March. Feed well when the flower spikes are first noticed forming. Flowering will be from late summer to autumn. After flowering gradually allow the pots to go dry, and then store them on their sides in a frost-free greenhouse over winter. The next year, tip out the pots and separate the rhizomes—which should have increased in number. Pot and start again as already described. During summer try to maintain a moist atmosphere, and shade the greenhouse well. Early started plants can be stopped to produce bushy plants, but this delays flowering for a couple of months. The many named varieties are described in the specialist growers' catalogues.

Sprekelia formosissima (Jacobean lily or Aztec lily)

This bulb has quaint, thin-petalled flowers, coloured rich crimson, borne on stems about 1 foot tall. Pot with neck protruding, as for hippeastrum, in February. A 5-inch pot is adequate. Try to maintain about 45/50°F (7/10°C) and water cautiously at first. The flower will usually appear before the foliage in June. When the foliage is growing well, give water freely and feed. In autumn allow the pots to slowly go dry and store the bulbs dry in their pots over winter until starting time the following year.

Vallota speciosa (Scarborough lily)

This species is best first acquired as large, flowering-sized bulbs. These should be potted in August, one to a 5- or 6-inch pot with the tops protruding as for hippeastrum. Water carefully at first, increasing as growth becomes vigorous. Flowering is in autumn, the trumpet-shaped scarlet flowers being borne at the top of strong stems. Each stem may carry as many as ten buds with about four or five open at the same time. They are large and showy. Vallotas are best treated as described for hippeastrum (page 150), and kept slowly growing in winter in the cool greenhouse. They usually produce off-sets which can be separated during repotting. These may take three to four years to reach flowering size.

Veltheimia capensis

This species has an attractive rosette of foliage from the centre of which rises a flower like a small red hot poker. It is a very easy bulb and of interesting appearance, but the flower colour is a rather drab pinkish shade. Pot in autumn in 5-inch pots leaving about half the bulb above the compost surface. The pots can be put directly on the staging of a cool greenhouse and kept just moist. Flowering is sometimes erratic and may occur from winter to early spring. Continue watering and feeding until summer and then rest the bulbs by keeping almost dry until autumn.

Zantedeschia aethiopica (arum or calla lily)

This is the well known arum 'lily' of the florist—although it is not a lily. The rhizomes should be potted from September to October, one to each 6-inch pot or about three to a 10-inch pot. It is an advantage to mix some crushed charcoal with the potting compost since it will have to be kept very moist. Just cover the rhizomes and keep the pots in a cool greenhouse, making sure the compost is kept nicely moist. Flowering is from March to June but depends on the greenhouse temperature. In warmer conditions, giving slight forcing, flowering can be considerably

TABLE FOUR

MORE SUMMER TO AUTUMN FLOWERING BULBS FOR POTS

Plant		Flowering time
Acidanthera	May	July
Brodiaea	Autumn	June
Calochortus	Spring	Summer
Camassia	Autumn	July
Chlidanthus	Spring	July
Crinum	Spring	July/September (1 per 10-inch pot)
Crocosmia	Spring	July/August
Galtonia	Spring	July/August (3 per 8-inch pot)
Habranthus	March/April	June/July
Iris	September/October	May/June (Dutch, English, Spanish)
Ixolirion	September/October	May/June
Lapeyrousia	Spring	Summer
Lycoris	Spring	August
Ornithogalum	September/November	Summer (Chincherinchee)
Oxalis	September/October	May/July
Ranunculus	Early Spring	June/August
Sternbergia	September/November	September/October
Zephyranthes	February/March	September

Pot five to seven to each 5-inch pot or *pro rata* according to bulb size unless otherwise stated.

earlier. After flowering and during summer, stand the pots outside, gradually reducing watering until the pots are allowed
to go dry in autumn. Until this time, however, always water
very generously indeed. The plants should also be well fed when
growing vigorously. The dry pots can be turned out in September and the rhizomes, which should have multiplied, repotted
as already described. There are several other ways that this plant
can be grown, but this is the easiest.

CHAPTER TEN

Favourite Greenhouse Plants for Flowers

THE following plants are generally best obtained as small specimens from nurseries or as rooted cuttings. Some are sold as 'house plants' and they will be found to grow to their full glory in the greenhouse. Remember that it is better to buy small plants rather than large, mature ones. This is not only cheaper, it also gives the plants a chance to get used to the conditions of your greenhouse. The more tender plants are best acquired during the warmer months of the year. Beware of buying plants that have been standing outside flower shops during chilly weather. Reputable nurseries send out plants at the right time of year. The plants are carefully packed and may be in pots or wrapped in moist paper. Pot up immediately the plants are received, but be careful not to over-water at first. Damaged roots may rot if waterlogged. It should be noted that there is a vast range of greenhouse plants and that it is only possible to make a selection here. I have therefore concentrated on subjects that should be freely available. Too often plants are recommended that are almost unobtainable. See appendix for suppliers.

Acalypha hispida (red-hot cat tails)
This is sometimes sold as a house plant, for which it is hardly suited. Its attractive feature is the long, catkin-like, pendent, crimson flowers. Unfortunately, without warmth and a very high humidity it rarely succeeds. It also likes an abundance of moisture during the summer and should be well shaded. Minimum winter temperature: 55°F (13°C). Add some crushed charcoal to the compost. In ideal conditions it will eventually reach a considerable size and it flowers from spring to summer.

Aeschynanthus speciosus (trichosporum)

This is also sold as a house plant and if kept on the dry side it will survive a winter minimum of about 45°F (7°C). This species is good for hanging pots or baskets. It is better in the latter because it likes an aerated compost. Some fibrous peat and moss should be added to a peat grit potting compost. It should be sprayed often with water during summer and well shaded; it will grow best in warmth and humidity. Groups of bright orange tubular flowers are borne from summer to autumn and at odd periods at other times.

Agapanthus (African lily)

Although there are several agapanthus that can be grown, the Headbourne hybrids, which are practically hardy, make excellent greenhouse plants. They are ideal for the unheated greenhouse where they will flower earlier and remain in good conditions longer. Give each plant a 10-inch pot. Water and feed well in summer, but keep on the dry side over winter. They bear large umbels of beautiful blue flowers from July to September, and the plants are noted for their neat compact habit, which makes them especially good for pots. These hybrids are available from any good garden centre or hardy plant nursery.

Astilbe

The hybrids are fine plants for the unheated greenhouse, but given slight warmth it will produce graceful feathery plumes from April to May (compared with June to July in the case of outdoor plants). Not all astilbes are suited to pot culture. The low-growing types are best, and for forcing the varieties 'Fanal' (red plumes) and 'Deutschland' (white) are especially recommended. Five-inch pots are suitable and it is wise to include some crushed charcoal with the potting compost since plenty of water is needed the year round, and they are semi-aquatic. Plants are best potted during autumn and kept in a cold frame until December. From then on the plants can be taken into the greenhouse and forced for early bloom at temperatures from 50/60°F (10/16°C) allowing the maximum temperature to be reached slowly over a couple of weeks. Cut off faded top growth in autumn and propagate by dividing the roots before repotting.

F

It has been found that roots that freeze during dormancy can be forced earlier.

Azalea

Beginners often confuse the tender and the hardy azaleas grown in pots. Most of the hardy evergreen outdoor dwarf types make excellent plants for the cold or unheated greenhouse where they will bloom earlier. These are available from any good garden centre, and a wide selection of varieties is usually stocked. They are usually container-grown and merely need transferring to proper flowerpots using a lime-free potting compost. Flowering is extended to several weeks during the spring months. Unfortunately the Indian azalea, *Rhododendron indicum*, is often also expected to be hardy. This is the azalea that appears in florists' shops at about Christmas time, and is only suited to the warm greenhouse. Moreover, the plants that come on to the market in flower have been forced commercially by special techniques. Sometimes, owing to chill and sudden temperature changes, bought plants may drop their flowers and foliage. To save these plants they should be kept warm and humid and shaded until summer. They can then be stood outdoors in a shady place and kept well watered. If in autumn the plants are placed in a greenhouse with a temperature of about 55°F (13°C), they may flower once again in December. At lower temperatures flowering will be later. A winter minimum of about 40/45°F (4/7°C) is desirable. Water with clean rainwater and always use lime-free potting composts, or acid-type composts. Repot when necessary in autumn.

Begonia (tuberous, see page 144; from seed, see page 116)

There are very many species with delightful flowers often combined with decorative foliage, and many are sold as house plants. Easy and impressive is *Begonia corallina*, and very similar is *B. x lucerna*. These have heart-shaped olive-green leaves spotted white above and flushed with red below. The flowers are borne very freely from spring to autumn on established plants and in large clusters. Their colour is deep pink and they have conspicuous winged seed-pods attached. Small plants will flower well. After some years in the cool greenhouse a height of several feet can be reached and viewed from below the hanging flowers look most impressive. B. *fuchsioides* is a compact, winter-blooming shrub, with fuchsia-like flowers as the name implies. B. *coccinea* grows very tall and has flowers similar to B. *corallina* but bright scarlet in colour. It flowers from spring to autumn. Its hybrid, 'President Carnot', has spotted foliage and more vigorous growth, but the flowers are paler. B. *haageana* has foliage coloured dark green on top and red below, and pretty pale pink flowers. B. *boweri* has foliage edged with chocolate-coloured streaks. It is somewhat hairy and has pale pink flowers in spring. B. *manicata* bears delicate panicles of pink flowers in winter. The foliage is also interesting with tufts of red hairs below and red borders. All these species are happy in 5- to 8-inch pots and with a winter minimum of about 50°F (10°C). For some the temperature can fall considerably, but they will usually suffer by dropping foliage and taking on a leggy, scruffy appearance. However, they usually recover with the warmer conditions of spring. Keep well watered in summer and shaded, and maintain humidity. In winter keep only just moist depending on the minimum temperature. The lower this is, the less water should be applied. Propagation can be carried out using stem cuttings or leaf cuttings, or by simply dividing the roots or rhizomes.

Beloperone guttata (shrimp plant)

Frequently seen on sale as a house plant, the common name is derived from the strange appearance of the bracts surrounding the insignificant flowers, which flourish from spring until late winter. Young plants should be given 5-inch pots and the first flowers and bracts removed to encourage general growth. Although it is often recommended that shade be given in summer, in fact the plants can be put outside in full sunlight—provided watering is not neglected. The sunlight develops a fine rich colouring. The plants can be returned to the greenhouse in early autumn. A winter minimum of about 45°F (7°C) is advisable to keep the plants in good condition, and watering should then be slight. Overwintered plants that have deteriorated can be cut back in early spring. They will usually grow to large specimens during the summer.

Bougainvillea

Some of the most showy climbers or wall shrubs are to be found
among the species of this genus. Again it is the highly coloured
bracts that give the display and the actual flowers are very
modest. It is not often realised that although the plants can
eventually cover large areas they will in fact make very attractive plants when quite small, even in 5-inch pots. By constant
pruning they can be kept as neat shrubs if you have limited
space. However, they are seen at their best when grown against
the wall of a lean-to or trained along wires up in the greenhouse
roof. For this purpose the plants are best set in large pots or
small tubs. When grown against a wall, a trellis or plastic netting should be given for support and the plant's stems tied to
this. Water well in summer and keep up humidity by frequent
spraying with clean rainwater. In winter keep on the dry side
and try to maintain a minimum temperature of about 50°F
(10°C). *Bougainvillea glabra* has mauve bracts and flowers well
as a very young plant, so also will *B. x buttiana*, of which the
finest variety is 'Orange King'.

After flowering, some pruning can be carried out, but February is the time for close pruning and the removal of all weak
growth.

Callistemon (bottle brush)

A number of species can be grown. The one usually recommended is *Callistemon citrinus* which eventually takes up considerable room. In fact *C. linearis* is much easier and more
practical for the home greenhouse. It is also hardy in mild areas
and is ideal for the unheated greenhouse where its bright red
'bottle brush' flowers will not become bedraggled owing to rain
—a common trouble when grown outdoors. This plant can be
kept to a neat shape, although the less pruning done the better.
It can be trained to form a short standard if desired. Flowering
is in July. It is available from some garden centres grown in
containers and it should be potted in a 10-inch pot. Water well
and give maximum light and air. In winter give less water to
keep conditions just slightly moist. The roots should not be
allowed to dry out completely. Ultimate height can be kept to
about 4 feet.

Camellia

These well-known evergreen shrubs are splendid for the cool or
unheated greenhouse and, contrary to widespread belief, they
flower freely as quite small plants, sometimes even in 5-inch
pots. There are very many named varieties, usually derived
from *Camellia japonica*, and a specialist nursery should be consulted before you make your selection. Although mostly perfectly hardy, under glass they bloom earlier, unblemished by
weather, and also last longer. The pot size depends on the size
of the plant purchased, but camellias can be grown in pots that
seem far too small provided they are fed well. An acid compost
is best. In alkaline conditions the foliage may become yellow
and growth poor. Never allow the roots to dry out, especially
when the buds form. Erratic watering, with extremes of dryness
and wetness, is a common cause of bud dropping and leaf fall.
Beginners often experience this trouble, which may result from
ill-treatment the plants have received months before. Shade the
plants well under glass where the temperature can easily rise
too high. Like all hardy plants under glass they object to 'oven
temperatures', and must be well ventilated. The plants benefit
from spraying with clean rainwater in summer, and they should
also be watered with this in hard-water districts. Flowering
usually takes place from February to May but in the greenhouse
can be considerably earlier. The plants eventually need pruning
to maintain shape and convenient size. This should be done
after flowering and before the commencement of active growth.
At this time any necessary potting-on can also be done. It is
usually advisable to stand camellias out in the garden during
summer to give more room in the greenhouse. Choose a shady,
sheltered place, stand pots on shingle to prevent worms entering,
and do not forget to water and feed.

Other species are sometimes available. The early flowering
C. sasanqua narumi-gata is very fragrant. The large white
blooms are borne from October to November. There are a
number of varieties derived from *C. saluensis* x *C. japonica*, all
of which are even less tolerant to lime. The late flowering
C. reticulata semi plena has exceptionally huge flowers in salmon-
red. Waxy white flowers are borne by *C. taliense*.

Campanula

Most greenhouse campanulas can be grown from seed (see page 118). The one most usually purchased as a plant is the very old-fashioned *Campanula isophylla*. This is an outstanding plant for hanging baskets, or for pots at the edge of the staging, where it will form a cascade of bloom from late July to autumn. It is happy in a frost-free greenhouse provided that it is kept on the dry side over winter. The blue form is probably the most attractive, but there is also a white form. Often leaf variegation occurs spontaneously, the foliage becoming edged cream. If a piece is removed and treated as a cutting a new variegated plant will result. However, in my experience such plants are less vigorous and the flowers are smaller. Propagation of *C. isophylla* can only be carried out by taking cuttings or by division of the roots in spring. It cannot be grown from seed.

Citrus (orange, lemon, grapefruit, lime, etc.)

Many people try to grow these from seed and are disappointed with the outcome. Success cannot be guaranteed because in commerce special techniques are used to produce plants suitable for cropping. These do not always come true from seed. Lemon and grapefruit are the most likely to give satisfaction from seed. Quite good lemon trees can sometimes be grown in only a frost-free greenhouse if there is enough space. Sometimes citrus species appear on the market, but they are not common.

By far the best investment is *Citrus mitis*, the dwarf orange, also known as Calomondin orange. This is generally easily obtainable since it is sold as a 'house plant'. Best results with the dwarf orange will be obtained in the cool greenhouse with a winter minimum of about 45°F (7°C). In these conditions the waxy, fragrant white flowers, and little oranges in various stages of ripening, will be on the plant almost the year round. Initially the plants are expensive, but they are well worth the money and will give pleasure for many years. They are best purchased in early spring. Shade only slightly to protect from intense sunlight, and keep well watered during active growth from spring to summer. Keep only slightly moist in winter. If subjected to sudden changes or allowed to dry out, the foliage may turn yellow or fall. Overwatering will also cause yellow foliage, as will also a compost that is not acid enough. Potting-on should not be done too frequently and not until the roots are slightly pot-bound. An acid compost must be employed. It may be an advantage to water the plant with a solution made by dissolving a pinch of aluminium sulphate (from a chemist's shop) in a pint of water. Clean rainwater is also best used for general watering, and the aluminium sulphate treatment only given if there is a tendency for leaf yellowing. Scale insects can be killed by dabbing with methylated spirit. Fortunately the dwarf orange is remarkably resistant to misfortunes, and even if all the branches become bare it will usually spring to life again when correct treatment is given. It can be very vigorously pruned if desired and trained to shape easily. Even if cut back severely it will usually grow new shoots soon.

The little oranges, about the size of walnuts, can be preserved in syrup and used in cocktails, and a well-established and well-grown bush will give an excellent crop. The seeds are few, but they will germinate at a temperature of about 65°F (18°C).

Clivia

For some unknown extraordinary reason clivias are sometimes described as grown from 'bulbs'. The plants actually have fleshy roots. The species usually grown is *Clivia miniata*, but this has several varieties. It is an easy but extremely impressive plant, with bold strap-like foliage and enormous umbels of large, erect, trumpet-shaped flowers borne in spring. These are coloured in showy orange shades. If small plants are purchased they should be given 10-inch pots. Plants can be grown from seed but may take at least three years before flowering. Splendid plants can be grown in a cool greenhouse, but over winter they will survive in a frost-free house if kept fairly dry. When in active growth they should be well watered and fed. Once established, they grow vigorously and soon fill their pots with roots and form side growth. When this happens the plants should be turned out of their pots after flowering and repotted after separating the side growth. This should be done as carefully as possible by disentangling the roots. If there is difficulty it is better to cut through the roots with a *very sharp* knife, or razor blade—this will not cause bruising of the tissues. After repotting, water very cautiously until the plants are seen to be growing well.

Daphne

The daphne most suited to the greenhouse is *Daphne odora* which is suited to just frost-free conditions and is a neat evergreen. It bears heads of very pale purple flowers from January to April and these have a delightful spicy fragrance. This species is usually obtainable from garden centres, particularly in the south and west where it is hardy in sheltered places. Once potted in 10-inch pots it needs little attention apart from watering and an occasional feed when in active growth.

Erica (heather)

Several greenhouse species come on to the market at around Christmas time. The most common are *Erica gracilis*, which has pink flowers and a white form, and *E. hyemalis*, which has long foliage and pink tubular flowers. These may have been forced for early flowering. The plants should be potted on when necessary in an acid potting compost (see page 98). They can be stood outdoors in summer when they should be watered and fed generously. They can be returned to the greenhouse in September where a temperature of about 45°F (7°C) is adequate. Water with clean rainwater.

Erythrina crista-galli (coral tree)

This is a spectacular shrub with herbaceous habit that has recently become more widely available. It should be potted in 10-inch pots in spring. A temperature of about 50/55°F (10/13°C) should be maintained to start growth if possible, and when this occurs water can be given in increasing quantity until it is generously applied. From June to July the large, waxy-textured, pea-like flowers are freely borne. They are a glistening red and very showy and unusual. In summer, keep the house cool, shade slightly, ond spray the foliage from time to time with water. During a good summer the plants can be stood outside to give more greenhouse space. In autumn, return the pots to the greenhouse where the winter minimum should be about 40°F (4°C) and the plants should be kept fairly dry.

Faded top growth can be removed, since new growth is formed each spring.

Fuchsia

This favourite is so well known that no description is necessary. It is usually encountered as one of the many named varieties that can be grown as shrubs or standards, or as hanging basket plants. There are also types for training against greenhouse walls and some noted for beautiful foliage. Some fuchsias, especially those related to the species *Fuchsia triphylla,* may not always be instantly recognised as fuchsias. Their flowers are very long and tubular.

There are numerous firms specialising in fuchsias and their catalogues should be consulted when making a selection. In them will be described a fantastic range embracing the varieties of many famous breeders. In recent years the American fuchsias have been given much publicity because of their great size and often double form with marbled colours on the petals. However, our own developments have probably done the fuchsia greater service because the grace and beauty inherent in the flower has been preserved in most cases. Most varieties are conveniently and cheaply bought as rooted cuttings in spring. These should be potted in $3\frac{1}{2}$-inch pots as soon as received.

Fuchsias can be grown in several ways and when ordering some consideration should be given to this. Some varieties are ideal for training as standards, especially those with elongated single blooms, or for hanging baskets. Some are best kept to the bush shape and others can be formed into fancy shapes like pyramids. All good catalogues will help in selection. All fuchsias need some small amount of training to be developed for best effect. This may have to start with the newly potted rooted cutting.

To grow a standard the tip of the plant must be retained intact at all costs. The plant must be grown on and potted on as required with this as the object. All side shoots should be removed, a cane being provided as support for the stem, until the required height is reached. It may be necessary to grow the plant on over winter, and in this case a growing temperature of about 55/60°F (13/16°C) is essential to prevent the plants becoming dormant and to attain the desired stem height. When

F*

the required height is reached the top of the stem can be nipped off. Branching shoots will then form immediately below. These should be stopped also to encourage further branching, and so on, until a bushy head is developed. At this time, and not before, the foliage on the supporting stem should be removed.

Hanging baskets of normal size usually require about three plants set around the edge. Once the leading stem is well over the basket side it should be stopped to produce plenty of branching growth.

As ordinary pot plants fuchsias need only be stopped from time to time to encourage bushy growth and a neat sturdy habit. Weak and unwanted growth should be cut out promptly and without hesitation. Although the flowering period of fuchsias extends over several months training involving stopping should not be performed too long in case the plants fail to get a chance to flower. Plants are best left to grow unmolested for about eight weeks prior to the required flowering time. Where large plants are being trained, or in the case of standards, a whole year may have to be devoted to the process.

Many of the choice greenhouse fuchsias are not hardy, or they might be severely checked or damaged if left outdoors. All those, whether hardy or not, used to decorate patios or terraces and window boxes, and in portable containers, should be put into frost-free conditions for the winter. The plants can be trimmed back to save space and kept only very slightly moist in a winter minimum of about 40°F (4°C). When the natural temperature begins to rise in spring more water can be given and any repotting or potting-on needed carried out. When new growth is under way, some of the shoots may have to be cut out to secure a good or desired shape. These shoots can be used as cuttings for propagation.

Give as much light as possible with protection from direct intense sunlight to get the best flower colour. Slight shading with Coolglass gives excellent growing conditions. Do not neglect feeding or watering. Varieties with ornamental foliage particularly need good light to develop foliage colour. In summer overhead spraying is beneficial. Remove all faded flowers and their seed pods promptly.

Gerbera (from seed, see page 125)

When bought as plants, named hybrids should be obtained from specialist growers (see appendix). They should be potted into 3½- or 5-inch pots, depending on their size, as soon as received. Plant so that the crowns are very slightly above the compost surface as this lessens the risk of rot. Watering needs care. Water should always be applied thoroughly but only when necessary. In winter little is required—just sufficient to keep the compost slightly moist. Plenty of light is also necessary, but in summer protection from intense sun must be given. Do not expect to get masses of flowers the first year. It may take three years before a good crop is obtained, but the blooms are so beautiful that it is well worth waiting. There should be a plentiful supply during the winter months. When removing the flowers they should not be cut. Pull the stems sharply so that they come away from the crowns. If a piece of stem is left it may instigate a rot which can spread down to the crown. Gerberas can be easily grown in the cool greenhouse with a winter minimum of about 45°F (7°C).

Hydrangea

Most of the hydrangeas seen in pots are varieties of *Hydrangea macrophylla*. Also effective is *H. paniculata* which bears large creamy-white panicles of bloom during late summer and early autumn.

Greenhouse hydrangeas are frequently acquired originally as pot plants bought from florists and intended for home decoration. When flowering is over, dead flowers and any weak stems or growth should be cleanly cut off. The plants should then be stood outdoors in a shady place, with their pots plunged in moist shingle or peat. This should be well over the pot rim if plastic so that the compost is kept moist. During summer, cut out shoots that have flowered to a point just above the highest of any new side shoots that may have formed. The best flower heads for the following year will be borne on these new shoots. Give liquid feeds from time to time as the plants grow during summer.

Take the pots into the greenhouse in autumn when the foliage falls and give very little water during winter. Temperatures over about 50°F (10°C) should not be allowed since this may inhibit flowering later. During February, pot on if necessary, and raise the temperature slightly if early flowering is required. At this time more generous watering can begin.

A special technique is used to raise flowering specimens from cuttings. The cuttings should be taken from flowering shoots about 4 inches long. These should be treated in the standard way (see page 224). Roots will quickly form at 65°F (18°C). Pot on to 2½-inch pots of acid or lime-free potting compost. When the plants are well rooted stop them so that there remain only two pairs of leaves. After potting-on to 5-inch pots a few weeks later, plunge the pots outdoors as already described. In early July stop the plants by reducing all shoots formed after the first stopping to two pairs of leaves. This should result in bushy plants to produce about five heads of flowers in summer, or in spring if the plants are gently forced. To force, maintain a temperature of about 60°F (16°C) from late December.

To obtain plants with one enormous flower head, strike cuttings in early autumn and treat as described except for stopping so that one stem develops.

Most hydrangeas become too large for the greenhouse after a time and they can then be transferred to the open garden. H. *paniculata* should be treated differently from H. *macrophylla*. Remove blooms after flowering and do not prune until autumn when each growth should be cut back to about three buds from the base. Untidy growth, basal suckers, drooping shoots, and weak wood must be cut out.

Some varieties of H. *macrophylla* can be 'blued'. No attempt should be made to blue those varieties which are naturally pink, white, or red. Generally, blue varieties tend to turn pink, or become of poor faded colour, in alkaline soil or compost. This is why acid compost should always be used. Good blue colours can be attained by incorporating aluminium sulphate with the compost or by watering with a solution. Dissolve ½ ounce aluminium sulphate in one gallon of clean rainwater and water the plants with this every two weeks throughout the growing period. Normal watering should also be done with lime-free water.

A number of specifically coloured named varieties will be found described in nurserymen's catalogues.

Jasminum

The most common greenhouse jasmine is *Jasminum polyanthum* which has an extremely powerful scent and bears masses of white flowers late in winter. In the cool greenhouse it is ever-green and tends to be rather rampant if unchecked. It can be grown in 10-inch pots and trained up wires or a plastic mesh fastened to a wall. Do not hesitate to stop shoots to attain neat growth, otherwise this climber can get quite out of hand. The best minimum temperature is about 40/45°F (4/7°C). Choose a position of good light and water well during summer. Be care-ful not to overfeed or there will be much foliage and less generous flowering.

Lapageria rosea

This is not a common species, but I include it in the hope that some publicity will bring it to the fore. It is an extremely beau-tiful evergreen climber with large, elongated, waxy, bell-like flowers, usually bright red. There is a white form and recently a pink has been obtained. The flowers are borne from September to late November, and the plant is quite at home in merely frost-free conditions. It is easily grown in 10-inch pots and it is easy to train, requiring little attention apart from an occasional tie. The plant is stocked by some nurseries and garden centres, par-ticularly in the south and west where it is hardy in sheltered places.

Nerium oleander (oleander)

This easy evergreen shrub usually begins flowering in early summer and continues until late autumn. It can reach a con-siderable size in the cool greenhouse, but can be kept in check by severe pruning if desired. Normally the plant should be given plenty of water at all times, but in cool or frost-free winter conditions it should be kept on the dry side. Good specimens can be kept in 10-inch pots for many years. If the tops are cut off when too high, new basal growth will develop. Proper pruning is important. Shoots that grow from the bases of the flower trusses should be removed at as early a stage as possible. After flowering, shoots of the previous year's growth should be cut back to within 3 inches of their base.

There are single and double flowered varieties in white and

shades of red and pink. Cuttings usually easily grow roots if
just stood in a glass of water. Indeed, many plants are acquired
from friends in this way. Considering their ease of culture and
their lovely showy flowers, borne in profusion over a long
period, oleanders ought to be more popular.

Pelargoniums (see also page 130)
These can be divided for convenience into three groups: zonal
pelargoniums (the so-called 'geraniums'), ivy-leaved pelargoniums, and regal or show pelargoniums. The last are particularly suited to greenhouse decoration. Some of the ivy type
are ideal for hanging containers or for trailing from shelves or
the staging edge.
Zonal pelargoniums During the summer there is little point in
growing these in the greenhouse. Under glass they will flower
well in winter—which is not generally known. Take cuttings
early in the year from plants that have been overwintered in
the greenhouse. For rooting the cuttings use a propagator at
about 60°F (16°C) and follow the general procedure (see page
224). Pot on the rooted cuttings into 2½-inch pots, and later
pot on as required. In summer, plunge the pots outdoors in a
sunny position, but taking care to keep the compost moist. Stop
the central stem when about 4 inches high and remove any
premature flower buds. In autumn, take the plants into the
greenhouse where, with a minimum temperature of about 45°F
—though preferably about 50°F most of the time—a good
display of bloom should be had all winter. Ventilate the greenhouse well whenever outdoor temperatures permit, and keep a
watch for *Botrytis cinerea* (grey mould, see page 85). Plenty
of winter light is desirable.
Ivy-leaved pelargoniums Varieties with variegated foliage are
particularly attractive—'L'Elegant', for example. Depending on
the hanging container size, three or four plants will be needed
for each. Little attention will be needed after planting except for
occasional stopping to promote branching growth and dead
flower removal.
    Ivy-leaved varieties can be trained up the wall of a lean-to,
or up the side of a greenhouse, if some plastic netting to which
the stems can be tied is provided. If given a 10-inch pot, the
plants will grow to a considerable height.

Regal pelargoniums The very showy and exotic blooms of the regals make them especially suited to greenhouse protection, but after flowering they should be plunged outside as already described for zonals. Cuttings can be taken during July and August and rooted, also as described; these can be kept over winter in 2½-inch pots at a temperature of (preferably) about 50°F (10°C). Rapid growth will commence in spring and the plants should then be stopped to encourage branching and potted on to 5-inch pots. Old plants from which cuttings have been taken should be drastically pruned back—don't be afraid to do this. Place the cut-back plants in a frame and give frequent overhead sprays of water rather than applications to the roots. This treatment induces much new growth, and then is the time to repot using the same size pot after reducing the root ball. This process will result in very nice bushy neat plants of show standard.

Often, one sees pelargoniums of all types which are straggly and untidy because the growers are afraid to cut back and prune severely when necessary.

Plumbago

The favourite is *Plumbago capensis* which has very beautiful phlox-like masses of bloom from spring to autumn. It is best described as a wall shrub and is seen at its best when trained against the wall of a lean-to. However, with constant pruning it can make a neat, bushy shrub. In both cases a 10-inch pot will ultimately be needed. If allowed to grow unchecked it will reach a height of about 12 to 15 feet and become a very impressive sight when in flower. It is very easy to grow in the cool greenhouse, where it should be kept just moist in winter and well watered in summer. After flowering, pruning should be carried out by reducing all growths by about two-thirds. In the cool greenhouse this species is evergreen, but if chilled it may lose its foliage in winter. In a warm greenhouse the flowers often appear over a longer time.

Roses

Roses grown in pots in the greenhouse can be flowered in early spring. Procure high quality H.T. roses in October in the usual way. Clean the roots under running water to remove soil, and pot into a potting compost using 8-inch pots. Trim the roots to fit the pot if necessary and cut away cleanly any that are damaged. After potting, stand the pots in the open garden on a layer of shingle until December. Return the pots to the greenhouse and prune the plants if necessary, with the object of getting several good shoots rather than lots of weaker ones. Drastic pruning will give better results than a hesitant, cautious trim.

Only cool conditions are required: temperatures over about 50°F (10°C) should be avoided. Ventilate whenever possible. In these conditions flowering should commence during April. Some growers prefer to stand out the pots for a year, removing most of the flowers in the early bud stage so that the plants' resources are directed to development. When they are stood out all summer the pots are best plunged (see page 59). Plants so treated can be returned to the greenhouse earlier, in November, and gradually forced in January. Again, 50°F should not be exceeded and the plants should be pruned, but this time much more leniently. Some of the floribunda and polyantha roses also make good pot plants. Some climbers can also be used on walls of lean-to houses or conservatories. There are of course innumerable rose varieties and the catalogues of the specialists, usually beautifully illustrated, should be consulted.

Saintpaulia (African violet) (see also page 133)

In recent years African violets have become very popular house plants. With the right conditions—a congenial temperature and moist atmosphere—they will continue to flower almost the year round. It is a waste of time to try growing them in chilly, draughty, or very dry surroundings. Special cases with thermostatic heating and artificial lighting supplied by a fluorescent tube are available to provide just the right growing environment. In the home and in cold or cool greenhouses these can be used for best results. A large enclosed propagator also makes a suitable home for the plants which are always neat and take up little space (see page 60).

Very many fine named varieties can be had from specialist nurseries (see appendix). You can also grow from leaf cuttings begged from friends (see page 228), or from seed (see page 133). In the latter case colour and form are very limited. The plants will not be despatched from a nursery until the weather is warm enough for safe delivery. Be careful about buying from florists and garden shops in case the plants have been chilled. Pot size depends on the size of the plants obtained. Generally a 3½-inch pot will accommodate a flowering plant for a long time, but a 5-inch may be needed for large specimens. The plants usually look better in half pots when they reach an appreciable size.

Mature plants often produce suckers a short distance from the parent plant. These can be removed by tapping the plant out of its pot and cutting away the sucker, leaving some roots attached. Both the parent plant and the sucker are then repotted. Another method of propagation is from 'side crowns'. These are also produced by mature plants and appear as tiny rosettes of leaves formed between the leaf axils. These side crowns should always be removed whether wanted for propagation or not. This encourages flowering and maintains a neat shape, and the removal is best done with a pair of pointed tweezers or by close snipping with vine scissors. The side crowns root very easily if just pressed into compost in a propagating case.

All propagation is best done at about 65°F (18°C). In general, African violets like warm, shady conditions in the greenhouse and a high atmospheric humidity. A winter minimum of about 50°F (10°C) will be endured if the plants are very carefully watered, but it is safer to keep choice varieties warmer and in a propagating case if necessary. During active growth, spraying overhead with a fine mist of clean rainwater is beneficial. Hard tap water will mark the foliage. If plants are exposed to sunlight when the foliage is wet, brown marks may appear.

Schlumbergera (Christmas cactus)
Several species are grown including the often confused, but very similar, Easter cactus, *Rhipsalidopsis gaertneri*, once included in the genus *Schlumbergera*. The plants have succulent flattened stems and bear very showy pagoda-shaped flowers. The Christmas cactus, *S. x buckleyi*, blooms from December to February and is magenta in colour. *S. truncata* (crab cactus) is

also winter flowering but there are several colours including white and blue shades. All have a trailing habit and are useful for hanging containers, although they are often grown to trail over the sides of ordinary pots. Rhipsalidopsis is considerably more erect in habit and the flowers are usually bright red. All these species are often sold as house plants. They are of easy culture provided that a winter minimum of about 50°F (10°C) can be maintained. Do not allow the compost to dry out at any time, but keep only slightly moist during winter. In summer, the plants benefit from standing outdoors in a partially shaded, but not too shady, place. Propagation is usually very simply carried out by breaking off pieces of the succulent stem and inserting in a cutting compost during summer. A case can be used to keep in moisture but no extra heat is required.

Stephanotis floribunda

This is another plant that can be obtained as a 'house' plant, when it is often trained around a wire hoop. It is a delightful twiner which, given a free run in the greenhouse, will attract much attention and fill the house with fragrance. The foliage is evergreen and the flowers tubular with starry petals at the end and creamy white. These are borne from early summer to autumn. It is usually much more successful in the greenhouse because it enjoys a very high humidity. It should be sprayed frequently with water during summer and slightly shaded. In winter see that the compost is moist and maintain not less than about 50°F (10°C). The plants flower best after they have matured for about two to three years. They can be given 8-inch pots and trained up wires and into the greenhouse roof so that the flowers hang down. Pruning, if necessary for large plants, should be done in February. Leading shoots can be reduced by about half their length, and lateral shoots reduced to about 3 to 4 inches.

Streptocarpus (see also page 135)

Beginners may prefer to buy the streptocarpus hybrids as small plants. They are sometimes advertised by nurseries in the gardening press. The best time to buy is in autumn. If these plants are kept in a cool greenhouse over winter with a minimum temperature of about 45/50°F (7/10°C), they will make rapid growth in spring and should then be transferred to 5-inch pots. In summer, keep the plants well watered and shaded. An overhead spray with a fine mist of clean rainwater is beneficial to maintain humidity. Feed when you first detect buds forming. After flowering, gradually reduce watering and keep only very slightly moist in winter. Plants that have been saved over several years can be propagated by simple division of the roots in early spring. If the plants are left too long without division they may become so leafy that flower production is impeded and obstructed. Propagation can also be carried out from leaf cuttings. A beautiful named variety to look out for is 'Constant Nymph'. This has an abundance of flowers, smaller than in the hybrids, and the colour is lavender with the throats of the trumpets a darker purple.

Strelitzia (bird of paradise flower)

Strelitzia regina is a greenhouse treasure and perhaps one of the most highly prized plants. Unfortunately, its unique exotic flower and tropical-looking foliage have made many people associate it with high temperatures and difficult culture. This is in fact nonsense, although even today one frequently sees it described as a warm-house or stove-house plant. I have had excellent flowering plants in little more than frost-free conditions over winter, and I have also had it as an indoor house plant on a large kitchen windowsill. Indeed, it is a very accommodating plant, which will even put up with some neglect.

The flowering-sized plants are expensive, but sometimes advanced seedlings come on to the market. It is possible to grow strelitzias from seed easily (germinate at 80°F), but they take at least four years to reach flowering size, depending on overall growing temperature. For flowering, the plants can be slightly pot bound, and 12-inch pots or small tubs or some other drained ornamental container will be necessary. The plants need plenty of water in summer and very little in winter. The lower the winter temperature, the dryer they should be kept. In the cool greenhouse or in the home they flower twice a year: in early summer and from November onwards. Sometimes there may be Christmas flowers.

Strelitzias are best left in their flowering-sized pots for as long as possible. Eventually, growth becomes fan-shaped and the plants can then be divided, each segment of the 'fan' being potted as a new plant. The dividing of such a large specimen is a mammoth job, but not difficult. It may be necessary to break the pot away from the roots if these have penetrated the drainage holes. Use a very sharp knife to cut through the fleshy roots. This does less damage than trying to disentangle them. The best time to divide is just after flowering in early summer. The plants enjoy slight shade in summer and their foliage, which is large and spade-like, can be sprayed with clean rainwater during warm weather. The flowers are coloured bright orange and rich blue like the plumage of an exotic tropical bird, the shape of the flower also resembling a bird's head. S. parviflora is worth growing too. It is generally smaller and thus more suitable where space is limited. A so-called 'dwarf' form of S. regina is now available from seed.

Tibouchina semidecandra (T. urvilleana)

This is another superb shrub for the cool greenhouse with a winter minimum temperature of about 45°F (7°C). The plant actually sold under this name is in fact Tibouchina urvilleana but this error seems to have persisted in all catalogues. The true species, T. semidecandra, is very rare. Plants are often sold as rooted cuttings. These should be potted on and have their growing tips removed. A further stopping should be performed on the laterals that form when they are about 4 inches long. Pot on as required to 7-inch pots. A stout cane will eventually be needed for support. Water well and maintain a humid atmosphere while the plants are actively growing. Keep only just moist in winter. The magnificent violet flowers, like enormous pansies, are borne freely from July to November. The attractive foliage often turns red in autumn. In late February, the plants can be cut back severely. Leading shoots can be reduced by half and laterals to two pairs of leaves. To take cuttings, choose non-flowering lateral shoots, about 4 inches long, from March to April. These will root easily by the usual methods (see page 224) at a temperature of about 65°F (18°C). Seed is also available now.

TABLE FIVE

MORE RECOMMENDED FLOWERING PLANTS

Abutilon megapotamicum Easy climber. Lantern-like red/yellow flowers.

Acacia armata Mimosa-like flowers. Compact and better pot plant.

Acacia dealbata Mimosa—only suitable for spacious greenhouse.

Clerodendron thompsoni Climber. Red/white flowers. Warm only.

Columnea Several species for baskets. Red/orange flowers. Warm.

Euphorbia fulgens Stems of orange/red flowers in profusion.

Euphorbia splendens Thorny plant. Scarlet flowers.

Gardenia jasminoides White fragrant flowers, but not easy. Warm.

Globba winitii Stems of rosy bracts long-lasting.

Hibiscus rosa-sinensis Variously coloured showy flowers.

Hoya carnosa Climber. Pink flowers. Shiny bronze leaves. Scented.

Hypocyrta glabra Semi-trailing. Orange/yellow flowers.

Isoloma amabile Orange-red tubular flowers. Hairy edged foliage.

Ixora Heads of showy orange to pink flowers. Small shrub. Warm.

Jacobinia carnea Heads of rose-coloured flowers. Showy. 50/55°F.

Jacobinia pauciflor Yellow/red flowers, pale green foliage.

Jacobinia suberecta Orange flowers, grey felted foliage.

Manettia bicolor Climber with tubular orange flowers.

Medinilla magnifica Spectacular pink flowers. Warm/humid only.

Pentas Various hybrids with starry flowers. Pink to white.

Spathiphyllum wallisii White arum-like flowers. Warm only.

These plants are suitable for a cool greenhouse unless otherwise stated.

CHAPTER ELEVEN

Beautiful Foliage Plants

OWING to the popularity of house plants we are now fortunate in being able to acquire very many delightful foliage subjects that were at one time very difficult to obtain. There are so many that I have concentrated here on describing some of the most beautiful, mostly with coloured or variegated foliage, and those especially suited to greenhouse culture. In most cases, house plants will grow much better under greenhouse conditions. Some are ideally suited to shady places and for growing under the staging. All will respond well and give great satisfaction if given the general care and feeding outlined in Chapter Six.

Aphelandra (zebra plant)

The most common species is *Aphelandra squarrosa louisae*. This has very striking foliage, the large, dark-green, glossy leaves being contrastingly veined with creamy white. When the plant is established and slightly pot bound, it produces curious yellow flowers of angular appearance. When these flowers turn green they should be removed, and afterwards many new shoots usually grow which can be used as cuttings. Although this plant likes warmth and will grow with great vigour in such an atmosphere, it can be acclimatised to survive very low temperatures. In the winter at a minimum temperature of about 40°F (4°C) it may look unhappy, turning its foliage down, but in spring when the temperature rises it will soon recover. In winter, very little water should be given. In summer, water generously. Never let the roots dry out completely. It likes a position with good light.

Aglaonema

There are a number of species and all are attractive plants often sold as house plants. Generally they prefer warm conditions but will survive a winter minimum of about 50°F (10°C). One of the easiest and most vigorous is *Aglaonema robelinii*. This has very large spear-shaped foliage of silvery green with a dark border. In cool conditions in winter aglaonema should be kept almost dry.

Aralia elegantissima (Dizygotheca) (spider plant)

Although often listed under the name *Aralia*, this plant has now been consigned to a new genus: *Dizygotheca*. It has very thinly serrated foliage of great delicacy and a well grown specimen is very beautiful. Unfortunately as a house plant it commonly fails by promptly dropping most of its leaves. It will do the same if subjected to sudden temperature changes. Unless you can provide a congenial warmth fairly constantly, winter minimum about 55/60°F (13/16°C), and maintain a high atmospheric humidity, it is a waste of time trying to grow this species. However, given the right conditions it is no trouble at all and will reach the proportions of a shrub, producing much side growth.

Begonia

There are innumerable begonias with ornamental foliage, many with delightful flowers too (see page 116). One of the most popular is *Begonia rex* with large, heart-shaped leaves beautifully marked and coloured. Another favourite is *B. masoniana*, called the Iron Cross begonia because of its characteristic leaf marking. A begonia that could be more extensively grown is *B. cathayana*. The foliage is reminiscent of *B. rex*, but the veins are red and the stems covered with red hairs. In the greenhouse this house plant usually grows to make a splendid specimen. For the descriptions of the many other foliage begonias, consult the catalogues of the specialist nurseries. Most of the plants prefer some shade and cool greenhouse conditions in winter. Plenty of water when in active growth is required, with just moist roots in winter. A humid atmosphere is always beneficial.

Caladium

These magnificent plants are mostly sold as named hybrids. They are grown from tubers started into growth in March in a propagator at 75°F (24°C). Pot into pots large enough to take the tubers and keep as warm as possible until there is a good head of growth. They may be kept in the greenhouse or used as house plants during the summer, but they quickly deteriorate in cold conditions. The large, showy leaves are somewhat arrow-shaped and very strikingly coloured or striped in green, cream, or bright red. In autumn the foliage dies down and the pots should then be stored almost dry—but not quite—over winter, and at a temperature not lower than about 55/60°F (13/16°C). Often the plants can be bought already in leaf growth during summer, and it is then possible to select the finest colours. This is not an easy subject unless you have a warm greenhouse, especially if you intend to grow the same plants year after year.

Calathea

There are a number of species of this genus with the most wonderfully coloured foliage. The leaves are also usually beautifully marked with stripes and blotches. *Calathea zebrina* is so named because of its stripes. *C. ornata* has cream veins lined with pink against a dark-green background. *C. backemiana* has vivid green blotches contrasting with silvery grey-green, and *C. picturata* has bright green bordering with a rich maroon colour below. The culture of this genus is almost identical to maranta (page 188). The plants are similarly ideal for the under-stage area and shady places.

Cissus

The most popular and easy of this genus is *Cissus antarctica*. The most beautiful is, however, *C. discolor* which unfortunately is less amenable. It needs a winter minimum of about 55°F (13°C) if it is to remain in good condition and not shed foliage. It is a delightful climber with bright green foliage marbled with a variety of lovely colours including pink, crimson, purple, and white. The undersides of the leaves are coloured a rich crimson. This species makes a splendid plant for a hanging basket. It is a good choice for a small greenhouse run at a higher temperature for a special collection of sub-tropicals, but in a cool green-house it will certainly be disappointing.

Ctenanthe

For some obscure reason these often appear on the market labelled calathea, which they resemble although they have a closer upright habit. They are likewise similar to maranta (page 188). Of the several species, *Ctenanthe lubbersiana* seems the most common, probably because it is a comparatively easy plant and will survive in a cool greenhouse with care. The foliage is mottled light and dark green and cream and is borne on longish stems. It enjoys quite gloomy conditions and is excellent under the staging.

Codiaeum (croton)

The plants sold in florists' shops under the name of 'croton' are usually *Codiaeum variegatum pictum*. It is very variable indeed, but the foliage is nearly always exotically coloured with various combinations of orange, red, and pink. Most varieties have long oval leaves rather like *Aucuba japonica*, the well known 'laurel', but there is one with quite different thin foliage. Again, these plants are not suited to conditions where the temperature can fall below about 55°F (13°C) in winter. Wide temperature fluctuations are also to be strictly avoided or the foliage will fall. Those varieties with narrow foliage are generally easier than the others. Unlike the majority of the foliage plants described here, the codiaeums should be given plenty of light, especially when they are achieving active growth. If, through an accidental drop in temperature, the foliage should fall, cut the plants right back. New growth will form if the temperature is restored. Do not buy these plants during the winter months.

Dieffenbachia picta

There are a number of varieties with handsome, spade-shaped leaves in various shades of green, usually marked or mottled with cream and sometimes veined. All are suited to partial shade rather than full light or the gloom under the staging. They are also all rather tender and should have a winter minimum of 55°F (13°C). A moist atmosphere is also essential to maintain reasonably fast growth and the production of new foliage which does not remain in its best condition for long. All parts of the plants are extremely poisonous. Ingestion of the sap is said to prevent the power of speech for some days.

Dracaena

Most dracaena species are happy with a winter minimum of about 50°F (10°C). They mostly have narrow or strap-shaped leaves and may eventually take on a palm-like appearance. *Dracaena parri* is sometimes used outdoors in summer for sub-tropical bedding effect. The foliage of most species is usually coloured or very attractively striped. During summer, growth should be encouraged by maintaining warm and humid conditions with good watering and feeding. In winter keep the plants on the dry side. Slight shade is required in summer, but in general the species like bright conditions. They can be grown in from 5- to 10-inch pots depending on species and size. Cuttings can be taken from basal shoots in spring. These root at 75°F (24°C) in a propagator. It is of interest to note that the first leaves that form on the cuttings are usually plain green, the true colours forming later.

Ferns (see also page 124)

Many ferns are valuable for the cool shady greenhouse, such as one that has to be overshadowed by a house or a lean-to faced north. *Pteris quadriaurita argyraea* is unusual for its silvery variegated fronds. *Nephrolepis exaltata*, the ladder fern, is ideal for hanging baskets, but it is important not to let it dry out in winter when it has lost its fronds. This fern can be easily reproduced from runners which it forms freely. *Athyrium filix-femina*, the lady fern, is hardy although deciduous. *Dryopteris filix-mas*, the male fern, also makes a beautiful pot plant and is indigenous to this country. *Polypodium vulgare* is hardy and a fine pot plant too. A tiny graceful species is *Davallia mariesii* and this is also hardy, at least in the south. This species can be made into 'fern balls' by being wound in moss and formed into a sphere by fastening with fine wire. The balls can be hung from the greenhouse roof. During summer they must be kept sprayed with water. In winter the fern is deciduous and the balls can be dried off and stored in a dry place.

For the warmer greenhouse the strange stag's horn fern (or

elk's horn) *Platycerium bifurcatum* can be entwined in moss and fastened to cork which can be hung from the greenhouse wall or from the wall of a lean-to.

Ferns like a moist but well-drained compost at all times. Most prefer shade or make it an essential requirement, and a moist atmosphere. An overhead misting with clean rainwater from time to time in summer is beneficial. Although most ferns will grow well in the potting composts described in Chapter Seven (page 92), they generally prefer acid conditions. Some also benefit from the addition of some sterilised leafmould with the compost.

Ficus

The popular rubber plant is *Ficus elastica decora*. The variety 'Doescheri' is beautifully variegated in pale green and cream. It has been said to be more difficult, but I have not personally found it so. Both, if ill-treated by erratic watering and wide temperature change, will drop their lower leaves. Although these plants are often grown in very small pots, more even conditions of moisture at the roots will be attained by keeping their pot size in relation to plant size. Best results are had when the temperature can be kept reasonably within the range 55 to 60°F (13 to 16°C). *F. benghalensis* is easy and very resistant to cool conditions, also simple from seed, but not so decorative. *F. diversifolia*, the mistletoe fig, is so named because it bears yellowish berries. A very impressive plant is *F. lyrata*, the fiddle-back. This has large foliage shaped like a violin. All these grow to a considerable size in a warm greenhouse. Should the lower foliage fall, the tops of the plants can be cut off to encourage new growth from the base. Most people are reluctant to do this, in which case air layering (see page 230) can be tried. Most varieties seem to grow best in partial shade, but not excessive shade (with the exception of *F. pumila*, a small creeper which is almost hardy).

Fittonia

Among the smaller foliage plants *Fittonia argyroneura* is one of the most charming. It has oval-shaped green leaves with the intricate network of veins strikingly contrasted in creamy white to give a lace-like effect. Unfortunately it is essential for this delightful species to be kept warm, but being small and compact this is easy to do with the aid of a propagating case. It is a good plant for bottle gardens or plant cases where a moist atmosphere, a winter minimum of about 60°F (16°C) and moderate shade will maintain the plant's beauty.

Maranta (prayer plant)

The marantas, like most other members of the family, are very beautiful plants. When making active growth they all like warmth, humidity, and shade. They are excellent for under the staging, and do not grow as tall as the calatheas. The name 'prayer plant' is due to the fact that at night the leaves fold and become erect, like hands closed in prayer. Several varieties of *Maranta leuconeura* are commonly grown. 'Massangeana' has large chocolate-brown spots on the foliage. 'Kerchoveana' has a 'herring-bone' marking. Both these are easy and will survive in a cool greenhouse over winter. Indeed, I have had them in only a frost-free greenhouse and they have grown again with the natural increase of warmth in spring. However, in the cool they will become very tatty and may lose all their foliage. The most beautiful is 'Erythophylla' which has larger foliage flushed with red. This is far less tolerant to cold and needs a winter minimum of about 55°F (13°C). All marantas and the other members of the family should have plenty of moisture and a humid surrounding when actively growing. Overhead misting with water is beneficial. In winter, water according to prevailing temperature. The cooler it is, the less water should be given, and in very cool conditions keep the plants almost dry. If the fleshy tuberous roots rot they will not grow again with resumption of warmer conditions in spring. For marantas, 3½- to 5-inch pots are usually adequate.

Monstera

Monstera deliciosa and M. *pertusa* are sold as house plants. The latter is often incorrectly given the name of the former, but is easily distinguished by much more compact habit and more rounded foliage. The leaves are large and have perforations or slits. Owing to the size of the plants they are best seen in their full glory in the space of a greenhouse or conservatory. Fortunately, the plants will survive a winter minimum of about

45/50°F (7/10°C) if kept only slightly moist in winter. They will begin growing vigorously when the temperature reaches about 65°F (18°C) so that in the greenhouse they can reach a considerable size. They may, in fact, even flower and fruit. The flower is an arum-like spathe and the fruit like a small elongated pineapple without the crest of foliage. The fruit, which takes at least a year to ripen, is said to be delicious, hence the name *deliciosa*, but I have found it unpleasantly fibrous. M. *deliciosa* is an impressive plant to train up a roof support or up a trellis on a lean-to wall. It will produce aerial roots which should be trained back down into their 12-inch pots or small tubs. Monsteras are quite unsuited to a small greenhouse unless you want to grow nothing else!

Palms (see also page 130)
The palms are among the most graceful and elegant of all foliage plants. Unfortunately, in the relatively small greenhouses of today it is rarely possible to show them to their best advantage. The nomenclature of palms is often confused and species appear on the market with a variety of names, frequently incorrect, and with an assortment of common or fancy names such as 'fan palm', 'Chinese palm', and so on. This makes identification difficult, particularly since many palms in the very young stage can look alike. Usually sold as 'Kentia' palms are *Howea belmoreana* (curly palm) and H. *forsteriana* (flat palm). Both are splendid greenhouse or house palms and they will be happy with a winter minimum of about 45°F (7°C). *Phoenix roebelinii* (dwarf date palm) has also come on to the market as a pot plant (see page 130), but the true date palm, *Phoenix dactylifera*, which some people grow from date 'stones', is not recommended. It grows too large and demands too much warmth. *Neanthe bella* is an attractive palm in the young stages and takes up little room. It is probably the most compact palm for the home greenhouse, and quite easy.

Most palms prefer plenty of light, and they do not mind pots that appear far too small. They like plenty of water, but perfect drainage. The compost should be acid. The John Innes with the chalk omitted, and a more fibrous peat used, has given good results with the palms I have grown. Some crushed charcoal added also is an advantage. During summer a spray with clean rainwater or a wipe with wet cotton wool keeps the fronds in good condition. When repotting choose a pot to give only about one to two inches of extra compost around the root ball. I prefer clay pots. These can be plunged in a larger container, ornamental if you prefer, of moist peat.

Peperomia

There are numerous species giving a remarkably wide range of leaf variation. All are charming and excellent for a small greenhouse. Most, with the exception of unfortunately one of the most delightful, *Peperomia sandersii*, are of easy culture and will thrive in a greenhouse with a winter minimum of 45/50°F (7/10°C). *P. sandersii* has delightful spear-shaped leaves banded silver and green. It needs careful watering or it may rot, and it prefers a draught-free, moist atmosphere, and a little extra warmth. It is a good bottle garden or case plant. *P. caperata* has tiny corrugated dark-green leaves borne on small, bushy plants and catkin-like creamy-white 'flowers'. *P. glabella* is a trailer with smooth oval leaves. The variegated form is the best. *P. scandens* is similar but has larger foliage. Its foliage tends to drop when the plant is young, but this is less likely as the plant matures. *P. magnoliaefolia* has large, oval, variegated foliage in green and cream. There are several others similar to those described but sufficiently different to be well worth collecting. In general they like shade and careful watering. Water well when necessary, but do not keep the compost too moist all the time. In winter, special care is required, and in cool conditions just enough water to prevent drying out should be provided.

Pilea cadierei

This is one of the most attractive house plants of easy culture, and it has become popular. The dainty foliage is prettily marked with glistening silver. In the greenhouse it can be grown to form a large specimen in a 5-inch pot, but to keep a neat habit it is wise to propagate new plants from time to time. Cuttings root with extreme ease. For best results water and feed well during active growth. It is liable to suffer from magnesium deficiency and watering occasionally with a solution of Epsom salt, about 1 ounce per ½ gallon of water or *pro rata*, will ensure excellent leaf colour and prevent crinkling or distortion. Shade is essential. A minimum winter temperature of about 40/45°F (4/7°C) is desirable.

Another pilea sometimes seen is *Pilea muscosa*, the artillery plant. This is completely different from *P. cadierei* in appearance, having delicate, very 'ferny' foliage. It has flowers which may not be noticed. These distribute pollen in clouds when the plant is shaken, like smoke—hence the popular name. It needs the same culture as *P. cadierei*.

Rhoeo discolor vittatum

This is an attractive plant forming a rosette of strap-shaped leaves, although in the greenhouse it can become fairly tall. The upper side of the leaf is boldly striped with cream and the lower side a deep rose colour. It prefers slight shade and needs careful watering in winter or it may rot at the base. The flowers are hardly showy, but are of interest because they are formed in little cup-shaped structures at the base of the stem. A winter minimum temperature of about 50°F (10°C) is desirable. When well grown the plant will form offshoots around the base which can be separated and used for propagation.

Sansevieria

The most common species is *Sansevieria trifasciata laurentii*. This is often lost through overwatering in winter, when it should be kept almost dry, particularly if the temperature is low. In summer it can be watered freely, but even then should be allowed to go almost dry between waterings. With very careful watering, the plant can be grown in a cool greenhouse, but it is really better suited to a winter minimum of not less than about 55/60°F (13/16°C). Propagation is easily done in summer by cutting up a leaf into pieces and inserting each in the usual cutting compost in a propagator covered to retain moisture. Plants so obtained will be unlikely to have the same variegation, and to get identical plants it is necessary to separate offshoots from mature plants. These and plants from cuttings must be kept very warm until the young plants are well established. Well grown sansevierias, with their tall spiky leaves bordered in cream, are very attractive.

Setcreasea purpurea

This is one of the easiest to grow of all beautifully coloured foliage plants. It will even survive months of neglect and has been recovered from empty houses and brought to life again on watering. Although it will endure merely frost-free conditions and erratic watering, it is best given care. It will then prove extremely decorative the year round. If badly grown it often becomes leggy and untidy. To keep it as a pot plant it can be frequently propagated from cuttings or by root division, when the young plants will retain an erect bushy habit for a long time. However, it also makes a fine trailer for hanging containers if fed and watered properly, and stopped from time to time.

The plant has the habit of tradescantia but the leaves are very long and pointed, slightly hairy, and a glorious purple colour. Small magenta flowers are also produced. This species prefers slight, not too heavy, shade. In excessive gloom the colour does not develop so well. It has been used for outdoor sub-tropical bedding during the summer months.

Tradescantia

Various forms of *Tradescantia fluviatilis* are well-known house plants, but they are often of poor colour or variegation through being overwatered and kept in conditions which are too dark. For the greenhouse, the species *T. blossfeldiana* is a better choice and a good hanging basket plant. It is, however, not so tolerant of ill-treatment and it prefers a warm, moist atmosphere, although it survives in a cool greenhouse over winter. The leaves are larger and covered with white hair, dark green above and purple below. The stems are also purple. It prefers slight shade. Well grown plants flower from spring to summer, their colour being purple to rose pink. A form with cream variegated foliage is sometimes also available. Young plants can make neat pot subjects and they can be grown on for hanging containers if desired.

Zebrina pendula

This is another easy trailer and a popular house plant. In the greenhouse, it is of special value because it will grow under the staging. Unlike the tradescantias, it develops its best colouring in poor light. It is also a marvellous hanging basket plant for a shady greenhouse. Gardeners often tend to overwater, which is not conducive to best colour development. If you desire to grow it as an ordinary pot plant it should be frequently propagated from the easily rooted cuttings. The young plants usually retain an erect habit for some time. 'Quadricolor' is probably the best known variety. Its leaves are above striped with rose-pink, silvery white, and varying shades of green, and are coloured purple underneath. However, this variety should be given plenty of light for the best colour contrast to develop.

CHAPTER TWELVE

Fruit and Vegetables in the Greenhouse

THERE are a number of fruits and vegetables which are ideally suited to the greenhouse. However, it should be realised that to grow well they will need space and often special environmental conditions. Trouble often occurs through attempting to grow them with a variety of other plants and ornamentals. A further point to bear in mind is that low-growing vegetables, like lettuce and early salad crops, can just as well be accommodated in frames (or cloches in some cases), which saves much valuable greenhouse space for crops needing the extra height.

Tomatoes
This is undoubtedly the most important of all greenhouse fruits and extremely popular, so I am giving a little extra detail here. For best results, the crop should be given a house of its own. A glass-to-ground house is preferable. There must be good light and ventilation.

Although basically an easy plant to grow, the tomato is subject to all manner of setbacks in the form of pests, diseases, and cultural problems, which can spoil the plants and the crop during the growing season. With care, and the selection of modern vigorous varieties, most of these problems can be avoided.

The first thing to remember is to *avoid growing the plants in the greenhouse ground soil and the use of crude animal manures of an unsterilised nature.* The great majority of disasters can be traced to these origins. To overcome soil problems it was customary in the past to sterilise the greenhouse soil each year before planting, or change it for fresh. This was time-consuming and not always satisfactory. Nowadays, the home grower is advised to use special tomato composts, available from most

garden shops, or potting composts in 9- to 10-inch pots. Fibre
or composition pots are good enough, and all pots should be
stood on plastic to isolate them from the greenhouse ground soil
and to prevent roots penetrating. Tomato pots which can be
thrown away at the end of the season can be obtained from
most garden shops. Fibre rings for ring culture (see below) are
also available. Disposable pots and the use of composts that are

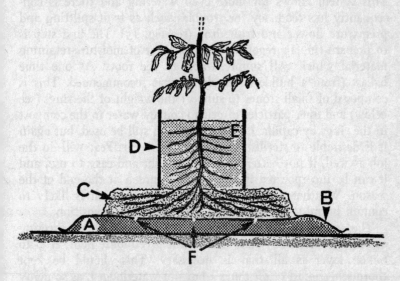

Fig. 15   THE PRINCIPLE OF RING CULTURE

For large installations spread layer of gravel (A) on greenhouse
floor and cover with sheet polythene (B), holed for drainage at
intervals (F). For small installations the gravel and holes in the polythene can be omitted. C: 4 to 6 inches of peat. D: Ring pot. E:
Tomato compost.

discarded at the end of the season, together with care over
general hygiene, will prevent carry-over and build-up of diseases
or pests over the years, and a satisfactory crop can usually be
guaranteed. A simple new method is to grow the plants in 'tom
bags'. These are plastic bags of special tomato compost. A bag is
laid flat on its side, sections cut out with scissors as marked, and
the tomato plants set in the spaces. As the plants grow, a few
slits are cut low on the bag's sides for drainage. At the end of

the season the top growth of the plants should be removed and burnt. The used compost in the bag can be dug into the outdoor garden to provide a source of humus. It should *not* be used again: this should be the rule with all tomato compost of any description.

Ring culture

This system allows for more even watering and there is consequently less tendency for troubles such as fruit splitting and premature flower and fruit drop (see Fig. 15). The first step is to prepare the 'aggregate'. This is a layer of moisture-retaining material which will supply water to the roots. At one time ballast (from a builder's merchant) was recommended. This is composed of small stones to support the weight of the rings (see below) and finer particles of grit to convey water to the compost in the rings by capillary action. This can still be used, but again it is desirable to sterilise or change each year. Peat will do the job as well, if not better. It is lightweight and easy to use, and it can be incorporated in the outdoor garden at the end of the season. Weathered ashes have been used, but ash is likely to contain harmful chemicals and is of variable composition.

The aggregate should be spread out over polythene sheeting or other material to isolate it from the greenhouse floor. A 4- to 6-inch layer is all that is necessary. This should be kept thoroughly moist *at all times*—but not waterlogged, as so many people suppose. One of the automatic systems described in Chapter Five is highly recommended (see pages 67–9). To prevent water–logging a few slits in the polythene sheet will be necessary, and the ground should be well drained below so that any excess water can run away freely.

The rings should be stood on the aggregate and filled with potting compost. Any proper potting compost will do, but a special tomato compost, or the John Innes No. 3 which in trials has given first-class results, should be used. After planting, the compost in the rings must be kept moist until the roots have reached the aggregate, if necessary (although, if the system is working properly, sufficient moisture should be taken up by the ring compost automatically). When it is seen that the ring compost is staying moist, no further water should be applied to the rings—only liquid feeds.

General tomato culture

Although tomato plants can be bought, it is a simple matter to grow your own from seed. For suggested varieties see Table Six. Seed sowing and germination should be carried out as described in Chapter Eight with a temperature of about 60°F (16°C). The time for sowing depends on the required earliness of the crop, which in turn depends on the temperature that can be maintained in the greenhouse. If a winter minimum temperature of about 50°F (10°C) can be maintained during the coldest weather, and the greenhouse is in a light, open position so that it benefits from all the sunshine available, sowing can be commenced during November. However, most home gardeners prefer to wait until February onwards, since maintaining the necessary warmth is then an easy matter. Even so, a November sowing should result in fruit ready for picking in spring, when tomatoes are expensive. With winter warmth, a late sowing in July to give pickings in December is also possible.

The seedlings should be pricked out into 3½-inch pots and grown on for a while to form sturdy plants before permanent planting. During this period, throw out any seedlings of abnormal appearance, especially those showing dwarfing and the production of numerous side shoots, those showing deformity of any kind, and pale, yellow or mottled specimens.

The young plants should be set in the pots or rings spaced so that from stem to stem there is a distance of about 15 inches. A string or cane must be provided for support as the plant grows and the plant led around this in a clockwise direction as its length increases. Strings should be firmly anchored to a short stout stick thrust into the ground (and through the aggregate if this is used). The tops of the strings can be fastened to the glazing bars or to a wire run along the greenhouse roof from end to end.

All side shoots which form where the leaves join the main stem must be promptly removed. This should be a daily routine. After the fourth truss has formed begin feeding with a high potash tomato feed, of which there are several on the market. A liquid feed is preferable, and should be used according to label direction. When the first truss has yielded its fruit and ripened, the foliage below can be removed. This tends to reduce disease problems, but the defoliation should not be drastic—the leaves are vital to the plant's life and functions. Defoliation can be continued upwards as the trusses crop, but if the leaves appear healthy and flourishing it is wise to leave some.

Pollination and setting of the fruit can be assisted by shaking the plants when in flower, preferably on warm, bright mornings. Spraying with a mist of water also helps. In obstinate cases the use of a special hormone tomato set can be tried. These are available from garden shops, and should be applied as directed on the label.

During August, or before this time if they have reached the greenhouse roof, the plants should be stopped. This directs the plants' resources to developing and ripening the existing fruit. It has recently been found that watering the plants with a Cycocel solution at the time of planting reduces the length of stem between trusses. This means that more can be grown to any given height and cropping is increased. There is also evidence that better and more disease-resistant plants result with the Cycocel treatment (see appendix).

During summer, it is vital to keep the greenhouse temperature below about 80°F (27°C). Above this, the fruit will not ripen properly to give a good red colour and flavour. The red pigment cannot form and usually the fruit becomes blotchy or patchy. With too much sunlight 'greenback' can result, which causes the fruit tops to remain green or yellowish. In recent trials excellent ripening has been attained in houses lightly shaded with Coolglass. Avoid heavy shading.

There are various other techniques which can be used in tomato culture. These include grafting on to disease-resistant rootstocks, tiered trough culture, and straw bale culture. It is doubtful whether any of these are an advantage for the home gardener compared with the easy pot and ring systems given here.

TABLE SIX

SOME POPULAR TOMATO VARIETIES

Ailsa Craig   Old favourite for flavour, but prone to ripening and other troubles.

Alicante   Fine quality fruit of good flavour and texture. Relatively free from ripening and other troubles. An excellent amateur tomato.

Big Boy F1   Enormous fruit, but of good flavour. Fleshy texture. Fairly easy culture. Deserves greater popularity.

Gardener's Delight   Very small fruit, but tangy flavour many people like. Very easy to grow and relatively trouble-free.

Kingley Cross F1   Compact for the small greenhouse and a good cropper. Relatively disease-resistant.

Maascross F1   Very early good quality fruit. Good disease resistance. Has proved very successful among amateur growers.

Seville Cross F1   Fruit of fine quality, and good disease resistance. Also has given good results among amateur growers.

Supercross F1   Good crops of excellent quality. Exceptionally good disease resistance—especially to tomato mosaic virus.

Tangella   Tangerine-coloured fruit of excellent quality and flavour. Relatively free from ripening troubles.

Ware Cross F1   Very vigorous plants. Large fleshy fruit of good flavour. Relatively easy and trouble-free.

Yellow Perfection   Rich yellow fruit of excellent quality and superb flavour. Early, easy, and prolific. This tomato ought to be far better known and appreciated. Relatively disease-resistant.

Cucumbers

It is usually recommended that tomatoes and cucumbers should not be grown together because their cultural requirements differ. Should there be pest trouble, many pesticides that can be used on tomatoes with safety will harm cucumbers. Cucumbers also prefer a more humid atmosphere and heavier shading. In spite of this, in practice numerous amateur growers do in fact manage to grow the two in the same greenhouse and get reasonable crops, so it is evidently worth a try. Success is more likely if one of the easier cucumber varieties is selected. Examples include Improved Telegraph, Conqueror, and particularly the 'all-female' types such as Femspot and Rocket (both F1 hybrids). The all-female cucumbers produce few or no male flowers. This means pollination cannot occur (with cucumber, pollination is undesirable). If ordinary varieties are grown the male flowers must be picked off each morning. They are easily recognised because they have no tiny cucumber attached. If pollination is allowed to occur, the fruits become swollen and club-shaped, they 'go to seed' and often develop a bitter taste. The outdoor varieties (Ridge types) will also do well under glass in company with other plants, but again the F1 hybrids are recom-

mended. The apple-shaped varieties are worth trying too. These
are easy, delightful for salads, and deserve to be better
known.

General cucumber culture

To begin with, this is much the same as for tomato. The old
weird and wonderful composts containing animal manures should
be strictly avoided. Use any of the modern sterilised composts
or the John Innes No. 3. Both pots and ring culture can be
used as described for tomato. However, the training is quite
different. Cucumbers are best trained along wires stretched from
end to end of the greenhouse. These wires should be spaced
evenly along the greenhouse roof or from 6 to 8 inches apart.
For the average small greenhouse about five wires will be sufficient. The pots are stood on staging and the plants trained up
and underneath the wires. When the plants reach the last wire
they should be stopped. In the meantime, and also after stopping, side shoots (laterals) will be produced. These must be tied
to the nearest wire and trained along. The laterals usually
develop at least four leaves before female flowers appear. After
the formation of a fruit the lateral must be stopped two leaves
further on from where the fruit is growing. From these laterals
will form secondary laterals, and these should be treated similarly, and so on. It is an advantage to remove tendrils and it is
essential to remove all male flowers.

The plants must be kept moist at the roots at all times, but
not waterlogged. Too much water may cause the young fruits
to go rotten and fall prematurely. Try to maintain conditions
that encourage fast development of the fruit, and do not leave
the cucumbers on the plants for long after they have reached a
suitable size, otherwise a bitter flavour may be produced. For
feeding, use any proprietary liquid or soluble feed according to
label instructions. The greenhouse, or the part of the house,
where the cucumbers are grown must be shaded. Coolglass has
given excellent results when used to shade cucumber houses.

It is best to grow your own cucumber plants from seed, which
germinates well at about 65°F (18°C). When to sow depends
on the greenhouse temperature you can maintain. Less than
about 55°F (13°C) is undesirable, and about 65°F (18°C) ideal.
The average greenhouse gardener will usually find April a con-

venient sowing time for economy in heating and for a good crop of fruit during the summer months.

Melons

In the greenhouse the Casaba melons are usually grown. Varieties to choose include Hero of Lockinge, Superlative, Ringleader, Emerald Gem, and King George. However, the Cantaloupe type, generally much smaller, can be grown if desired—though these give perfectly good crops in frames. Melons can be grown in a similar way to cucumbers but there are certain important differences. The wires should be spaced further apart, about 10 to 12 inches preferably. The house need not be shaded unless it is exceptionally hot and sunny, and when the fruit has reached full size the humidity should be lowered by increasing ventilation and reducing the watering. The best sowing time is March, to yield fruit from July onwards.

The most important difference from the growing of cucumbers is that in this case the female flowers *must* be pollinated. This is done by picking a male flower, removing the petals, and transferring pollen to the female flowers all at the same time. Again, the females have a tiny melon attached, and after pollination this will begin to swell quickly. Do not allow more than about three or four melons to develop on each plant. Usually the secondary laterals give the most fruit. The large fruits will need support with nets available from garden shops. Do not pick until they are absolutely ripe. This can be ascertained by pressing the end furthest from the stalk with the finger. If it is soft and resilient the fruit is ripe.

Grapes

Grape vines require little or no heat in winter and their culture is such that they make difficult companions for the majority of popular greenhouse plants. For this reason they are best given a vinery of their own, and special greenhouses are available or can be built. A south-facing lean-to is ideal. The plants are best planted outside the greenhouse in a well-drained border running alongside. The stems (called 'rods') are then led into the greenhouse, through gaps in the base of the side, and trained up on wires under the roof. Potted plants should be obtained from a nursery and planted in January about 4 feet apart. After plant-

G*

ing, reduce the rods to about 1½ to 2 feet. The first year one leading shoot should be encouraged vertically as far as possible. If only one vine is being grown, two leading shoots can be selected and trained horizontally and in opposite directions. From these, top laterals can be trained vertically and others removed. All side shoots from vertical growth should be stopped when about 2 feet long and cut back entirely in winter. Also in winter, cut back the main leading vertical shoot, or shoots (if several are being grown from a single vine), to ripe hard wood. During the second year, the side shoots should be secured to wires run in a similar manner as in growing cucumbers and melons and a number of bunches of grapes may be produced. Winter pruning during the second and subsequent years consists of reducing all laterals to one or two buds. In the third year there should be a good crop.

Only one bunch of grapes should be allowed to each lateral, any others being removed at as early a stage as possible. To get a good shape to the bunch, and prevent overcrowding of the berries, thinning is usually necessary. This is done carefully with a finely tipped pair of scissors, called vine scissors, and without touching the young bunches with the fingers.

To avoid mildew problems, care should always be taken over ventilation. Although in winter no extra warmth is necessary, from spring onwards a congenial warmth will aid good fruiting. During flowering a minimum temperature of about 55°F (13°C) is desirable. After the fruit is gathered there is no need for warmth at all and the vines can be exposed to frost without damage. Watering should be aimed at maintaining moist conditions at all times and at providing adequate moisture when the plants are making active growth. Waterlogging of the roots must be always avoided. A limited number of grape varieties is available.

Grapes in pots

In the small home greenhouse it is fun and convenient to grow the plants in 12-inch pots. The best varieties for this are Black Hamburgh and Royal Muscadine. Vines grown in this way can be trained up canes, but they cannot be expected to yield more than about six bunches and their life is also limited.

Pot one-year-old plants in December to January. Use clay

pots and plunge them outdoors in an open position—the plants are perfectly hardy. During late winter bring the pots into the greenhouse and start the vines into growth at a temperature of about 50 to 55°F (10/13°C). Two 4- to 5-foot canes should be thrust into the pot, one each side, with another cane tied across the tops to form a loop. The vine is then trained up one, across the top, and down the other, as it grows. The lateral shoots must be limited by removal so as to leave about 1 foot between those remaining. Each of these should be stopped two leaves beyond the place where grapes develop. The following winter when the plant is dormant it should be pruned by removing half the cane formed the previous season, and reducing laterals to two buds. After three years it is not worth retaining the plants and a fresh start should be made. When pruning, some of the laterals can be used for propagation. The lateral should be cut up so that a well-formed bud with a length of stem about an inch long on either side occurs on each piece. Press these into a cutting compost in small pots so that the bud just protrudes and root in a propagator at about 70°F (21°C). Pot on as required and plant as already described after the first year.

Vines in pots are most decorative as well as giving a useful number of grapes.

Peaches, nectarines, and apricots
For worthwhile crops these are all best grown as fan-trained specimens on the rear wall of a lean-to facing south. It should be realised that considerable space will be necessary. In this case a well-prepared border at the wall base is required. It should be well drained and the ground treated much the same as if the plants were for outdoor culture. Any good general gardening book will give details. Training is also similar to that of outdoor wall-grown fruit, but more care is needed to encourage lower growth and avoid excessive height. An important difference is that under glass the flowers must be pollinated. Do this with a tuft of fluffed-up cotton wool tied to a stick, lightly dusting from flower to flower, at around midday if possible.

In the greenhouse a good atmospheric humidity must be maintained, but do not spray blossom or the ripening fruit with water. If a lean-to is not available the plants can often be grown up the side of an ordinary house and led along wires under the roof espalier fashion. The selection of suitable varieties and suitably trained trees to start off with is vital to success. A specialist nursery should be consulted. Easy peaches for under glass include Duke of York and Hale's Early. For nectarines, Lord Napier and Early Rivers are recommended. The apricot Moorpark is the one generally grown. Apricots need special care to ensure good ventilation, and high temperatures should be avoided during blossom formation and flowering, otherwise it is likely to drop. Dwarf bush peaches suitable for growing in 12-inch pots are now available.

Figs

Figs are best grown in large pots since they can become rampant if unrestricted. The variety Brown Turkey is easy. It can be fan trained if desired. Under glass good crops are usually obtained since fruits form on both the current and the previous year's growth. However, for quality the fruits are best restricted to about three or four per shoot. All weak and straggly wood must be kept cut out, and watering should be generous during active growth, but reduced slightly when the fruit is ripening. Plants in pots can be stood outdoors in summer to give more greenhouse space.

Strawberries

These are essentially frame and cloche crops, and the height of a greenhouse is not really necessary. However, a few pots can be grown among other plants if desired. For decorative effect, special strawberry urns can be planted up. The aroma of strawberry fruit under glass is also delightful. New plants should be obtained each year and grown outside until January when they can then be brought into the greenhouse in a temperature of about 45/50°F (7/10°C) minimum. The plants should by then be in 5- to 7-inch pots. The flowers should preferably be hand pollinated. A strawberry specialist should be consulted for suitable varieties (see appendix, page 245). The old favourite Royal Sovereign is, however, still an excellent one.

Miscellaneous fruits

Apples, pears, plums, and cherries are sometimes grown under glass for early crops, but for modern greenhouses it is very doubtful whether the space needed makes them worth while. However, it is now possible to get dwarf fruit trees (especially apple, pear, and peach) that can be easily grown in large pots, although even in this case the plants can usually be stood about the open garden for normal fruiting.

As curiosities, several species of physalis can be grown in small pots. They yield grape-sized fruits of very pleasant apricot flavour. One of the best is the sugar cherry, *Physalis ixocarpa*, which can be easily raised from seed as an annual.

A decorative plant producing pots useful for flavouring soups is okra, *Hibiscus esculentus*. Pot on the seedlings to 5-inch pots and pick the elongated pods before they are fully ripe—or they may become woody.

Sweet peppers

The correct name is pimiento, from the Spanish. The fruits sold in the shops are also often called capsicums, an incorrect name which leads to confusion with true capsicums from *Capsicum frutescens*. Sweet peppers are from *C. annuum* and, incidentally, this has no relation to the true peppers.

Seed should be sown early and as described for the ornamental varieties (see page 119). Pot on to 5- to 7-inch pots, and keep warm and well watered. Feed as soon as the fruit is seen to be forming. As many as thirty fruits can be had on well grown plants, but when pot grown it is usually best to restrict the number. The plants need a position of good light and they will need support. Fruit is usually ready by autumn. Green fruits will turn red after picking if kept in a warm place indoors.

From November-sown plants it is possible to get crops by the following April, but only if considerable winter warmth is provided.

Aubergines (egg plant)

Culture is similar to pimiento in that a long season is desirable for growth and ripening. Sow not later than March germinating at about 65°F (18°C) and pot on to a final 7-inch pot. A stout cane will be needed for support, since the fruit is large and heavy. If desired the plants can be stopped at an early stage to encourage bushiness, but they can be allowed to grow to about 3 feet if preferred. Only two or three fruits should be permitted to develop on each plant. Water and feed well as soon as the fruit is seen to be forming. The variety Early Purple does particularly well in pots and has a fine purple colour.

Lettuce

This is really another frame crop, but it can often be grown with other plants in the greenhouse to make the most use of space. Obviously lettuce to crop when there is nothing from outdoor sources is desirable, and for this the choice of variety is of the utmost importance. The following varieties are recommended (all are cabbage lettuce types):

Name	Sow	Ready
Kweik (cold greenhouse)	August	November/December
Kloek (cold greenhouse)	October	March/April
Sea Queen (cold or cool)	August/February	December/April
Emerald (cold or cool)	August/February	December/April
May Queen (cold or cool)	October/March	March/June

It should be realised that *not all lettuce varieties are suited to culture under glass*, and a number of greenhouse types will be found described in the seed catalogues.

The technique of sowing and pricking out is similar to that of bedding plants (see page 233). A germination temperature of about 55°F (13°C) is adequate. Although it is customary to plant in the greenhouse ground soil, excellent lettuces can be grown in pots, troughs, or beds of potting compost isolated from the ground soil by polythene sheeting. The great menace to lettuce is botrytis (see page 85). Good ventilation is of the utmost importance.

Beans

Climbing French beans can be grown in the greenhouse and make good use of the height. Runner beans are rarely successful. There are a number of interesting and tasty climbing French varieties. These include Purple Podded and Violet Podded, both attractively coloured, almost stringless and of excellent flavour,

Romano, which is stringless and delicious, and Coco, which has broad pods and seeds that can also be used in the manner of haricot beans.

Germinate the seed at about 65 to 70°F (18 to 21°C) and transfer first to small pots. In the home greenhouse it is best to sow late February and plant out in March. Earlier planting can be done but this means maintaining the winter minimum temperature of about 55°F (13°C) for a longer period. Good light is also most important.

Culture is very similar to that of tomato: the plants can be set out in pots or rings. Alternatively, troughs of compost can be used using polythene sheeting held in place by boards or some similar arrangement. The plants can be spaced about 15 inches apart, and trained up strings. A high humidity should be maintained and the plants kept well watered, but on no account waterlogged. To obtain a good crop it is necessary to stop the laterals at the third joint. Secondary laterals should be similarly treated. For best flavour it is important to pick the beans when young and not to leave them on the plants too long. Picking can be expected to commence around April or May.

Dwarf French beans can also be grown, especially in the company of cucumbers, because they like a similar environment. However, in the home greenhouse it is usually convenient to sow from January to February to avoid maintaining a high temperature for so long. Three to four plants can be set to each 8-inch pot and a few canes given for support.

Miscellaneous vegetables

Depending on space available it may be worth growing a few early- radishes, carrots, turnips, and beetroots. Again the seedsmen's catalogues should be carefully consulted for varieties suitable for growing under glass and gentle forcing. However, these are all best given frame culture if wanted on a larger scale. Similarly there is usually space for mustard and cress, and the odd pot of herbs, such as mint, to provide for winter requirements.

An area under the staging can often be used for forcing and/or blanching. Rhubarb can be easily forced in winter in a blacked-out place under the staging. A few three-year-old roots can be planted in boxes and subjected to a temperature of about

50°F (10°C). Chicory and seakale can be similarly forced, and details of varieties and the initial garden work involved will be found in any outdoor gardening book. To black out an under-the-staging area, black polythene will be found useful. The blackout must be perfectly lightproof.

CHAPTER THIRTEEN

Specialist Greenhouse Plants

THERE are a few types of plant that warrant specialisation
because of special interest or outstanding beauty. Often it is
worth devoting a greenhouse entirely to their culture so that
any special conditions they like can be exactly fulfilled. However,
this does not mean that anyone with a mixed greenhouse cannot
grow them very well indeed if they are prepared to exert a little
extra care. A number of plants already mentioned sometimes
capture the interest of people to the extent that they devote
a whole greenhouse to them. Begonias, ferns, and foliage
plants of various temperature requirements are examples. Here,
some of the more popular specialisations are described more
fully.

Alpines
It may be thought strange that these plants so used to adverse
weather conditions could benefit from greenhouse protection. In
this country their enemy is cold coupled with wet, which can
cause rotting of the roots. Many alpines are frozen and buried
under snow in their native environment. The snow blanket pro-
tects the plants from excessive cold; but in the open here, they
are likely to be subjected to many degrees below freezing when
there is no protective snow. For this reason, a greenhouse kept
just above freezing is an ideal environment—provided there is
plenty of ventilation and light. Special alpine houses are available, designed to give the best possible growing conditions, but
any well ventilated house can be used if sited in an open position.
There are also numerous alpines that will be at home among a
mixed greenhouse collection.

The low growing and dainty nature of alpines means that
they are best displayed on staging rather higher than usual,

which brings their beauty nearer the eye. They are usually grown in well-drained pans or half pots. The usual potting composts can be used, but it is generally necessary to add more grit for drainage and in some cases stone chips to give a more coarse texture, or limestone for those liking alkaline conditions.

The great majority of alpines flower from spring to early summer. This means there may be few flowers the rest of the year and the plants can then be accommodated in frames if desired. This leaves room for growing annuals in pots or similar plants that enjoy the airy, light conditions of the alpine house. Under glass, many alpines will need protection from intense sunshine. This is best given with a weak mixture of Coolglass applied to the glass, unless slatted blinds are fitted.

Nearly all the rock garden plants grown outdoors in the garden can be accommodated in the alpine house, but there are many choice species that can be displayed to better advantage. There are certain alpines that can be extremely difficult to grow, and these may be best avoided where the beginner is concerned. It is essential to get a catalogue of alpines from a specialist grower (see appendix). It should be appreciated that there are a vast number of species and a whole book would be needed to do justice to them. A number of other plants can be grown in company with alpines. The dwarf spring-flowering bulbs make a wonderful show, and the taller kinds can often be put at the back of the staging. The dwarf conifers are splendid evergreen foliage plants and you might like to try bonsai too. A collection of the charming *Primula auricula* varieties (show auriculas) will also thrive in alpine house conditions.

Many alpines can be grown from seed, but this may sometimes need exposure to frost before it will germinate.

Bromeliads

These plants belong to the pineapple family and have soared to popularity in very recent years—so much so that people are beginning to collect them. However, they are very amenable and generally happy in the company of a wide range of other plants if care is taken. There is no need for a special greenhouse. The pineapple itself, *Ananas comosus*, is not really a practical proposition, since it needs more warmth and space than can usually be provided economically by the amateur greenhouse. However, pineapple tops can often be rooted in warmth during summer and grown on, even producing fruit if there is sufficient warmth and humidity.

Bromeliads from warm parts of Central America grow well in the greenhouse and are little trouble. Species from the mountains of South America are usually very easy, because they are resistant to wide temperature changes, typical of their home environment. There are two types of bromeliad: epiphytic and terrestrial (as with orchids). The former grow above ground in moss or debris that collects in the forks of trees and the like. The latter root into the ground like ordinary plants. The two can often be distinguished because the epiphytic types have smooth-edged leaves and the terrestrial types have barbed leaves like pineapple tops. The leaves are arranged in a star or rosette shape and are often very exotically marked or coloured, sometimes with very dramatic effect. Many species have a cup-shaped hollow at the centre, called an 'urn', which should generally be kept topped up with water. This built-in 'reservoir' makes watering an easy matter for beginners.

Not all bromeliads have spectacular foliage. In some it is plain green. Curiously though, these give the most flamboyant flowers. Those with exotic foliage often have flowers of little interest. A bromeliad flowers only once and then forms several new plantlets around the base. These should be removed and potted. The epiphytic types can be planted in moss wound around pieces of tree trunk to give a natural effect (see also page 74). A general compost recommended by T. Rochford Ltd, the famous house plant firm, is equal parts of pine needles, peat, and leafmould, but when pine needles are difficult to procure various mixtures of sterilised leafmould, peat, and grit can be used. Large pots should be avoided. I prefer clay for these plants. Most bromeliads will be happy with a winter minimum of about 50°F (10°C) and often the temperature can fall much lower for short periods without harm, provided the plants are kept on the dry side. Good light is preferred in winter with slight shading in summer. A moist atmosphere in summer is also desirable.

Owing to their popularity as house plants there are now very many species available. To save space the reader is again recommended to get a catalogue from a specialist grower for a detailed description. Although bromeliads can be grown from seed sown in a warm propagator, their development is usually slow. It is more convenient, and quicker, to buy small plants from a nursery.

Cacti and succulents

This is another wide-ranging subject for which thousands of species could be collected. Many are not as particular as other plants over watering, so they are a good choice for those who cannot be in constant attendance. It is nevertheless a mistake to think that cacti and other succulents can be neglected and ill-treated. If they are given reasonable care they frequently reward you with the most beautiful flowers. It is also a common mistake to think that they need hardly any water. This may be true in winter: but in summer, or when active growth is being made, they can be watered generously, as long as the compost is well drained and watering is only done when the compost has become almost dry again.

A glass-to-ground greenhouse is ideal for cacti and succulents. It will give the good light they need and with staging and shelving a vast number can be accommodated in quite a small house. A winter minimum temperature of about 40°F (4°C) is generally sufficient, but an airy, dry atmosphere should be the aim at all times. However, many cacti and succulents are happy in company with other plants in a mixed greenhouse.

Most cacti and succulents are not fussy over compost provided that it is well drained. Most of the potting composts suggested in Chapter Seven (see page 92) can be used if a generous addition of grit is made to make drainage perfect. Although the plants like plenty of light, the intense summer sun may cause damage under glass and slight shading with Coolglass is then advisable. This group of plants is remarkably free from pests and diseases and should be found very easy. Once again there is such an enormous number that a specialist's catalogue should be studied for plant descriptions. Many interesting species are now also sold as house plants for windowsill culture.

Epiphyllums must be singled out for special mention. These are notable for exceptionally brilliant and large showy flowers, and many people make special collections of them. Numerous fine named hybrids exist. Being tall growing, these plants need a cane for support. They also require more summer shade than other cacti.

Many cacti and succulents are easy to raise from seed sown by the normal methods (see page 108). When handling spiny plants for potting it is usual to hold them with a strip of folded newspaper to avoid discomfort to the hands.

Carnations

Although some of the garden carnations, such as the Chabaud type, can be taken up in autumn, potted, and flowered in winter under glass, greenhouse carnations proper are the perpetual flowering kind—called PF for short.

A few PF carnations can be grown in pots in the mixed greenhouse, but their blooms are so pleasing and often delightfully scented that it is worth devoting a small greenhouse to growing them to perfection—particularly since flowers can be had nearly the year round. Any glass-to-ground house will do provided there is good ventilation, but special carnation houses are available. PF carnations grow to a considerable height and they are usually quite vigorous. They must be bought from a specialist nursery (see appendix), and are best obtained as rooted cuttings of named varieties from December to March. These should be potted into 2½-inch pots when received and then potted on as required to final 7-inch pots. It is also possible to obtain plants in 2½-inch pots that have been stopped by the nurseryman. These should be put into 5-inch pots on arrival. Alternatively, established plants can be had, from September to November, in 5-inch pots. These will flower the following winter and can also be used as a source of cuttings.

PF carnations like plenty of light and air and a winter minimum of about 40/45°F (4/7°C) for a good production of winter bloom. Special carnation compost with a high potash content can be had from nurseries, but the John Innes No. 2 will give good results.

Young plants should be stopped when they have grown about ten pairs of leaves, and all side shoots that subsequently develop stopped similarly leaving about five pairs. Stop the longest or fastest growing shoot first. Do not try to stop all shoots at the same time. The first stopping is done when the plants are about 8 inches tall, and the second stopping is done when the plants are in their final pots. Further stoppings can be carried out if desired to obtain continuity of bloom. The best stopping procedure can vary with the variety and has to be learned by experience.

The plants will require support and although canes and various improvisations can be used, there are proper wire carnation supports on sale. Watering should aim to maintain a nicely moist compost at all times. High potash feeds, as used for tomatoes, also work well for carnations.

To obtain fine blooms it is necessary to disbud. The unwanted side buds should be removed as soon as possible to leave only the crown bud to develop. Slight shading, preferably with Coolglass, is needed during periods of brilliant sunshine.

It is not advisable to retain old plants after about two to three years. Young stock should be propagated from cuttings taken from December to February. It is best not to use the old plants as a source of cuttings. Take them from young plants using side shoots about 6 inches long with about six pairs of leaves. The cuttings root easily by the usual methods (see page 227), or in pearlite, at a temperature of about 65°F (18°C).

PF carnations do not make very good decorative pot plants and they are of most use for cutting. There are many exquisite varieties described in the specialists' catalogues (see appendix). More suited as pot plants are the American spray carnations. These are scented and require no disbudding. Their culture is otherwise identical to the ordinary PF types. They are generally available only as rooted cuttings.

Chrysanthemums (see also pages 120 and 235)
These are among the most magnificent blooms worthy of specialisation and easily within the scope of the home greenhouse. The late flowering types can conveniently be accommodated in a greenhouse after clearing tomatoes. Growing these chrysanthemums gives great satisfaction and the blooms are among the most long-lasting of all cut flowers.

The late-flowering chrysanthemums are grown in pots outdoors during the summer and transferred to the greenhouse for flowering from about October to December. There are a number of different types classed according to their bloom structure as follows: Exhibition and Exhibition Incurved ('incurved' refers to petals that turn inwards to form a ball-shaped bloom); Reflexed Decorative (petals turn outwards loosely); Intermediate Decorative (some petals turn out and those near the centre turn inwards); Anemone-Flowered; Single; Pompom; Spray; Thread-petalled; and Spidery. The Exhibition types are those bearing the enormous blooms seen at flower shows. These, the Decoratives, the Anemone-Flowered and the Singles are also divided into large- or medium-flowered forms.

General cultivation

A glass-to-ground greenhouse giving the maximum light and air is desirable. A winter minimum temperature of about 45°F (7°C) is all that is necessary. The first step is to obtain a catalogue from a leading chrysanthemum specialist (see page 245) so that you can make your selection of varieties. New varieties and novelties appear each year and any recommended list soon becomes out of date. For a rough idea of how to assess the number of plants needed, calculate that about twenty-five can be accommodated comfortably in a small 10 × 6 foot greenhouse and pro rata.

In the beginning, rooted cuttings of named varieties should be bought from a chrysanthemum specialist. These should be put into 3½-inch pots on arrival from February to March. Although the standard potting composts described in Chapter Seven can be used for chrysanthemums, the John Innes No. 2 is particularly recommended. Subsequent feeding can be done with Woolman's chrysanthemum plant food, described below, and all potting should be done as described in Chapter Seven (see page 92). After the initial potting, stand the pots on the staging and see that the temperature does not fall below about 40°F (4°C). As the plants become established, ventilate freely whenever weather permits, and keep the compost just moist.

By late March to April the plants will be ready to pot on to 5- or 6-inch pots depending on development. Some varieties are more vigorous than others, but the plants must not be allowed to become pot bound. For this potting, and for subsequent pottings, the John Innes No. 3 is recommended or a peat/grit compost for reasons given below. From now on no artificial heat will usually be required unless some freak weather prevails. When the plants have become established in their pots they should be transferred to a cold frame for hardening off (see page 234). Here they should be given as much air as possible, but a watch must be kept in case of night frost when the lights must be closed if necessary.

By early June the plants should be ready for transfer to their final pots, either 8- or 9-inch ones. Take particular care over drainage of the pots at this stage (see page 102) because the plants will now be standing in the open for the summer, and rains can waterlog badly drained pots.

The next stage is to find a suitable place outdoors for standing the pots. It should be well away from trees or light obstruction, but should be protected from the direction of prevailing winds—this is most important. The pots should be stood on a run of plastic sheeting, or any other material that will prevent worms or soil pests from entering the drainage holes of the pots and the roots from entering the ground soil. It is usual to stand the plants in rows, spacing the pots 3 to 4 inches apart from rim to rim, and leaving a space between the rows of about 4 feet. Into each pot must be inserted a strong 5-foot cane. The John Innes composts and the peat/grit type usually give fairly sound anchorage for the canes. These composts are also reasonably heavy and give a more stable base to the plants. At each end of the rows a strong stake must be thrust into the ground and a wire run along to which must be secured the tops of the canes. This is essential to prevent wind from blowing the plants over. Long rows of plants will need more stakes at intervals so that all the plants are held really well. Should there be any problem in securing the canes to the pots, Woolman's special wire clips should be used (see page 245).

During their standing-out period the plants will obviously need careful watering, and a trickle feed automatic system is worth considering (see page 67). No feeding should be necessary until about July, when a top dressing of some fresh compost given, or Woolman's chrysanthemum fertiliser should be applied according to the supplier's recommendations. Overfeeding must be avoided. During hot spells an occasional spray of the foliage with water, after the sun has gone, is beneficial. Keep a constant watch for pests and take instant action if they are seen. Chrysanthemum leaf miner is a common one, its presence made evident by the appearance of meandering lines on the foliage. Close inspection will reveal a tiny grub burrowing between the leaf surfaces and this can be killed merely by pinching with the fingers. Routine spraying with Hexyl Plus will deal with this and other common pests.

The time for transferring the plants to the greenhouse is generally about mid-September. Make sure that the greenhouse is thoroughly clean and cleared of all tomato debris if this crop has recently been grown there. After removal to the greenhouse the plants must be given free ventilation to get them used to greenhouse conditions. Should there be late strong sunshine the house may need slight shading with Coolglass which can be instantly wiped off when not required. As the plants come into flower watch for *Botrytis cinerea* (see page 85) and take precautionary measures. Stand the pots on plastic sheeting and avoid overcrowding.

Training and stopping chrysanthemums
Left to grow naturally, a chrysanthemum first forms a solitary bud at the top of its stem, called the break bud. This will not develop, but below, a number of shoots will grow from the stem: This is called a natural break. These shoots will produce buds called first crown buds and these will flower if left. Other breaks will occur and produce second crown buds giving more flowers, and so on. However, if things are allowed to proceed naturally the time of flowering and the quality of blooms may not be what we desire. For this reason, both the breaks and the number of buds allowed to develop are controlled by stopping, securing buds, and disbudding.

Stopping is done by merely removing the break bud or about ½ to 1 inch of the growing tip of a shoot. The time to carry out these operations varies considerably from variety to variety and chrysanthemum type. It is therefore essential to arm yourself with a grower's catalogue, such as Woolman's, which gives a detailed timing and stopping key for each variety, including a diagram to illustrate stopping procedure. Stopping and timing can never be exact because of variation of the climate from north to south-west. The correct timing for shows can only be assessed by experience and trial and error.

Securing a bud means the opposite to stopping—the bud at

the end of a shoot is left to develop and any side shoot or buds below removed at an early stage.

Exhibition chrysanthemums   For best results some varieties are flowered from the first crown buds and others from the second. Only one to three of the enormous flowers are allowed to develop to each plant. Buds usually begin to form on the two to three stems permitted to grow during about late July and should be secured in August by removal of lower side shoots as already described. It is also possible to employ the 'single stem method'. This entails stopping the plants in early June and securing only one bud on a single stem, all other shoots being removed.

Exhibition incurved   Three to four blooms (sometimes six) are allowed for each plant. Secure buds from late August to mid-September, removing any that appear earlier. These chrysanthemums enjoy a little shade when they are stood out during summer, and they should be fed adequately—but take special care not to overfeed.

Decorative types   These are very popular. They have flowers of pleasing size, and very wide range of lovely colours. As many as eighteen good-sized blooms can be borne by each plant.

Stop the plants when in their 3½-inch pots and when about 6 to 9 inches tall. From the shoots that result retain only three to four to grow on. These shoots should be stopped again from late May to June.

Other types   The anemone-flowered can be treated similarly to decoratives. The plants are so named because of the anemone shape of the flowers. Single chrysanthemums are of easy culture requiring little stopping, and certainly not after early April. Do not secure buds until after the first week in September. Other varieties grown in pots can generally be left to grow naturally without any stopping. A recent introduction is the 'Mini-Mum' from the Wye College of Horticulture. This dwarf species is excellent as a flowering house plant being only about 8 inches high. The flowers are single, sometimes with thin 'spoon-shaped' petals, and they have an attractive colour range. They are purchased as rooted cuttings, potted into 3½-inch pots in which they will flower, and kept at about 45°F (7°C). From March to October the plants must be blacked out for twelve hours in each twenty-four. This can be done by removing the plants, which can stand on trays for convenience, to an under-stage area blacked out with black polythene sheet. Alternatively, boxes can be placed over the plants. The black-out should be provided each evening and removed each morning. Flowering usually takes place about ten to twelve weeks after potting and continues for about six weeks.

Cascade and Charm chrysanthemums are described on page 120. Dwarfing methods, using various chemicals, are described in technical literature issued by the chemical suppliers (see page 245).

Treatment of greenhouse chrysanthemums after flowering
When flowering is over, the plants should be cut down to about 2 feet and in January cut down further to about 3 inches. At a temperature of about 45 to 50°F (7/10°C) a good supply of new shoots should form, and these can be used for cuttings, which need only about the same temperature for rooting. See also pages 224–7 and 235. Exhibition types are usually rooted from January to February, the latter being early enough for incurved forms. Decoratives can be rooted from February to March, and singles during March.

Orchids
It is easily possible to grow several kinds of orchid among the plants in a general mixed greenhouse collection. As far as the home gardener is concerned, a special greenhouse is not essential. However, the fascination of orchids could well make this desirable eventually. Although there are groups of orchids to suit different temperature conditions, the cool-house types are obviously the most popular and the easiest as far as heating is involved. Few orchids are really difficult to grow, given the right conditions and temperature. Their culture is merely a little different from other greenhouse plants.

In general, orchids require a very open fibrous compost. Composts were at one time based on sphagnum moss, osmunda fibre (from osmunda fern), various forms of leafmould, and similar ingredients. Today, synthetic materials have been used with considerable success, including forms of plastic. It is therefore best to get your compost from the nursery supplying the plants. If possible, always try to see your plants in flower before buying if you are paying a fair sum. However, unflowered seedlings are inexpensive and fun to grow if you are prepared to wait a year or so to see results.

Undoubtedly the most popular orchids are the cymbidiums. These have showy sprays of large butterfly-like flowers which can be picked and used individually as 'buttonhole' blooms if desired. They are easily grown with a winter minimum temperature of about 45°F (7°C). Very exotic, and giving the impression of being difficult, are the cattleyas. These have huge, richly-coloured blooms, but they do need a congenial temperature. However, the plants are far more compact than cymbidium and a large collection can be accommodated in quite a small greenhouse. Laelias are similar: there are some suited to warm and some suited to cool conditions. Vandas are also variable in their temperature preferences. Most odontoglossums and miltonias are suited to cool conditions, and both are very beautiful.

Popular orchids too are the paphiopedilums (once known as cypripediums). Unlike most orchids these have no pseudobulbs (the swollen part at the base of the stems). There are two types: those with plain foliage which are usually suited to cool conditions, and those with mottled foliage which prefer warmth. The flowers are 'slipper'-shaped, waxy and often curiously marked, and they last a very long time.

There are thousands of orchid species and as many named hybrids, so this is another case where the interested reader must obtain a grower's catalogue for details and descriptions. Nearly all those grown in the greenhouse are named hybrids, but there are a few species well worth adding.

General culture of cool-house orchids
Although the orchids like a moist atmosphere, the air should never become stagnant and ventilation must be given whenever weather permits. Bottom ventilation is particularly useful, but draughts must be avoided. Temperatures below about 45°F (7°C) should also be avoided, but most plants will survive drops to almost freezing for short periods. You cannot expect to get best results if this happens too often. In summer the temperature must be kept down. It has recently been found that excellent conditions can be obtained if Coolglass is used for shading.

In winter, good light is essential and the glass must be kept clean, but from February onwards when many plants will be coming into flower, shading should again be applied as necessary if the sun is intense. Again, the easy adjustment of shade density and removal is possible with Coolglass.

Watering of orchids must always be really thorough, but no further water should be applied until the compost has become almost dry again. Clean rainwater is usually advised, but filthy water must never be used and where clean rainwater is not obtainable (see page 78) it is better to use mains drinking water even if it is hard. In winter, watering may be greatly reduced or in some cases ceased. It is rarely necessary or desirable to feed orchids. There is sufficient plant food in the compost to last until the next repotting.

Usually the best time to repot is just after flowering or in spring. Pseudobulbs are often produced in a one-sided manner. When repotting, plant off-centre with the new growth and roots facing the greatest compost area and volume. Old back bulbs can usually be cut away and discarded. It will be necessary to push the compost down and between roots with a potting stick (see page 105). It is important to pot firmly but not so that roots are damaged. Special care must be taken over new, succulent-looking roots. Old shrivelled ones can be carefully cut away. Newly potted plants should not be watered for a week or so, otherwise there is risk of root rot.

The reader seriously interested in orchids, and perhaps having had success with cymbidiums, should try some of the many other exciting types. One of the best books dealing with all the popular kinds in detail is *Popular Orchids* by Brian and Wilma Rittershausen (David and Charles).

Hardy orchids

The most rewarding hardy orchid that can easily be grown in the alpine house, or in any cold or cool greenhouse, is *Pleione formosana*. There are several named varieties available and the flower resembles a small cattleya bloom. Pleione is best planted in a large half pot using a compost made from equal parts of peat, loam, grit, and leafmould, with a little bonemeal added. Left alone, a pseudobulb will multiply and form a clump in the pot. When the flower dies, new pseudobulbs are produced at the side of the old, and the old one shrivels. Before this happens, some tiny pseudobulbs may be formed at the apex of the old. These can be detached and planted. In winter give very little water, but keep the compost moist when active growth is taking place. Flowering is usually in early spring.

CHAPTER FOURTEEN

Propagation

THERE are several reasons for propagation apart from the obvious one of increasing the number of your plants. Sometimes old plants can become untidy and 'leggy', or they may become too large for convenience. In certain cases old plants may deteriorate and flower badly. These circumstances call for a fresh start to be made, and often the existing old plant will be a rich source of material for propagation—such as cuttings of various descriptions, offsets, side growths, and so on, described in this chapter.

Often gardeners desire to produce more from a particularly pleasing plant. Extensive propagation may be necessary if plants are to be used for outdoor bedding, but there is little point in propagating just for the sake of sheer numbers. A greenhouse full of the same kind of plant can be very dull unless there is a good reason for it.

CHOOSING PROPAGATION MATERIAL

It is important to be very fussy about the selection of plants for propagation. Undesirable characteristics can be reproduced as well as desirable ones. It is therefore necessary to choose plants with the best habit, flower colour, flower size and quality, good foliage, and so forth. The methods of propagation described here will reproduce exactly the plant's characteristics except when propagating from seed (see below, page 224). It is vital that sickly plants of any description should not be used. Virus diseases are a great menace, since they are incurable and are easily spread by insects—and often by the mere handling of plants. They are of course passed on during propagation. Plants with yellowing and particularly mottled foliage, distortion of any description, strange-shaped (undesirable) flowers, or flower colours abnormally striped should not be used. Neither should plants that seem backward or stunted. All these are possible symptoms of virus diseases.

Plants that have suffered some form of disaster such as wilt through lack of water or pest attack, or suffering from chill or neglect, may also be best avoided as sources of propagation material except in dire need—for example, if it is thought the parent plant may die. Material from such plants may not propagate so readily. However, a plant that has had an accident such as being damaged or dropped is an obvious case where immediate propagation can restore the plant to your collection.

PROPAGATION FROM SEED

It should be realised at once that the majority of the choice hybrids, F1 hybrids, named varieties, and so on, cannot reliably be reproduced from seed. This applies to the great majority of the plants described in Chapter Eight, and the seed must be freshly bought each year. Such seed is usually produced by expert crossing, selection and pollination, often by hand and by special techniques. It is neither possible nor necessary to enter into the genetical reasons here. However, in some cases where pure species are concerned you can collect your own seed. To be viable (that is, to be able to germinate) the seed often has to be ripe and to have matured on the plant. For a rough guide as to when seed is ready for collection, watch for the time when the plant itself is ready to shed it. If you specially desire to collect a particular seed, it is often a good idea to remove all but a few flowers so that the plant's energy can go to developing a limited number. The general technique for growing from seed is described in Chapter Eight. (See also page 210 for comment on the seed of alpines.)

SOFT-WOOD CUTTINGS

The great majority of greenhouse plants can be reproduced by removing suitable shoots, inserting them in a rooting compost, and when roots have formed potting in the usual way. In the greenhouse, cuttings can be taken nearly all the year round except from plants undergoing a dormant period. However, the best time to take most cuttings is when the plants are just about to begin an active period of growth. This means that spring can be a busy time. However, there are numerous popular plants that can also be propagated from cuttings taken in early autumn.

The compost used for rooting cuttings of all kinds is a mixture of equal parts by volume of moss peat, well teased apart, and sharp washed grit. This can be put into pots or seed trays depending on convenience and the quantity of cuttings to be rooted. When pots are used, it is a curious fact that better rooting often occurs if the cuttings are inserted around the

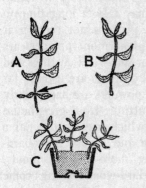

Fig. 16 TAKING A SOFT-WOOD CUTTING

A: Shoot of plant selected. B: The shoot prepared for rooting, the final cut being made just above root node (arrowed). C: Cuttings inserted around edge of pot, ready for the propagator if necessary.

edge and close to the side. Usually a number of cuttings can be put in each pot. Cuttings should always be as small as possible. Large pieces of plant are of no advantage and are much more difficult to deal with.

Rooting is always quicker with a source of bottom heat (see page 60). A propagator is desirable and often essential for those plants that originate from warm countries. However, many of the hardier greenhouse plants may root well during the summer with no extra warmth.

For successful and fast rooting it is also necessary to reduce water loss from the foliage of the cutting. This means that the cuttings must be covered with a 'light', plastic film, or other transparent enclosure to keep in moisture. A modern way of preventing water loss is mist propagation (see under this heading,

H

page 231). For hardier plants, cold frames can be used with advantage to save greenhouse space. On a larger scale, frames can also be fitted with warming cables if heat is required (see page 61).

For the occasional job of propagation, polythene bags can be used. A little moist cutting compost should be put at the bottom of a bag, one or more cuttings inserted, and the bag suspended in a warm place. When rooting occurs it will be seen through the polythene and the cuttings can then be removed and potted. This very simple technique is remarkably effective with many greenhouse plants.

The ease with which cuttings root varies very considerably according to the nature of the plant. Some, like nerium, tradescantia, and even some fuchsias, will root merely on standing in a glass of water. Some plants may take a long time to root or present considerable difficulty, perhaps not rooting at all. To accelerate the rooting of cuttings hormone powders are often used. There are two types: one for soft-wood cuttings and one for hard-wood cuttings. Hard-wood cuttings are usually far more difficult to root, and the hormone powders are particularly suited to them. However, nearly all cuttings from greenhouse plants will be of the soft-wood type which are, as the name implies, from soft or immature growth and shoots. Semi-hard-wood cuttings are taken from rather more mature shoots, especially in the case of many shrubs. Hard-wood cuttings come from most trees and woody shrubs and are mostly taken when the plants are dormant. Although both semi-hard-wood and hard-wood cuttings are rarely used for greenhouse plant propagation, they may be taken from outdoor plants and rooted and grown on under greenhouse conditions for a time. (See Chapter Fifteen, page 241.)

To use the hormone powders, merely dip the prepared cuttings into the powder, tap off the excess, and insert the stem in the cutting compost in the usual manner. There is no point in trying hormone powders on plants the cuttings of which are known not to root at all.

To take a cutting, choose a small, vigorous shoot and cut it cleanly from the parent plant. Carefully break off the lower leaves so as to leave foliage originating from about three nodes. Then cut cleanly through the surplus stem close to, and underneath, the highest node from which the foliage has been removed. This is best understood by reference to Fig. 16. In most cases, it is best to avoid taking cuttings from shoots carrying flowers or buds. If this cannot be avoided they should be cleanly removed. Always use a very sharp knife in taking and preparing cuttings, to avoid bruising the plant tissue. A razor blade in a holder or a surgical scalpel is useful.

Since the rooting compost contains no fertiliser, the cuttings should be potted as soon as roots form. Some growers do include fertiliser; others are of the opinion that the presence of fertiliser may retard root formation. Personally, I have been happy not to include fertiliser.

LEAF CUTTINGS

This is another technique of special value to greenhouse gardeners. Many plants, particularly of the *Begoniaceae* and *Gesneriaceae*, can be propagated by leaf cuttings taken in various ways (see Fig. 17). The *Gesneriaceae* include such plants as gloxinia, streptocarpus, saintpaulia, and aeschynanthus.

Large leaves can sometimes be cut up into small pieces. The veins on the underside should be slit with a very sharp knife —but not so that the leaf is penetrated—and then the sections placed flat, vein side down, on the cutting compost already described. If preferred an entire leaf, with the veins cut in several places, can be similarly treated and weighted down with small pieces of broken clay pot or the like. Many begonias can be propagated conveniently this way, and also by cutting the leaves into small triangular sections. (See Fig. 17.)

Plants with long leaves can sometimes be cut up into sections, for example streptocarpus. The sections are inserted vertically in the cutting compost in the same way as soft-wood cuttings. In all these cases the roots will grow from the place where a vein is cut, and little plantlets will grow up from them. When large enough to handle they should be immediately potted in a nourishing compost.

In the case of plants with small leaves it is often necessary to use an entire leaf taken with the small leaf stalk attached, for example in the case of saintpaulia. The leaf stalk is inserted in the cutting compost vertically so that the base of the

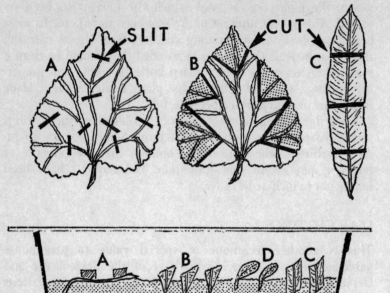

Fig. 17   VARIOUS TYPES OF LEAF CUTTING

A: Removed leaf with slits cut across leaf veins as arrowed. B: Triangular pieces of leaf cut out (shaded) with leaf vein at apex. C: Long leaf cut into sections. D: Some leaves can be pulled off and inserted in the rooting medium directly (e.g. saintpaulia).

leaf just reaches the compost surface, and a new plantlet will form at this point. All leaf cuttings must be covered to keep in moisture, as described for stem cuttings.

DIVISION

Most perennial pot plants can be simply multiplied by division of the roots in the same way as outdoor herbaceous perennials. The division is best done just as the plants are expected to begin active growth. For plants that have been dormant, or resting, most of the top growth can often be advantageously removed and the roots divided up into as many pieces as convenient. Obviously, plants that only form one stem cannot be divided satisfactorily. The best subjects are those which form a clump and have numerous growing shoots. Division is then best done to allow one shoot at least to each piece separated. In cases where the roots become entwined and matted, it is often best to cut through them with a very sharp blade. If roots are severely disturbed, bruised or otherwise damaged they are much more liable to rot. After potting divided plants, watering should always be cautious at first.

Tuberous plants can be multiplied by cutting up the tubers so that one shoot is left to each piece. The tubers are started into growth in the usual manner, by immersion in moist peat (see page 142), to encourage shooting before division is made. Again, a very sharp blade should be used. Loss of sap from the cut surface can be prevented by dusting liberally with finely powdered charcoal. This also helps to protect against disease.

OFFSETS

Numerous greenhouse bulbs form tiny bulblets around the side when they reach a mature size or after flowering. These can be carefully separated when repotting and potted individually in small pots. Although this is usually a quicker method of propagation than from seed in the case of bulbs, the bulblets often take at least three years to reach flowering size.

Some tubers, rhizomes, and similar storage organs reproduce themselves during the growing season. The new storage organs can be separated and potted when it is time to start into growth again. Examples are achimenes, smithiantha, and gloriosa.

LAYERING

This is a convenient method for training plants and climbers, but it can also be done with some upright growing species if the stems are supple enough to be bent. A length of stem is bent down and led just under the surface of some potting compost contained in a separate pot. The stem can usually be kept in place by a staple made by bending a piece of stiff wire into a 'U' shape. When roots have formed, the new plant is severed from its parent. Rooting is accelerated by removing a tiny

Fig. 18   PROPAGATION BY LAYERING

A : Wire staple to hold down stem (alternatively, a stone can be used). B : The rooted stem severed from its parent.

section of the outer coating of the stem underneath the compost; alternatively a slit can be made in the stem. (See Fig 18.)

AIR LAYERING

This is particularly useful when plants growing as a single stem drop their lower leaves, a typical well-known example being the rubber plant, *Ficus elastica*. An upward slit is made in the stem below the existing foliage. Into this is wedged a small tuft of sphagnum moss after dusting with hormone rooting powder. Some compost consisting of sphagnum moss, peat, and grit is then formed into a ball around the site of operation and held in place with fine florists' wire. The sphagnum moss will help to consolidate the compost. Around this is then wound polythene sheet to retain moisture, and the polythene secured with wire around the stem at the bottom and top of the compost ball (see Fig. 19).

When roots have formed, they can usually be seen through the polythene. For this method to be successful it is often necessary to have a reasonably high temperature in the greenhouse. For this reason, it is best done during late spring so that benefit is obtained from summer warmth. When roots are seen the stem should be cut just below and the rooted top potted.

MIST PROPAGATION

It has been pointed out that all cuttings must be covered with a transparent enclosure to keep in moisture. If cuttings lose much moisture by transpiration they will of course wilt and die, since they have no roots to make good water loss. In recent years, it has been found that if a film of moisture is maintained over the foliage of the cuttings, successful rooting is far more likely to take place (see Fig. 20). Many cuttings difficult to root by normal methods will root easily with this one.

The film of moisture is maintained from misting jets set above the cuttings. So that excessive saturation does not occur, the jets are operated automatically, usually by what is known as an 'electronic leaf'. This device activates the jets when a film

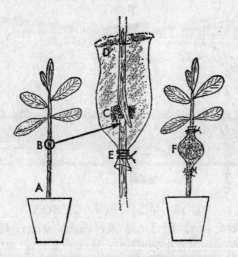

Fig. 19   AIR LAYERING

A: Original plant from which lower leaves have fallen off. B: Slit in stem made in upwards direction. C: Wedge of peat or moss dusted with hormone rooting powder. D: Thin polythene sheeting (transparent). E: Secure to stem with wire or tape. F: Polythene chamber filled with moist peat – when rooting has occurred it will show through the polythene.

of water has evaporated, and there are various designs of apparatus. Recently the photo-electric method has proved far superior and more reliable. In this case the water jets are controlled according to the light energy falling upon them, which in turn affects the rate of transpiration and water loss. Electrical control methods depending on conductivity of a film of water, or on evaporation, are liable to fail due to algae growth and lime in mains water. The photo-electric method is however independent of the water supply (see also page 69).

Although mist propagation was originally used by professional growers, small units suitable for the amateur greenhouse are now available. These are easy to set up and operate and most are reasonably priced. Mist propagation is particularly effective in combination with electric warming cables to warm the rooting medium.

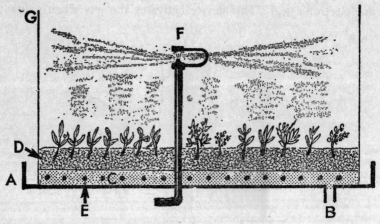

Fig. 20   MIST PROPAGATION

A: Waterproof tray. B: Drain for excess water. C: Layer of sharp grit. D: Rooting medium. E: Warming cable arranged as in Fig. 4. F: Misting jet connected to control system. G: Glass or plastic screen to confine mist.

CHAPTER FIFTEEN

How a Greenhouse Helps the Home and Garden

A GREENHOUSE can be so useful as an adjunct to the outdoor garden, and in supplying cut flowers and house plants for the home, that it is often worth having a small separate structure especially for this purpose. A small greenhouse used in this way will cover its cost very quickly. Moreover, you can grow cheaply from seed many choice and unusual garden plants that would otherwise be difficult or expensive to buy. There are also many wonderful bedding plants offered each year by the leading seedsmen that are not generally available from shops and nurseries.

BEDDING PLANTS

All the seed catalogues from the firms listed in the appendix, and others, should be obtained and your selection made as early as possible. Sowing in the greenhouse begins in January for slow-growing plants like antirrhinums and pansies, and continues until May for later flowering subjects. In the greenhouse, with the aid of the composts and techniques suggested in this book, growth will be rapid and vigorous. Do not sow too early or you will have many plants far too advanced for bedding out before the weather will allow. The majority of popular bedding plants can be sown from about March to April.

For sowing, the general techniques described in Chapter Eight are applicable. However, it is usually convenient to prick out into large seed trays, 14×9 inches. The plastic type are best for the home gardener. The old wooden trays are likely to harbour pests and diseases and are difficult to clean. Do not overcrowd the trays. As a rough guide, bear in mind that about twenty-four seedlings to each, spaced evenly, is suitable for

H*

most bedding plants, but their size will of course have to be taken into account. Nursery-bought bedding plants are often very overcrowded and this results in root disturbance—check when they are bedded out. Always water-in the seedlings with Cheshunt compound (see page 114).

A common recommendation is to put boxes of seedlings up on shelves near the glass, rather than on the staging, so that they get more light, but in fact there is no need for this if the greenhouse is uncluttered. Just as much light reaches the staging in a modern greenhouse as reaches the shelves. If the seedlings are too near the glass they may suffer from chill at night.

For mass production of bedding plants, it has been found more economical to use soil-warming cables to keep the roots warm, with a greenhouse air temperature as low as possible— usually 35/40°F (2/4°C) will be found quite sufficient, with a root temperature of about 50/55°F (10/13°C). Warmed benches can be constructed by covering a warming cable, spread out on asbestos sheet over the staging, with an inch or so of sand. On top of this is spread a layer of moist peat in which the boxes or seed trays of bedding plants are plunged. Temperature can be automatically controlled by thermostat. It has been found that with this method strong root systems can be developed without excessive top growth—which is a primary aim in bedding plant production. Plants with a sound root system will grow away much faster than those with weak roots and lots of top growth.

Choice bedding plants like shrubby calceolarias (F1 hybrids), petunias, the magnificent zinnias now available, polyanthus, and so on, can be pot-grown with advantage. It is also a good idea to retain some of these under glass to fill gaps that might occur in beds and borders during the year.

All bedding plants must be hardened off before planting out. This means exposing them gradually to the rigours of the outdoor climate. The majority of bedding plants will be set back or killed completely by frost, since they are mostly half-hardy annuals. Even some of the hardier plants are best gradually introduced to outdoor conditions. Hardening off is best done in frames. These need not be heated, and the frame lights should be closed at first, later opened a little during the day, then closed only at night, and subsequently fully exposed all the time prior to bedding out. This process should take about two weeks, and should be timed according to your district, so that at the end of the period there is no further risk of frost.

For plants to be set out in the garden it is often convenient to use pots of a special composition that can be planted with them. The composition is usually compounded from compressed peat or similar vegetable matter so that it decomposes on contact with the soil, providing a source of humus for the roots. The use of such pots avoids root disturbance and the plants will grow away very quickly after bedding out. Careful attention should however be given to watering. The composition pots may not rot down if conditions are too dry and this may cause the roots to become confined, with the opposite from desired effect on growth.

CHRYSANTHEMUMS (garden types)

There are a number of ways the greenhouse can assist in the growing of these beautiful plants. The roots of outdoor varieties, called 'stools', should have their top growth cut down to about 18 inches after flowering and any new shoots removed. The roots should then be carefully lifted with a fork and washed to free them from soil. The stools can then be 'boxed up', by planting them in boxes of any sterilised potting compost (see page 92). The boxes should be placed in a frost-free greenhouse for the winter after watering to see that the compost is moist—not wet. Little water will be subsequently needed, and in January the stems can be cut back again to about 5 inches. During or around March, a good supply of new shoots should appear that can be used as cuttings. The original roots are then best discarded. During winter, give the boxed stools a light, airy position and inspect them regularly for signs of fungi or decay. A temperature of only about 45/50°F (7/10°C) is required for rooting the cuttings.

Early-flowering Charm chrysanthemums can be sown in early February in a warm propagator and the plants grown on in pots for bedding out. Large mounds of bloom form from early autumn onwards and this type of chrysanthemum deserves to be far more extensively grown. Korean chrysanthemums can be sown similarly. They make fine cut flowers as well as decorative border plants, and grow to a height of about 2 feet.

DAHLIAS

After the top foliage has been blackened by frost it should be removed and the stem remains cut back to about 8 inches. The tubers should then be carefully lifted so as not to damage them, and as much as possible of the adhering soil removed on site. It is important not to damage the outer skin of the tubers or disease organisms may later gain entry. The tubers should then be put in a greenhouse and placed so that the stems left on them point downwards. This allows any moisture to drain away and assists drying off. After a few weeks the remaining soil should be gently brushed away and the old roots cut off. The stems are then reduced to about 2 inches and the tubers stored by immersion in dry peat or sand. The boxes containing this can go under the staging of a frost-free greenhouse, but care must be taken to see that the plunge material does not get wet over winter. The tubers should be inspected from time to time for signs of disease.

During February, plant the roots in boxes of moist peat on the greenhouse staging at a minimum temperature of 45°F (7°C), but preferably higher for quicker results. Shoots should soon appear and these can be used as cuttings when about 3 inches long.

Where sufficient warmth is a problem the tubers can be started during March in the same way as above. When 'eyes' begin to develop on the crowns of the tubers, the tubers can be divided so that each piece has an eye. Division should be done with a very sharp knife.

To get a very early show of blooms, tubers can be potted in 10-inch pots during March to April and grown on under glass to an advanced stage if there is room. The plants can then be planted out when all danger of frost is past in June to give a long period of bloom when dahlias are not normally seen.

ZONAL PELARGONIUMS (so-called 'geraniums')

From an early sowing of F1 hybrids it is now possible to produce fine plants for summer-to-autumn display (see page 130).

However, this is at present too expensive for quantity production of bedding plants, though a good way of obtaining initial stock for subsequent propagation by cuttings. Cuttings can be taken from plants in the beds during August to September. After rooting, the plants should be kept in the greenhouse over winter and care taken not to water excessively. A winter minimum of about 40/45°F (4/7°C) is desirable, and the plants should be potted on as required, to final 5-inch pots. Bed out when all danger of frost is passed and after hardening off.

Plants can also be saved over winter by lifting from the beds in late autumn, just before the first frost, and either potting or planting in boxes in the greenhouse. Such plants should be kept almost dry and also cut back to remove all unwieldy and straggly growth. In many cases the plants can be cut back very severely. Cut-back potted plants can be grown on for bedding out again. Alternatively, if there is a little extra warmth from January onwards, the plants can be started into growth with a slight increase in watering, and the shoots formed used as cuttings. The cuttings, rooted in a propagator and grown on in warmth, will yield new material for bedding out the same year.

To overwinter 'geraniums' safely in the greenhouse, take great care not to give too much water, keep out frost, and watch for botrytis (see page 85). Ventilate freely whenever possible.

SUB-TROPICAL BEDDING

With the aid of a greenhouse a number of plants can be used outdoors during the summer to give a sub-tropical effect to beds or borders. Sometimes they can be used in pots to stand on a terrace or patio, or one or two could be used as specimen or feature plants in a lawn.

Most of the palms can be used (see pages 189 and 130), especially when they have reached a fair size. Erythrina (page 168), abutilon (page 114), grevillea (page 126), jacaranda (page 127), canna (page 145), nerium (page 173), and strelitzia (page 179) are also possibilities.

An impressive plant is *Musa ensete* which can be raised from seed sown at 80°F (27°C) during summer and grown on over winter at a minimum of about 50°F (10°C) to form sizeable plants for the following summer. (It is important to obtain fresh seed: stale seed is unlikely to germinate. Seed that floats in water is invariably useless.) The *Musa ensete* species is also known as the Abyssinian banana. It has the most handsome banana foliage and makes a fine plant for the greenhouse if there is space. Good specimens can be had in 10-inch pots. When putting this plant outdoors, choose a spot sheltered from excessive wind or the foliage may become torn.

Easy to raise from seed to give decorative plants the first year are *Zea mays* and *Ricinus communis*. Ornamental varieties of both should be selected. The first is the source of maize, but its garden forms have coloured striped foliage and often decorative cobs with coloured seeds. The second is the true castor oil plant. Again there are some handsome forms, those with red foliage being especially attractive. Seed catalogues usually list several varieties. The castor oil plant will form spiky seed capsules during a warm summer and these will contain several prettily marked seeds. These should not be allowed to fall into the hands of young children who might be attracted to them: the seeds are extremely poisonous if chewed or eaten.

The more permanent plants for sub-tropical bedding are best put out in their pots, the pots being plunged. In this way they can easily be returned to the greenhouse before the frosts. Clay pots are best for such plants, since these will allow moisture to pass through when they are plunged. To deter the entry of worms, place some coarse shingle at the bottom of the plunging hole and over the top of the pot. Worms can be a nuisance because they disturb the roots. Should they gain entry, and their presence be suspected on returning the pots to the greenhouse for the winter, they can be brought to the compost surface by watering with potassium permanganate solution, ¼ ounce per gallon of water. The same treatment can be given to any other greenhouse plants, such as fuchsias, that have been used for garden decoration during summer with their pots plunged.

INSTANT GARDENING WITH POT PLANTS

Very many garden plants and the more hardy greenhouse plants can be pot grown under glass to give advanced and early flowering specimens. Dahlias are one example (see page 236), but many herbaceous perennials can be treated similarly. In addition, plants like begonias, pelargoniums, fuchsias, and impatiens can also be used for bedding and in borders as well as greenhouse pot plants. Of course, great care must be taken not to put the plants out too early so that they suffer from cold, and they should be properly hardened off. These and many other greenhouse pot plants are also suitable for planting in pots for terraces, patios or other paved areas, or in window-boxes, to give instant effect. It is always wise to have a few pot plants in reserve as the year progresses to fill any gaps that may occur in beds or borders.

CUT FLOWERS UNDER GLASS

It is doubtful whether it is worth while for the home greenhouse gardener to devote a whole greenhouse to the growing of flowers for cutting. However, the present popularity of floral arrangement could mean that some devotees might like to exploit the possibilities of the greenhouse in this respect more fully. Many greenhouse plants will of course provide some beautiful and sophisticated material for floral art. In addition, most popular cut flowers can be grown in pots to give earlier blooms and of a quality rarely attainable without weather protection. It should be realised that all outdoor flowers, when grown in the greenhouse, should not be subjected to excessively high temperatures, and conditions must be as airy, cool, and light as possible.

Roses can be grown in pots for early cut flowers (see page 175). Other notable cut flowers from the greenhouse include chrysanthemums (pages 214, 235), carnations (page 213), gerberas (page 171), spring-flowering bulbs (page 140), many annuals such as stocks, antirrhinums, and so forth (page 115), and orchids (page 219). Many of the foliage plants described in Chapter Eleven can yield cut material too.

Gladioli are often worth growing for cutting and very fine blooms can be obtained under glass. Planting can begin from mid-January onwards, but only a modest warmth of about 45/50°F (7/10°C) is necessary and desirable. Planting can be done in large pots or, if greater quantity is required, in poly-

thene-lined troughs dug in the greenhouse floor and filled with
compost. Provided great care is taken in supplying adequate
support, the corms need be planted only about 1 to 2 inches
deep so as to give plenty of depth for the roots. If they are not
supported well they risk toppling over.

One of the most important cut flowers is the sweet pea. These
can be sown in October so that the plants can be overwintered in
a frost-free greenhouse, or in January or February. In both cases
the plants are grown on under glass and hardened off for
early planting out and early cut flowers. If the sweet peas
are to be grown under glass to the flowering stage, sowing is
best done during September. In this case *some care is needed
in selecting suitable varieties*. The early winter flowering types
will flower under the restricted light conditions of winter and
spring. The large flowering Spencers flower well under glass but
it is difficult to get bloom before April and often there is a
tendency for buds to drop. The Cuthbertsons are easier although
smaller, but have good stems for cutting. For sweet peas the
greenhouse must have all the winter light that is possible and
be at least 5 feet high to accommodate the plants. All seedlings
grown under glass should be stopped, otherwise the general
culture to be found in any book on outdoor gardening
applies.

HOUSE PLANTS

A greenhouse with a propagator will provide an endless source
of exciting house plants to decorate the home. Many can be
raised from seed and grown on in the greenhouse until they
reach the decorative stage. The most pleasure from house plants
will be obtained if they can be changed about frequently so
that they can 'holiday' from time to time under greenhouse
conditions of light and humidity. For special occasions some
of the permanent greenhouse plants can be brought into the
home for a short while if a specially exotic display is required.
Most of the foliage plants described in Chapter Eleven make fine
house plants. A list of those easy from seed is given in Table 2,
page 137.

A popular house plant especially suited to greenhouse conditions is the poinsettia, *Euphorbia pulcherrima*. This often causes

disappointment through getting chilled. A minimum temperature of about 55°F (13°C) is essential, otherwise it quickly
becomes a very sorry sight. Purchased plants should be allowed
to slowly go dry, the top growth then cut back, and the pots
stored in the greenhouse until new shoots appear during about
May. These shoots are taken as cuttings. Rooting is easiest under
a mist propagator if you have one; otherwise a closed propagator at about 65°F (18°C) should instigate quick rooting. The
plants are then potted on as required and stopped when about
6 inches high to promote bushiness. Keep the compost nicely
moist at all times, without wide fluctuations, or the foliage may
tend to fall. Poinsettias so raised will generally be taller and
mature later than shop-bought plants. The latter are usually
artificially dwarfed (see appendix) and brought to earlier decorative stage by artificial light.

GENERAL GARDEN PROPAGATION AND SEEDLING
PRODUCTION

Innumerable garden plants can be conveniently propagated from
cuttings rooted under greenhouse conditions and grown on in
pots under glass for a time. Mist propagation is particularly
successful (see page 231). Very many choice, rare, or unusual
border, alpine, and shrub plants can be raised from seed obtained from specialists (see appendix). This is a specially interesting and exciting aspect of the greenhouse helping the garden
and the reader is urged to make exploration in this field. Too
often gardens tend to be full of plants that can be seen anywhere. The greenhouse can make yours different.

The greenhouse is also invaluable for raising vegetable seedlings. Plants such as lettuce, cabbage, cauliflower, and onion can
be conveniently sown in the greenhouse for subsequent planting out. For exhibition results it is sometimes worth growing
on vegetable seedlings in pots to quite an advanced stage before
setting out in the vegetable garden. The more tender vegetables
(correctly fruits), like sweet pepper and aubergine, must always
be grown under glass for a time before planting out in June.
Only by giving them a long season of growth will reasonable
crops be obtained. (See also Chapter Twelve, page 205).

APPENDIX

Major Suppliers

All the plants, equipment and materials described in this book
are available from one or other of the following firms. In some
cases several firms supply the same items and there are often
many others not mentioned here; it has been possible to make
only a selection. Most garden shops stock common items like
pesticides suitable for the greenhouse, Coolglass shading, Cheshunt compound, tomato fertilisers, tomato set (Betapal), peat,
potting composts, etc., and a selection of common equipment.

Greenhouses

The catalogues of the following firms illustrate all the types
described in Chapter Two. *Aluminium:* Crittall-Hope Ltd, Brain-
tree, Essex (also steel); Alitex Ltd, Station Road, Alton, Hants;
Edenlite Ltd, Hawksworth Estate, Swindon, SN2 1EQ. *Timber:*
Alton Glasshouses Ltd, Alton Works, Bewdley, Worcs.; Robert
H. Hall Ltd, Paddock Wood, Tonbridge, Kent; F. Pratten & Co.,
Ltd, Charlton Road, Midsomer Norton, Bath, BA3 4AG.

Electrical heating and automation

Simplex of Cambridge Ltd, Sawston, Cambridge, CB2 4J (also
warming cables, sterilisers, mist units, propagators, automatic
watering and ventilation, artificial lighting and electrical fittings).

Oil heaters (wick-type)

P. J. Bryant, Forest Road, Fishponds, Bristol; Aladdin Industries
Ltd, Kingsway, Fforestfach Industrial Estate, Swansea,
Glamorgan, SA5 4HB (also automatic filling, see page 41).

Natural gas heating

Bradley-Nicholson & Co., Brettenham House, Lancaster Place, Strand, London WC2E 7EN.

Heating, automatic aids of all descriptions, many accessories, gadgets, etc.

House and Garden Automation, 186 High Street, Barnet, Herts (also capillary watering matting, see page 67).

Fan heaters and electrical equipment, mist units, etc.

Autogrow Ltd, Quay Road, Blyth, Northumberland.

General Greenhouse equipment of all kinds

Humex Ltd, 5 High Road, Byfleet, Surrey, KT14 7QF (also instruments, thermometers, and Panasand, see page 67, blinds, propagators, etc.).

Hot water heating (oil and solid fuel)

H. E. Phillips Ltd, King William Street, Coventry, Warwicks, CV1 5JH; Metallic Heaters Ltd, Bridge Works, Alfreton Road, Derby.

Photo-electric irrigation (see pages 69 and 232)

Wright Rain Ltd, Crow Arch Lane, Ringwood, Hants.

Capillary sand bench units and trickle watering

Nethergreen Products Ltd, PO Box 3, Alderley Edge, Cheshire, SK9 7JJ.

Frames and irrigation equipment

Access Frames, Yelvertoft Road, Crick, Rugby, Warwicks.

Moisture meter

(Graduated with reference tables) (see page 57). J. M. A. Scientific Ltd, 152 Nelson Road, Twickenham, TW2 7BX.

General sundries, pots, tools, fertilisers, Coolglass shading, etc.

E. J. Woodman & Son Ltd, High Street, Pinner, Middlesex.

Horticultural chemicals, fertiliser mixtures for home compost making, plant hormones, dwarfing chemicals

Chempak Products, Brewhouse Lane, Hertford, SG14 1JS; Medlock Chemicals, 8 The Grove, Stubbington, Fareham, Hants.

Peat, peat composts, tom bags, acid and special composts

Alexander Products Ltd, Burnham on Sea, Somerset.

Seedsmen

Sutton & Sons Ltd, Reading, Berks (general); W. J. Unwin Ltd, Histon, Cambridge (general); Samuel Dobie & Son Ltd, Upper Dee Mills, Llangollen, Denbighshire, LL20 8SD (general and greenhouse plant seeds); Thompson & Morgan Ltd, Ipswich (general and very wide range of rare and unusual *seeds, palms, succulents, alpines,* etc.); M. Holtzhausen, 14 High Cross Street, St. Austell, Cornwall (*rare seeds* and *bulbs,* and *curiosities*).

Plantsmen

H. Woolman Ltd, Grange Road, Dorridge, Solihull, B90 3NQ (*chrysanthemum* specialists, *general greenhouse plants, fuchsias, pelargoniums, carnations, begonias, gloxinias,* and many *bulbs, tubers,* etc.); Thomas Butcher, Shirley, Croydon, Surrey (*exotics, palms, smithianthas, rare pot plants* and *seeds, nerines*); B. Wall, 4 Selbourne Close, New Haw, Weybridge, Surrey (*bromeliad* and *begonia species* specialist, many other *greenhouse pot plants*); Steven Bailey Ltd, Eden Nurseries, Sway, Hants (*carnation* and *gerbera* specialist); Blackmore & Langdon Ltd, Bath, Somerset (*prize begonia* specialist, also *cyclamen* and *gloxinias*); Wallace & Barr Ltd, Marden, Kent (*bulb* specialists, *rare greenhouse bulbs, nerines, lilies*); Walter Blom & Son Ltd, Leavesden, Watford, Herts (*general bulb* specialist); W. E. Th. Ingwersen Ltd, Birch Far Nursery, Gravetye, East Grinstead, Sussex (*alpine plant* specialist); Burnham Nurseries Ltd, Kingsteignton, Newton Abbot, Devon (*orchid* specialist); Thomas Rochford & Sons Ltd, Hoddesdon, Herts (*foliage plants* and *exotics*—their plants can be ordered from any florist. The firm does not supply direct); Holly Gate Nurseries Ltd, Billingshurst Lane, Ashington, Sussex (*cacti* and *other succulents*); Blackmore Nurseries,

Liss, Hants (*fruit*); Treseder's Nurseries, Truro, Cornwall (*camellias* and *half-hardy shrubs*); Hillier & Sons, Winchester, Hants (*choice shrubs, climbers* and many *half-hardy shrubs and plants* including *rare varieties*).

General Index

Plant Index